DATE		
JUL 8 '83		

GOVERNING ELITES

GOVERNING ELITES

Studies in Training and Selection

EDITED BY RUPERT WILKINSON

NEW YORK

OXFORD UNIVERSITY PRESS

1969

The Contributors

CORRELLI BARNETT is a free-lance military historian, and the author of *The Desert Generals* (1960) and *The Swordbearers* (1963). He is a Member of the Institute for Strategic Studies, London; a Fellow of the Royal Society of Literature; and an associate of the University of East Anglia. He served as a Historical Consultant to the BBC television series, "The Great War and the Lost Peace, 1918-1933."

ROBERT R. BOLGAR is a Fellow of King's College, Cambridge. He has contributed to the *Cambridge Modern History* and is the author of *The Classical Heritage and Its Beneficiaries* (1954). He is presently working on a history of medieval universities and a history of ideas during the early Renaissance.

MICHALINA VAUGHAN is a Lecturer in Sociology at the London School of Economics. She was born in Poland and educated in France, and has worked for UNESCO as a social scientist. She has published articles in a number of countries, and is the co-author of two forthcoming books, one on Irish government, the other a comparative study of British and French education in the nineteenth century.

JOSSLEYN HENNESSY is London editor of the *Eastern Economist,* New Delhi. From 1937 to 1946 he served in the Indian government. At the time of Independence, he was a correspondent for the *Sunday Times,* London, and reported on events following the partition of India and Pakistan. His books include *India and Pakistan in World Politics* (1949) and *India, Democracy and Education* (1955).

YOSHINORI IDE is an Associate Professor at the Institute of Social Science, University of Tokyo. He holds an LL.D. degree from the Faculty of Law at that university, and is the author of studies in public administration and related subjects.

TAKESHI ISHIDA is a Professor at the Institute of Social Science, University of Tokyo. He has done advanced study in the United States under a Rockefeller Foundation grant, and he has been a Senior Specialist at the East-West Center, Hawaii. He has contributed to various Japanese and American publications and has written five books on Japanese politics.

VERNON J. PARRY is a Senior Lecturer in History at the School of Oriental and African Studies, University of London. He has contributed to the *New Cambridge Modern History,* the *Cambridge History of Islam* and the *Encyclopaedia of Islam.* He is currently writing a history of the Ottoman Empire.

HENRY SELBY is an Assistant Professor of Anthropology at the University of Texas. A classicist, he came to anthropology via graduate work in Roman religion. For six years he taught in a large London secondary school. He is the author of *Kinship & Social Organization* (with Ira Buchler, 1968) and *The Other Side of the Soul: The Ethnography of Deviance in a Mexican Indian Community* (forthcoming).

RUPERT WILKINSON is a Lecturer in American Studies at the University of Sussex. He spent his early life in the Philippines and has worked in publishing and for a United States commission on alcoholism. He is the author of *Gentlemanly Power* (British title: *The Prefects,* 1964) and *Winchester and the Public School Elite* (with T. J. H. Bishop, 1967).

Foreword

All the contributions to this volume were specially written for it, with the exception of Correlli Barnett's essay which was first published in the *Journal of Contemporary History,* London, July 1967. I am indebted to Jean Floud, Ronald Dore, and Bruce Coward for advice and encouragement in the organizing of this collection, and to the publishers and authors for their patience over many delays.

R.H.W.

Falmer, Sussex
March 1968

Contents

Introduction

This book is historical and cross-cultural. It views some ways in which selection and education have shaped governing elites. For our purposes, the term "elite" means a distinctive group holding high status in its community and knit together by a strong group feeling, ethos and style. Not every contributor to this volume would necessarily choose that definition for his own, but as a common denominator it will serve.[1]

In two senses the term is relative. First, it is relative to the community. On the factory floor, a guild of skilled workers may constitute an elite; so, in an army, may a "crack" regiment. One of the ways, indeed, whereby the term passed from French into English

[1] In this definition, "high status" refers to high status in the eyes of non-elite and the community as a whole. Elite members often feel themselves to have high status and to be in some way superior as a group: group ethos becomes in-group ethos and a true esprit de corps. But I would not make this further, subjective element part of the definition.

Beyond this, some sociologists have given complex and varied definitions, including the notions of social influence and respected attributes that exceed specific skills. On the other hand, current dictionary definitions are somewhat simpler than mine. "Elite" and "elect" both come, via the French, from the Latin, *eligere,* "to elect" or "choose out." There are sociologists who would use the term "elect" where I use "elite," but in my opinion "elect" has too much connotation of either political election or divine appointment to have this use. There is also the tendency among political sociologists to apply "elite" to any range of leaders holding the same kind of high position—thus, "business elite," "political elite"—but this deprives the term of its specific value.

usage was the notion of a *corps d'élite*. In the second place, high status, and sense of group are themselves relative attributes. Although in general one may usefully distinguish between "elite" and "non-elite" groups, there are often borderline cases. In America, for example, it has been a matter of controversy as to whether Presidential appointees and the pools from which they are drawn constitute an elite "establishment." That they enjoy high status is beyond dispute. But do they have enough in common, and *feel* they have enough in common, to warrant the term "elite?" Certainly the common elements of their experience in office provide some group character, some tendency to a distinctive and shared way of life. Taken alone, however, the shared consequences of office would not provide a very strong elite unity, especially since virtually none of the Presidential appointees have unbroken careers as long-time civil servants. To the extent that the appointees do form an elite, it is as part of a larger elite based on several supporting institutions—not only government, but certain types of company and law firm, major university faculties, foundations, and so forth. As is now well-known, a number of men have the common experience of a "musical chairs" career, shifting from institution to institution and meeting on various committees, commissions, and boards, both public and private. But this common experience affects the individual most at a relatively mature stage of his life—on the whole, a less formative period than in youth. There is no great bond rooted in a common and distinctive family background or formal education. Harvard, Yale, even Yale Law School, educate but a tiny percentage of America's top government executives, compared with the "Oxbridge" proportion in Britain, and the Tokyo University proportion in Japan. It is not surprising that the Washington-centered "establishment" must remain in quotation marks. It is not enough of a social group to have strong elite markings.[2]

[2] In American government, members of the Senate, especially the Senate "inner club," are made an elite by sustained adult influences centered on the political institution itself. Likewise for the senior members of the House Appropriations Committee, a very corporate body. The "top brass" of each armed service also forms an elite, due to the combination of shared high status, long and similar careers, and special training which stresses group loyalties.

So much for the word "elite." A few words should be added about the term *"governing* elite." In some pre-industrial societies, with a simple basic organization, all elites may be governing elites: that is, their primary functions may include leading their political community in a direct way. But in more complex societies, particularly those with a clear division between public life and private occupations, one can distinguish governing elites from other sorts of elite. Indirectly and over the long-term, *non*-governing elites—for example, an academy or in-group of distinguished writers and artists—may lead the community by influencing the culture, but in an immediate sense it cannot be said that helping to run the community is their primary function. By contrast, military elites are often a form of governing elite, for defense is a part of government and war an instrument of foreign policy. Priests and religious interpreters may also form or belong to governing elites in those societies where notions of public order, the community, and its well-being deeply involve religion. The *shaman* magicians warding off supernatural threats, the *ulama* interpreting the law of Islam, the bishops at the coronation of a European monarch—all constitute governing elites. It remains to be said that some elites are quasi-governmental (Russian technocrats?); that a person may belong to more than one type of elite at the same time; and that a number of elites may, to a varying extent, comprise one comprehensive elite.

The systems described in this book vary considerably. For one thing, some of the educational institutions are or were much more specifically tied to the notion of a governing elite than others. Even within ancient Greece, as Robert Bolgar shows, there was an immense difference between the training of the Spartan ruling caste and the education given to Athenian elites. Likewise, the very term "education" acquires an elastic meaning when it covers entities that range from the curricula of the French *grandes écoles* to the informal influences exerted by British civil servants in India upon their Indian colleagues and subordinates. There was also, of course, great variety in the criteria by which elites were selected. In his anthropological essay, Henry Selby suggests that elite selection systems can usually be thought of on a scale, or continuum, running from pure "birth" criteria at one end to achieved "merit" at the other. But the corollary is that most elite systems have in varying proportions combined elements of both. A striking and curious example of this is described by Vernon Parry in his study of the Ottoman Empire. At its high period, the Ottoman Muslim government was largely run by elites selected in the first instance according to rigid rules of origin: they were drawn in childhood or youth from non-Muslim captives of war and non-Muslim subjects. Furthermore, those selected became, in a technical sense, special slaves of the Sultan. And so they remained; yet among themselves, their promotion to higher and higher offices was meant to depend solely on merit; and they were in general cut off from family connections.[3]

There are also other anomalies—or what may seem to be anomalies from a present-day democratic standpoint. A training system which is fairly open in its recruitment, yet very much focused on producing an elite, may sometimes appear more elitist in the bent of its education than a relatively closed system, devoted to the training of a hereditary leadership class. Correlli Barnett gives tentative support to this idea in his chapter on military elites. West Point, he notes, has retained a much more traditionally "Prussian" discipline than Sandhurst and St.-Cyr. One reason for this may be that West Point draws cadets from more varied social backgrounds; hence, more conditioning is needed to give its intake a common group character. But this *homogenizing* process is also a *distinguishing* process, for it gives the officer cadet an intense social experience shared only with select fellows. The same process has been attributed to British public school training in the late nineteenth century.

[3] It is not known how far differences of family background subtly affected promotion and selection. But then in any society, to the extent that the behavior of individual parents has distinctive influences on their children, there can be no complete equality of opportunity—that is, equal opportunity for those of the same inborn qualities to reach high positions. The offspring of those already in high positions will tend to learn best the kinds of thought and expression needed to reach high positions themselves. From this standpoint, the egalitarians of modern society should seek to separate children from their parents in infancy, if they cannot insure that all occupational positions are to be equally "top." The Ottoman system went some of the way toward this, for the non-Muslims recruited into the state elites were converted to Islam and their progeny usually disqualified from the same elites. (The fathers had often married Muslims of high birth.)

The main elaboration of public school custom, etiquette, and ritual, seems to have come after the schools began receiving large numbers from the rising bourgeoisie. In part, this elaboration may have originated with the new recruits themselves—the tendency of a certain type of middle-class mind to imitate and systematize the manners of gentry "birth and breeding." The apparent result, however, was a public school response to more open recruitment, a response which accentuated elitism in the actual training given.[4]

A final point of comparison and contrast lies in the approaches taken by the authors to their studies. On the whole, it is fair to say that the contributions represent various mixtures of the sociological and historical. But even this is a simplification. The disadvantage of such a variety is that it does not yield a plainly laid-out comparison of the different elite systems. It does, however, demonstrate some of the many ways in which elite selection can be viewed (even without much emphasis on the psychological dimensions of the subject: for instance, the impact of training and selection on personality).

In addition to describing the various systems, nearly all the authors mention some of the systems' successes and liabilities. That, in the main, they should only do so in a cursory way is not surprising. How does one judge the success of an elite selection and training system? Even if one applies only those criteria which would be respected in the culture concerned, there are a number of possible tests and therefore considerable leeway for subjective choice by the author. In the last essay, I examine some of these criteria of success, and show how they may be compatible in some ways but not in

---

[4] I have described further the curious ways in which rationalist devices for mobility and aesthetic devices for elitism may interlock, in my comparison of British public schools with Imperial Chinese education: *Gentlemanly Power,* Oxford University Press, New York, 1964, especially Chapter 12. (Published by Oxford University Press, London, as *The Prefects.*) The mystique and function of examinations are one important aspect: see also the Japanese and French studies in the present volume.

The systems described here are not the same as the mobile-elite societies described by Henry Selby, in which elites are selected from relatively formal training systems shared with the non-elite. In these cases, the marking out and molding of the elite does depend heavily on group influences after the period of training. To a varying extent, however, training overlaps social influences in adulthood.

others. Following this, a few general observations are made about the advantages and disadvantages of elitist education as a social and political institution.

Rupert Wilkinson

GOVERNING ELITES

HENRY SELBY

Elite Selection and Social Integration: An Anthropologist's View

Anthropologists often like to think of themselves as devil's advocates. As soon as a general statement about human beings is made, it is hotly contested by the anthropologist because "they don't do it that way in Basutoland." In this essay I will try to be more constructive. By using the anthropologist's knowledge of a vast range of societies all over the world, I will attempt to make some general statements about the formation and education of elites.

The anthropologist deals for the most part with what are often called "primitive societies." These societies are usually illiterate (though not always, especially these days), and generally at a low level of technology. They are, to be sure, very different from our own society, and perhaps for that reason we can gain a good deal of perspective both on them and, by comparison, on ourselves. Almost any outsider who has lived in one of these societies is shocked and, above all, bewildered by the difference between himself and the subjects of his investigation. Only with great difficulty can he make broad sense of the daily activities, ways of thinking, and modes of living of the people he is supposed to be understanding. Because he can only see things in broad outline the "woods for the trees" problem is for practical purposes solved for him. Those are all he can see and understand.

We will consider, then, two aspects of the whole complex of activities called elite education. First, there is the *selection* of the elite. What are the different ways in which a society can select its elite

3

members, and what effect does a particular selection process have
on the structure of the society as a whole? Second, there is the problem of *communication* between the elite and other classes of society. "Communication" is used in its broadest sense, meaning the
transfer of information between individuals or from one group of
people to another. Learning how to communicate, what to communicate, and learning the assumptions that underlie and guide proper
communication are exceedingly important in the education of any
elite class. Communication can take a myriad of forms, all having
the meaning that any society chooses to make of them. A punch on
the nose is sometimes a very effective means of communicating; so
is a gesture, a manner of speaking, or a way of carrying oneself.
Communication in an elite society serves two ends. It binds the society together, or *integrates* it, so that people co-operate in their
work and social activity to keep the society going economically and
ritually, and do not split off into separate groups. But at the same
time it emphasizes the necessary social distinctions between the
groups. We will be particularly interested in studying how the children in an elite society learn to communicate so that these two ends,
integration and maintenance of social distinctiveness, are achieved.

We can start the examination of elite society with the selection
process. When we talk about selection we are referring to the recognition of certain characteristics that a society declares to be important in distinguishing elite people from non-elite. Broadly, we can
say there are two kinds of characteristics: those that a person is
born with and those that a person acquires during his life. If the
elite is selected from a pool of people whose identity is determined
at birth, we will call the society an immobile elite society. And conversely, if the elite is selected from a pool of people, not determined
at birth, who have managed to acquire during the course of their
education and training a certain characteristic (or roster of characteristics), we shall call such societies mobile societies. Most elites
depend on both hereditary and merit criteria, but often they tend
to one or the other extreme. This distinction between two extreme
or "ideal" types, mobile societies and immobile, is important because each has very different problems in maintaining an integrated, cohesive society. We shall first discuss immobile societies,

reviewing the nature of various selection procedures and continuing with a discussion of two complex, immobile societies, the Inca and the Aztec; and then we shall discuss mobile societies.

Selection criteria vary widely, and take very unusual forms to our eyes. The Mundugumor of New Guinea, for instance, know who are going to be members of an elite artist class because all artists are born with the umbilical cord twisted around the throat. According to Margaret Mead:[1]

> Men and women born to the arts need not practice them unless they wish, but no one who lacks the mark of his calling can hope to be more than the clumsiest apprentice.

More often people are classified elite or non-elite according to their parentage. The Spartiate caste in Sparta, the Eupatridae in Athens, the first-born sons of Samoan chiefs, the royal princes in African kingdoms represent selection of elite members by birth.

Perhaps most interesting of all is the choice of people according to certain personality characteristics considered inborn and not the product of training. Societies exist with elite classes made up of very strange types of people; strange, that is, to our mind. Megalo-maniacs in Kwakiutl society,[2] paranoid misers in Yurok,[3] dreamers in Menominee[4] all formed elite groups.

The Chuckchee of Siberia[5] selected what we would call schizo-phrenics for their elite shaman class. They were a reindeer-herding people of the Siberian steppe who lived most times close to the margin of starvation. They had chiefs who were responsible for the executive decisions of the group, but above the chief was the shaman, the magician who controlled the spirits. On one famous occasion when a plague was raging among a group of Chuckchee, the shamans demanded the death of the chief. So popular was the chief that no one could be found to put him to death until the chief

---

[1] Margaret Mead, *Sex and Temperament,* New York, 1960, p. 135.
[2] An American Indian people of the Pacific Coast region.
[3] An American Indian people of California.
[4] An American Indian people of Wisconsin.
[5] The main source for the Chuckchee is Waldemar Bogoras, *The Chuckchee,* Anthropological Memoirs, American Museum of Natural History, New York, 1904-1909.

himself, bowing to an authority greater than his own, besought his own son to slay him. So strong was the fear of the shamans, and so deeply rooted the feeling that only they could shield the tribe from the evil spirits, that the luckless son plunged a knife in his father's heart and handed the body over to the all-powerful magicians.

Shamans were vital for the Chuckchee, for their spirit world was well populated with dangerous phantoms, thought to stalk the camp with gaping mouths, to enter the houses and kill the people. It was believed that shamans could control the spirits, and through this control bring death upon a person. Their skill in sleight-of-hand and magical tricks over-awed the people. They were a highly skilled professional class.

The young men most suited to this profession were the nervous and highly excitable. Waldemar Bogoras describes them as being near the point of constant hysteria; a few of them were, in his terms, "half crazy." Often extremely withdrawn, they were also highly sensitive; should the ghost of a sneer be exhibited during their performance they would simply stop. When they sat to converse they would stare into empty space and stay silent for long periods. If they were balked in their career by parents or relatives, they would simply sicken and die. The shaman spent a good deal of his time in sleep, but if by chance he should set out from the camp he would wander for days and lose himself in the steppe and be likely to die from exposure unless found by searching relatives. He was subject to visions. When called to his work he lost interest in ordinary affairs, ceased to do the herding work, ceased to talk to people around him, and would not even answer their questions.

In short the Chuckchee shaman was a roster of psychotic symptoms. In this society the very people whom we would relegate to the margin of society, and probably place in a mental institution, became in effect the ruling elite.

Since normally one does not study to be a schizophrenic, education would contribute very little to the formation of this elite class. To be sure the Chuckchee shamans had to perform prodigious feats of drumming, lasting for days on end, and they had to master a few magical tricks. But these feats were supposedly learned from the spirits themselves, and there was no socially recognized or institutionalized form of training. Shamans were recruited from a group of people recognized in childhood, people we would probably call mentally disturbed.[6]

Selection in immobile societies is a simple matter. Only a few well-marked people are available for elite positions, and the majority of them occupy these positions. The umbilically twisted New Guinean becomes an elite artist; the first-born Samoan becomes head of his lineage; the schizophrenic Siberian, a shaman. The content of education depends on a number of things. First, if there are specific tasks to be done, these must be learned. Second, if there is a specific kind of character to be formed, training must be undertaken to form that kind of character. In a complex caste system, as in pre-Independence India, each caste must teach its young members how to fulfill the caste's tasks; sweepers must learn to sweep, leather workers to make leather, and so on. Ritual observances that unite the caste and differentiate it from others must be learned. The bearing or deportment of each caste must be learned by its members so that they can express proper caste relations in everyday behavior. We will discuss all of these in the treatment of Inca and Aztec education.

But perhaps the most important problem that society as a whole must solve has to do with communication between the social groups, or social integration and cohesion. Ideally, everyone should believe that the social structure is "right," "natural," or "traditional," and that any deviation would be "wrong," "unnatural," or against the will of the ancestral spirits or established religion. Often societies are not able to obtain such a consensus from all members. The issues of communication and integration become most pressing in those cases where the distance between groups is very great, and the lower group feels that it is largely deprived of the means of satisfying bodily and spiritual needs. Maintaining great social distance and loyalty to the community is a difficult undertaking, and usually strong countermeans are necessary to prevent the socially

[6] This is not, of course, to contend that schizophrenic symptoms are always recognizable in childhood, or that schizophrenia, as defined in Western cultures, is solely and invariably inborn. The point remains that the Chuckchee *considered* their shamans' essential qualities to be inborn, not learned.

inferior groups from breaking away. These countermeans may take the form of terror or coercion, as with the Negro in nineteenth-century America. This example is particularly instructive because we can see a society maintaining itself despite drastic exertions on the part of outsiders to change it. When the formal, legal apparatus for maintaining social distinctions was removed with the abolition of slavery, new social groups were mobilized to apply informal pressures against change. Poor and uneducated whites, drawn largely from classes which had never owned slaves, were empowered, informally, to maintain the ante-bellum social structure through terror—lynchings and beatings. In this they were aided by practices which withheld from the Negro the right to vote, the chance of a fair trial, and other benefits of justice.

Stark coercion, unsupported by other devices, is usually unsuccessful over long periods of time. Its very violence breeds instability and tends to encourage counterviolence, which can destroy the society. Much more effective and much more common is the expression of differences in group status through ritual observances. When a Brahmin presides at the wedding of a sweeper and the latter clears the offal from the Brahmin's courtyard, we are witnessing more than a purely economic exchange of services. The symbolic aura of each of these offices affirms the ranking of each in relation to the other. The context of the exchange and the ceremony make the ranking of the castes quite explicit. This form of communicating status differences between recognized groups within a society is very common and can be seen in such acts as the dramatically symbolic custom of *jus primae noctis* (or *droit du seigneur*) where the villein of medieval Europe exchanged his bride's virginity in return for part quittance of the lord's authority over her. These ceremonies have an unmistakable meaning for both parties, symbolizing, or communicating, the differences in rank between them.

The elite class may communicate its superiority in various ways. It must carry out its valuable tasks effectively. A Brahmin must execute his priestly duties, a shaman his magical rites, a warrior his martial offices, and so on. Second, an elite class must so carry itself that in its meetings with people of a lower class it exhibits the qualities of manner and bearing that affirm superior status. A

Roman senator must so wear his toga that clearly he possesses the dignity that gives him his special authority. In training an elite, then, care must be exercised to ensure that members know how to do certain things and do them in specified ways, ways that are valued by the whole of society. These emphases can be seen quite clearly in the training of Inca and Aztec children of the upper classes.

The Inca were an immobile society. By A.D. 1100 they had established their domination in highland Peru and they maintained an empire, expanding and consolidating it, for 400 years until the arrival of the Spanish. The empire had four provinces, and within these provinces households were organized into hundreds, the hundreds into thousands, and an administrative official put in charge of each group. The pyramid of power went all the way up to the emperor, or Inca; and through this bureaucracy, taxation (in kind), forced labor, military conscription, and national enterprises were organized. The efficiency of the system has excited the admiration of most chroniclers and commentators.

There were two classes, nobles and peasants. There was extremely little mobility, and the marking characteristic of the upper class was one of birth—"blood." Training was of immense importance in the marking and maintenance of elite status. The Inca Rocca, who founded the first schools in the empire, was, according to Garcilasco de La Vega,

> opposed to all popular education and ordered that the children of the common people should not learn the sciences, which should be known only to the nobles, lest the lower classes become proud and endanger the commonwealth. The common people were to be taught the occupations of their fathers, which was enough for them.[7]

The schools were for the nobility. The upper class was schooled in its own traditions, the glories of empire, and the legends of their fathers' heroism. The aesthetic side was not neglected. Religion,

---

[7] Garcilasco de la Vega, *The First Part of the Royal Commentaries of the Yncas,* tr. and ed. by Clements R. Markham, London, 1869-71. Quoted in Joseph Bram, *An Analysis of Inca Militarism,* Seattle, 1941, p. 76.

astrology, music, philosophy, and history were included in the curriculum.

There were four years of instruction in the House of Teaching at Cuzco, the capital of the Incas. As Edward Hyams and George Ordish have described it:

> The word university is not altogether out of place, for the dons, *amauta-cuna,* and *haravec-cuna* lived in the college . . . and gave a set course of lectures; it might, however, be nearer the mark to compare this institution to the house of a teaching order of monks. The House of Teaching was an important national institution with a great influence in government circles.[8]

The general purpose of Inca education was described by Garcilasco de la Vega:

> The schools were not established for the teaching of letters, for these people had none; but to instruct the pupils concerning their rights, (the) precepts and ceremonies of their . . . religion, and the principles of their laws and customs, with their correct interpretation. It was intended that they should thus attain a knowledge of the art of governing and become more refined and assiduous in the military art. The pupils were also taught the methods of computing time, and of recording events by means of knots, as well as to converse with elegance and grace. . . . They were, then, instructed in the arts of poetry, music, philosophy and astrology.[9]

The first year of their training was devoted to the learning of the national language—Quechua, the second year to religion, the third year to the use of *quipus,* or knotted ropes which the Incas used for mnemonic devices, and in the final year the history of the nation was studied. During the whole period military training was emphasized, and justifiably so, because the relations between the nobility and peasantry were based on coercion and resembled nothing so much as the relations between the Spartans and their helots in seventh and sixth century Lacedaemon. Fittingly enough the four

---

[8] Edward Hyam and George Ordish, *The Last of the Incas,* London, 1963, p. 106.
[9] Garcilasco de la Vega, in Bram, op. cit., p. 76.

years of study were capped by a "Spartan" examination which Louis Baudin has described:

> The whole course of instruction culminated in an examination of a military nature called *huaracu,* which took place every year or two years at Cuzco, and made it possible for the Inca to assure himself that the future members of the élite were competent to be army leaders. The candidates were first put on a diet of pure water and raw maize, without pimento or salt for six days. Then they were properly fed, and took part in a race at the gates of the city under the eyes of the various families who encouraged them by their shouts, extolled the winners and flung reproaches at the laggards. After this the youths, divided now into two camps, would fight against each other with such zeal that occasionally some of them would be wounded or even killed. The physical exercises were concluded with wrestling and with archery, and slingshot matches. These were followed by moral tests. The candidate had to stand watch ten nights in succession and remain impassive even when the chief made a feint of smashing his skull with a club or running his face through with the point of a lance. Finally he had to prove his technical knowledge by making a bow, a sling, and a pair of sandals.
>
> The candidate who at any point whatsoever evinced fear or fatigue was eliminated in disgrace. On the other hand the youth who had been judged well trained and endowed with sufficient resistance to pain was received by the Inca, who, in the course of a magnificent ceremony, himself pierced the lobes of his ears. The young man had a right, from that time on, to wear enormous earrings, the dimensions of which were proportional to his social rank.[10]

In the light of the Inca example we can review the processes of selection, integration, and communication. Selection was very simple. Family indicated blood; nobility was hereditary. Since the Inca were immobile, relegating the peasants to a lower status, they were faced with the problem of keeping the society together—the problem of integration, as well as the problem of so communicating with

[10] Louis Baudin, *A Socialist Empire. The Incas of Peru,* tr. by Katherine Woods, and ed. by Arthur Goddard, Princeton, N.J., 1961, pp. 45-6.

the lower orders as to maintain the status difference. Loyalty to the social order was maintained by coercion. Bureaucracy backed by armed force administered the empire. In addition, the nobles wore distinctive clothes and ornaments, such as earrings. Their speech, elegant and refined, bespoke a training in culture and an upper-class tradition which were totally foreign to the peasant. They showed physical endurance in the face of danger, evenness of temper, and military skill. The fact that the nobility embodied the high tradition of the Inca empire and exhibited to a marked degree the martial traits that all admired, lent a feeling of "rightness" to their high position, and encouraged loyalty to the society by all. In this way the upper classes achieved a consent by the governed, which in turn made for stability. So well marked and distinctive was the nobility of the Inca state, that after the Spanish conquest the peasantry saw no incongruity or discontinuity in the change of masters, and continued serving another equally distinctive elite group in the same way as they had served their Quechua-speaking masters. The system could accommodate Spanish rule quite easily, and the structure of the Inca state remained practically unchanged down to the Peruvian war of independence.

Quite independently, toward the end of the florescence of the Inca Empire and a thousand miles and more to the north, the Nahuatl-speaking Aztec tribe rose to a sudden and meteoric eminence among the people of the Central Mexican Highlands. The Aztecs carried their distinctive form of war, "the flowery war," to their neighbors, terrorizing them by their ferocity, carrying their young men off to sacrifice on the altars of the savage war-god Huitzilopochtli, who demanded his sustenance of throbbing hearts torn from living bodies.

For the Aztecs the problems of the elite society were slightly different from those of the Inca. Whereas the Inca had over time consolidated their empire and stabilized their society, the Aztec appearance in history was so darting that our picture is of an immobile elite society in formation. The Aztecs lived among their enemies, a bully nation meting out stern revenge for disobedience or failure to render tribute, forever seeking new tribes to conquer in order to feed the ever-hungry god. In Aztec society and its methods of teaching the young we see the problems of maintaining a national elite in a dynamic, unstable situation of near constant expansion and extension. We are watching the birth of an empire.

Manhood was of supreme importance to the Aztecs. All man-power resources had to be used, and used well, if the empire was to be sustained and expanded. Within the state there were two social orders, an upper class of nobles (*tecuhtli*) and a lower military and commercial class of commoners (*maceualli*).

Each class had its own type of school. The *pilli* (sons of the *tecuhtli*) attended schools presided over by the god Quetzalcoatl. They became his priests, although they became many other things besides: warrior leaders, justices, civil servants, and government officials. The *maceualli* attended military schools presided over by Huitzilopochtli. Class barriers did not completely exclude the sons of the *maceualli* from entering the schools of the upper class *pilli;* in theory it was possible for a father to enroll his child in whichever school he wanted. Nevertheless, such mobility seems to have been rare. Government leaders, priests, and important merchants sent their sons to the elite schools, while the commoners, the soldiers, petty merchants, and non-administrative officials attended the schools of Huitzilopochtli, where education was practical and directed at training the youth for war.

The schools of the *pilli,* which trained the imperial elite, were very different. Quetzalcoatl, the supreme god of the Aztec pantheon, presided over them. He was the god of justice and moral probity, god of life, creator, and endless benefactor of mankind, discoverer of maize and jade, and inventor of the calendar. Under his aegis the students were schooled in ethics, morality, and self-discipline. They were trained to be calm and judicious, to hold themselves above the common people with a Roman *gravitas*. They were trained to speak well, to master the very formal speech patterns which were almost a language apart from the demotic Nahuatl spoken by the commoners. The children were proved and tested by being forced to carry out the most demeaning, menial tasks, and were sternly punished both by their senior students and by their mentors if they defaulted. The historian Bernadino de Sahagún describes the scholars' duties:

> They would sweep and clean the house at four in the morning.
> . . . The older boys would go out and look for maguey thorns.
> . . . They would bring wood that was necessary for burning in
> the house at night. . . .
>
> They would stop their work a little early and then they would
> go straight to their temple to attend the services of their gods,
> and the exercises of penitence, and to bathe first . . . The meals
> they ate, they cooked in . . . (the school). . . . At the setting
> of the sun they would begin to prepare the necessary things. . . .
> Every night at midnight they would get up to pray, and whoever
> did not get up would be punished by piercing his ears, his chest,
> thighs and legs.[11]

They had to perform the tasks of women, girls, and menials; they
learned to serve and humble themselves before people of wisdom
and authority. Discipline was severe, much more severe than in the
schools of the commoners. According to Sahagún, a boy entering
the school for the first time around the age of fifteen was told by
his father:

> Listen, my son, you are not going to be honored, nor obeyed,
> nor esteemed. You are going to be looked down upon, humiliated
> and despised. Every day you will cut agave thorns for penance,
> and you will draw blood from your body with these spines and
> you will bathe at night even when it is very cold. . . . Harden
> your body to the cold . . . and when the time comes for fast-
> ing, do not go and break your fast, but put a good face upon
> both fasting and penitence.[12]

Every night the boy's sleep was interrupted; often he was compelled
to join a procession to the mountains carrying incense and offering
prayers to Quetzalcoatl. For failure to work hard at whatever task,
however demeaning, for every error, he was punished.

The staple of his education was speech and rhetoric in the very
fine Nahuatl tradition, which has endured to this day. He learned
to carry himself with gravity, to be courteous and yet demand the

[11] Fr. Bernadino de Sahagún, *Historia General de las Cosas de Nueva
España,* Mexico, 1938, I, 327. Quoted in Leon-Portilla, *Aztec Thought and
Culture,* tr. by Jack Emory Davis, Norman, Okla., 1963, p. 139.
[12] Sahagún, op. cit. Quoted in Jacques Soustelle, *The Daily Life of the
Aztecs,* tr. by Patrick O'Brian, Harmondsworth, Eng., 1964, p. 176.

respect of others. And he learned how he was different from other, lesser men, how his class was different from and superior to the *maceualli*. In other words he was given a distinctive training which set him apart from the commoners, and he was educated in the rules of conduct which affirmed and maintained the social distance between himself and those of lower degree. He shared a stern initiation only with his fellow *pilli* and joined with them in the worship and cult of the all-high god, as befitted his station.

By comparison with the Inca upper class, the Aztec elite was more open. As we have already noted, *maceualli* could attend the schools of the *pilli*. The formal structure of the society was nevertheless immobile. Few of the *meceualli* in fact entered the elite schools and became members of the ruling class. Communication of elite status to the *maceualli* was based on distinctions of manner, dress, and ritual function. For the society as a whole education served two ends. First, it trained the upper class in its duties of administration and leadership in war, while training the lower classes to serve. Second, it educated all people in the social distinctions necessary for a stable military régime.

At the other end of the scale from the immobile Inca and Aztec societies are those where the opportunity of becoming a member of the elite group is open to all. In these mobile societies the pool or population from which the selection for elite status is made is relatively large, encompassing in its extreme form the whole society. Qualities which mark an elite person are not strictly the prerogative of a small group, but can be acquired by all. We might feel that, since mobile societies are closer to our notions of what a society should be, their criteria for elite status might be like our own. But, as in immobile societies, the range of criteria is very wide.

For example, among the Iatmul of New Guinea, studied thirty years ago by Gregory Bateson, there exists an elite of old men who have gained great power and influence through the memorization of totemic names. Bateson says these names are

> . . . all of them compounds, each containing four to six syllables, and they refer to details of esoteric mythology, so that each name has at least a leaven of meaning in it. The names are

arranged in pairs, and the names in any one pair generally resemble each other much as the word Tweedledum resembles the
word Tweedledee—with the notable difference that the altered
syllables generally have some meaning and are connected together by some simple type of association e.g. either by contrast
or synonymy.[13]

This pedantic elite is called upon in the debates of the clans and
also in the settlement of disputes of every kind, from initiation to
land tenure. Excellence in the recitation of totemic names gives the
speaker the authority to arrange the affairs of the people in practical spheres as well. In other words, there are few restrictions even
in mobile societies on the criteria that may be used for the selection
of elites.

But mobile societies encounter a different sort of situation when
they come to deal with the problem of communication and integration—as an extended analysis and example will show. Take a society in which everyone is permitted to strive for the valued goals
of the group (symbolized by elite status). Given any group of
human beings, there will be some who will overpass the goals, much
as the miser overdoes the middle-class ideal of thrift; there will be
some who cannot attain the goals at all because of indequate capacity; and there will be some who will combine the perfect mixture
of qualities which will enable them to reach the goal. Integration
in these societies is an exceedingly difficult problem because there
are no ritual barriers to constrain people within their allotted
classes; furthermore, the "mystique" of eliteness will be largely
eroded because each member has had a training or education which
is roughly the same. Since some will fail and others will over-suc-
ceed to the point of ineffectiveness, the problem is simply to deal
with failure. If the misfits, disgruntled from a sense of failure, become alienated from the society, then that society begins to break
apart. A satisfying role must be found for such people.

This is precisely the problem of pariah classes in liberal societies,
the problem upon which Gunnar Myrdal focussed the American
attention.[14] In a society where the goals are open, people who are

[13] Gregory Bateson, *Naven*, Stanford, Calif., 1958, p. 222.
[14] Gunnar Myrdal, *An American Dilemma*, New York, 1944.

deprived are a good deal worse off than in a closed or immobile society where goals are shaped for each group separately.

Rather than think that such problems are insoluble, let us look at one society which found solutions in a dramatic and startling way—the Plains Indian societies as they were known in the nineteenth century. Life on the American plains is harsh and requires an endurance that few can claim. The soil is fertile now, but before the introduction of the mold-board plow it resisted intensive agriculture. In the summer the rain is sparse and when it comes it often pours down in flash thunderstorms that are almost as damaging as drought. The wind is an enemy. There are no artificial or natural barriers to break its force, and when it blows across the flatness, the dust swirls and burns, the eyes smart, and the body aches with the impact. When the norther blows, the temperature can drop thirty to forty degrees in an incredibly short time, and an autumn day can turn into a winter's blizzard in a matter of hours. It is a harsh and forbidding climate.

Here, during the eighteenth and nineteenth centuries, lived the Plains Indians, tribes of famous name: Cheyenne, Crow, Arapaho, Comanche, Blackfoot. These Indians were known for their endurance, their physical courage, and their bellicosity. The Indian child was early indoctrinated into the beliefs and values of his people. While he was loved and greatly indulged by his parents in a way that white people still felt to be too pampering, he was also taught, and taught young, that whimpering and demanding brought no results.[15] Every manly exploit that a boy performed was richly rewarded. At about the age of five he was given a toy bow and arrow, fashioned by his father, and was sent out to shoot little birds and to practice for the hunt with his age group. When he brought in his first kill, relatives would present him with gifts, and his father would go about the camp telling of his son's deeds in a loudly rhetorical voice. When he was ten he would be taken along on the buffalo hunt, and if he managed to shoot a buffalo, a feast would be given and gifts presented, and again the boy's prowess would be proclaimed throughout the camp.

[15] In some of these societies a child who whimpered and cried was simply hung in its cradleboard on a tree, out of earshot, until he stopped.

The Indian boy learned that a man had to be enduring, coura-
geous, and generous and carefree with his property, even his wife.

> When an Arapaho chief was having a scalp shirt made for him
> (a very serious undertaking) word was brought to him that his
> wife had run off with another man. He merely filled his pipe and
> passed it to the other man saying he had no fault to find with her.
> . . . Chiefs, when such advantage is taken of them, sometimes
> show their superiority to the indignity by remarking most cas-
> ually . . . "A dog has pissed on my tipi."[16]

The Cheyenne chief embodied the virtues and values of his tribe.
Continence and self-restraint were important. A highly respected
warrior was known to have slept alongside his wife and had no
intercourse with her for twelve years (she had never conceived a
child though perfectly capable). This remarkable restraint earned
him the respect of all, and was felt to conserve his strength and
enhance his warriorhood. In the words of one who knew the Cheyenne early and well:

> A good chief gave his whole heart and his whole mind to the
> work of helping his people, and strove for their welfare with an
> earnestness and devotion rarely equalled by rulers of other men.
> Yet though simple, honest, generous, tender-hearted and often
> merry and jolly, when occasion demanded he could be stern,
> severe, and inflexible of purpose.[17]

The Plains Indians were warring tribes and their lives were in constant danger. They never knew when an enemy might sweep down
upon them or when, away from the camp, they would fall into an
ambush. They exalted the tribal virtue of manly excellence, and
especially honored a man who could leap inside an enemy's battle-
ments on horseback or on foot, and "count coûp"—that is touch an
armed enemy and escape unharmed. To exhibit bravery was far
more important than to kill. The man who had counted coûp many
times was the most highly regarded of all and was granted special
privileges within the camp. The man who had never counted coûp
was no man at all.

[16] E. A. Hoebel, *The Cheyenne*, New York, 1960, p. 38.
[17] George Grinnell, *The Cheyenne Indians*, New Haven, Conn., 1923.

Among the Cheyenne the elite was formally recognized in the "Council of Forty-four." The members of this Council were chosen by co-optation.[18] They were men who best embodied all the virtues that the society emphasized. The Council made the important tribal decisions, and debated on such matters as moving camp, undertaking a tribal war, or seeking an alliance with another tribe. Sometimes there were wide differences of opinion, yet the debates were conducted with a courtesy, respect, and gravity that precluded any wrangling or depreciation of others. This elite Council also debated important criminal cases, and made legislative and judicial decisions of the highest order of complexity. Their sagacity and prestige were so great that no decision taken by them could be combatted.

Yet not all men could embody the values of the Cheyenne. Not all could be judicious warriors of great courage in battle and prudence in council. Some lacked judgment, while demonstrating courage to the point of foolhardiness. Others were timid, by the measure of their society. The foolhardy would rush imprudently along the line of the enemy, or throw themselves into the fight in such a way that only with singular good fortune would they escape death. In some of the Plains Indian tribes it was thought that such men no longer cared to live; the Crow called them "Crazy-Dogs-Wishing-to-Die." But among the Cheyenne they were thought to have received assurance from the spirits in a dream or vision, that they were fanatics in battle and pledged to recklessness. Whereas most Indians under attack felt obliged to do no more than stand their ground, the Contraries (as they were called in Cheyenne) deliberately courted death, recklessly dashing up to the enemy, often to be killed in the space of one season. Deviants they were in the sense that they exaggerated the warrior's code of their society and lacked the calm judiciousness that was also prized, but they were given an honorable place in the group, though excluded from its councils and its leadership. Though they had lost the race for pre-eminence in the society they could still exercise their special talents in an honorable way.

The Cheyenne also gave a dramatic role to deviants at the other end of the scale of manly valor—the timid. These persons (again

[18] Election by existing members—*Ed.*

interpreting a vision) donned women's clothes and took up women's labors, often becoming homosexuals and at times "wives" to other warriors. They were called *berdaches* and held an important place in the society.[19] Sometimes they were credited with greater spirit-vision or they were acknowledged masters (or mistresses) of women's skills, such as quilling or beading. At the most important dance of the year a *berdache* was called upon to plant the first pole of the Sun Dance Lodge. Their voices sometimes changed to a shrill effeminate tone, and if they chose to become homosexuals, they always took the passive role in sexual intercourse. Theirs was an honored place, and women would send their girls to them to learn the trades from those who knew them best. They were, of course, liberated from the dangers of the battlefield, but war parties liked to have their company, not only for their medical skill, but also because they were socially graceful and entertaining. Young people sought them out because they possessed the most powerful love medicines. In short, though deviant in the sense that they were incapable of carrying off the role of the judicious warrior, they were not relegated to a place of dishonor among their fellows; on the contrary, they were given a place of esteem and tasks of difficulty.

In examining the society of the Plains Indians we can see that a tremendous emphasis was put upon manly courage and enterprise in every facet of their training. This emphasis received constant testing and reinforcement in their everyday lives. The elite of the society were those people who embodied the values of bravery, fortitude, steadfastness, dash, élan, tempered with a judicious concern for the preservation of the tribe, continence, self-restraint, and respect for others. Those who deviated from these values either by exaggerating the warrior at the expense of the statesman, or by failing to meet the warrior's code at all, were given useful and respected roles. People who might have been social wreckers performed functions which benefited society as a whole.

The Cheyenne serve as a particularly good example of a highly mobile society that chose its elite on merit and performance. They solved the problem of educating all while relegating none, of estab-

[19] Hoebel, op. cit.

lishing ties between elite and non-elite groups. Through these ties —or through this communication, to use our more general term— the co-operative basis of the society was maintained in the joint pursuit of goals which were common to all. They had solved the central problem of specialized function, co-ordinated with integrated action, while admitting all to the striving for goals.

In conclusion, we can look at these matters from a slightly different point of view. Every society has the problem of social integration. It has to arrange its affairs so that the society hangs together and everybody does what he has to do to keep the society going. In a tiny homogeneous society where the division of labor and resources is simple, there are few problems. Every adult male does approximately the same thing, as does every adult female. But when the society becomes more complicated, begins to divide up its essential jobs among different groups of people, distributes its resources in unequal proportions, and establishes an elite group, then the problems of maintaining an integrated society become acute. Using examples studied by anthropologists, we have suggested two contrasting types of elite society. Immobile, or caste, societies solved this problem both by coercion and by weaving between groups a network of ritual ties that were accepted by all. They devised specialized training so that a different set of skills, and a separate ideology would be learned by each group. Mobile societies created satisfactory positions for those who did not "make the grade." They educated all for the highest places in a common educational program and then provided satisfactory alternative roles for those who were excluded from elitehood.

But no society, not even those we have described as examples, is a pure type in the sense that it is completely mobile or completely immobile. Societies lean to being one yet include characteristics of the other. Birth and merit are always considerations in forming an elite. Sadly for social utopias, genes will out, personality and capability are in part genetically determined, and in virtually any social system the son of an elite father has a better chance of becoming a member of the elite than the son of a non-elite father, provided the selection criteria do not change. Using the simpler societies as illustrations of certain principles of elite selection and training, we have arrived at the following tentative conclusion. To the degree that a society recruits members for elite positions from a restricted group of individuals (immobile societies), special training, separate ritual functions, special knowledge, and distinctive deportment will be emphasized in the training of the young. And conversely, to the degree that a society recruits members for elite positions from all the people (mobile societies), training will be directed at instilling elite values in all; but separate-but-equal roles may be provided for those who do not "make the grade."

ROBERT R. BOLGAR

The Training of Elites in Greek Education

Our histories of ancient education begin with the *Iliad*. They cite the relationship between Phoenix and Achilles and use it to prove that the Homeric heroes made special provision for the upbringing of their young. They ask us to believe that way back in the Dark Age of Greece, if not in Mycenaean times, there were privileged groups who employed tutors to secure the transmission of their skills and beliefs; and that this practice then set its stamp on all that followed.

The thesis that Greek education had aristocratic beginnings and never lost its aristocratic orientation was forcefully stated in Werner Jaeger's *Paideia* and has received a great volume of support since it was first formulated:

> For many centuries, indeed we might say to the end of its history, the education of antiquity was to retain many of the features which it received from its knightly and aristocratic origin. . . . Even when these (i.e. the Greek) societies wanted to be democratic and thought they were so, they lived in a tradition which was noble in origin. . . . It is not difficult to see here a parallel with the development of French and modern Western civilization, which had progressively extended to all social classes, and perhaps vulgarized, a culture whose origin and inspiration were indubitably aristocratic.[1]

[1] H. I. Marrou, *A History of Education in Antiquity,* tr. by G. Lamb, London, 1956, p. 8.

23

Jaeger's view—with its romantic overtones—has come to be so widely held, that the thinness of its supporting evidence necessarily takes one by surprise.

The Homeric poems were composed—in something like their present form—between the close of the ninth century and the early decades of the seventh.[2] They had behind them a massive oral tradition accustomed to celebrate the Mycenaean past as a heroic age. But this past was not clearly remembered. The centuries which had intervened between the fall of Troy and the poetic exploitation of its story had been sufficient in the absence of written records to obscure not only the events and personalities, but also the social conditions of the vanished Mycenaean culture. The author of the *Chanson de Roland* knew more about the historical Charlemagne than Homer about Agamemnon.

Consequently, when a bard found himself ignorant of Mycenaean conditions, he filled the gap by depicting the customs and artefacts of the world he and his listeners knew; or deliberately archaizing, he made use of a less remote past which was still remembered. We find in the *Iliad* and *Odyssey* three types of data: the distortions of legend, contemporary detail, and a residue from the earlier part of the so-called Dark Age. Dating the references that the poems make to social conditions is therefore a hazardous task without evidence from outside sources.

The historian who wants to use Homer's statements about education must come to terms with this difficulty. He must also take into account the fact that the relevant texts can be interpreted in a variety of ways. Take the passage about Phoenix[3] which is supposed to show that the sons of the Homeric aristocracy had tutors to educate them. What we are told is that Phoenix, who owed a debt of gratitude to Peleus, occupied himself with Peleus' infant son; and the instance we are given to illustrate their relationship is that the man helped to feed the young Achilles at table. No one who has performed this office for a friend's child will feel that it suffices to establish Phoenix's tutorial role. It is true that, at a

---

[2] Since this essay ends with the Hellenistic Age, it has seemed unnecessary to place the letters B.C. after the dates mentioned.

[3] *Iliad* IX, 434 seq.

later stage, when Achilles came to Troy as an adolescent, the old man was charged with the task of teaching him "to be both a speaker of words and a doer of deeds."[4] But that situation was an unusual one. Achilles went to war at an exceptionally early age; and we have no guarantee that the measures which his father took to meet this emergency represent what would have happened if the boy had stayed at home. Even if we accept (as we have some reason to do) that the Phoenix passage describes conditions obtaining during the eighth century, we cannot be sure that princes at that time normally received the systematic training that the employment of a tutor would suggest.

As for Achilles' other legendary instructor, the centaur Cheiron, his teaching is mentioned only once in Homer, at the end of *Iliad* XI[5] where we hear that he had taught Achilles the use of simples. And this is scarcely enough to establish him as the hero's tutor in our sense of the word. One can learn from a casual acquaintance; and the very same passage which mentions Cheiron tells us that Achilles had passed on this knowledge to Patroclus. But no one suggests that Patroclus was Achilles' pupil.

The validity of the Homeric evidence needs careful consideration, because if we cannot draw firm conclusions from it—and it would seem that we cannot—then the case for the historical priority of aristocratic education falls to the ground, and the resulting picture is very different from the one drawn by Jaeger or Marrou. If we refrain from making the *Iliad* and the *Odyssey* say more than they properly do, then it is the seventh century which stands out as the age when men first started to think about education. But by that time we find traces not only of aristocratic tutors, but also of more popular forms of schooling given to the children of citizens in the emergent city-states.

Turning therefore to the beginning of this new age, and first to the aristocratic class in society, we can feel fairly certain that by the seventh century the teacher-pupil relationship, whose Homeric existence is open to doubt, had become a familiar one, familiar enough to be a theme in art. The sons of the nobility were by then

4 Ibid. 442-43.
5 *Iliad* XI, 830-32.

evidently expected to learn their skills from older men of experience. It is also well attested that the nobles of the period subscribed to the Homeric ideal of personal excellence; and about one hundred years later we have the verses of Theognis to show us that aristocratic circles knew those special friendships where the mature partner feels responsible for his junior's development. These are the facts which taken in conjunction have been held to justify our likening the seventh-century aristocratic education to the training of a medieval knight. But the parallel is of doubtful validity. The knightly ideals of the Greeks were not linked to any institution of knighthood. We hear nothing of standards to be achieved; and Theognis' paternal care of his Cyrnus had little concern with systematic teaching. Pindar, moreover, the authentic voice of aristocratic prejudice, refers to those who learn their skills with the greatest contempt. Would he have done so if organized expert instruction had played a major part in the upbringing of the aristocracy? The evidence at our disposal is again far from conclusive. That so-called knightly training, which has been represented as originating in the Homeric Age and then influencing the whole subsequent development of education, may never have had a substantial existence. What we know on the subject would accord with the less startling hypothesis that the skills an aristocrat required were mastered casually through haphazard instruction, imitation, and practice, and that the aristocratic code was assimilated in the course of everyday living.

The popular origins of Greek education are by contrast much better attested, and organized instruction seems to have arisen first of all in the emergent city-states. That awareness of civic unity which came to characterize Greek communities during the eighth and, more particularly, the seventh centuries found expression in religious rites and in the needs of defense. Processions, choral song and dance, military exercises and maneuvers were the activities which drew the citizen body together; but these were all activities which required group rehearsal and training. They also required a degree of physical agility beyond what is normal even among people leading an outdoor life, and which could come only through regular physical instruction.

It is in Sparta that we meet for the first time a man training a group in music and dance. The poems of Alcman were obviously intended for public performance of an elaborate sort, and they evoke delicately the relationship between the trainer and his pupils.[6] Military exercises must have made their appearance also in the seventh century with the new hoplite armies that had to maneuver in unison.[7] As for gymnastics, the introduction of children's competitions in the Olympic Games of 632 is, as Marrou points out, sufficient proof that facilities for physical training existed by that time in many communities. And finally there is the legend that Tyrtaeus was an Athenian schoolmaster. This legend, for which a Scholiast on Plato's *Laws* is our main authority, has little biographical value but may be held to reflect a common belief in the antiquity of an organized educational system.

It is plain, moreover, that we have here evidence of a new departure. Athletic contests, dancing, and singing had been traditional activities among the Hellenic peoples and their Mycenaean predecessors, but the organized and elaborate forms they assumed during the seventh century were without parallel. The Homeric epics have numerous references to singing and dancing, but there is nothing to suggest that these activities called for special instruction. We cannot carry Alcman back to the court of Menelaus. He would have had no place there.

The differences between the old world and the new emerge, however, most clearly in the field of athletics. At the funeral of Achilles' friend, Patroclus, three champions offer themselves for the running; two box, and two wrestle. This paucity of competitors contrasts sharply with the conditions which prevailed in later times when the

---

[6] Alcman frag. 26.

[7] The hoplites were heavily armed soldiers carrying a pike and large shield who fought in a compact mass or phalanx several ranks deep so that there were always replacements for those who fell in front. Nothing short of massed charge could overcome a phalanx and its evolution put an end to the period when battles were decided by the feats of a hero better armed and more agile than the rest. This had important social consequences. States now depended for their military power on those citizens who could afford the hoplite equipment—small farmers and those equivalent to them in wealth—and that class tended to gain political importance at the expense of both the nobles and the poor.

average stadium contained sixteen or twenty places for runners, while the number of entrants for boxing, wrestling, or the *pancration* appears to have varied from twelve to over two hundred.[8] The Homeric pattern plainly fits the kind of informal contest we have on our village greens. The poet did not expect from his warriors the response usual from people challenged to display a skill for which they had been trained, and the impression that the Homeric athlete relied largely on the strength and speed given him by nature is further supported by the boasting of Nestor and Ulysses. Both claim pre-eminence over a wide field: boxing, wrestling, running, throwing the javelin or the discus. Such versatility was unusual once habits of training had become firmly established. It is true that the Pentathlon combined discus and javelin throwing, the long jump, running, and wrestling; but its exponents rarely counted among the serious challengers in the main races and bouts. Few of them, moreover, sought to specialize in more than three of the possible five events. Classical athletics had no room for a Nestor.

When Pindar, who wrote at the beginning of the fifth century, vaunts the superiority of natural endowment over mere training, he seems to be laboring a distinction which could have had little meaning by his day. The victors he celebrated had all availed themselves of extensive professional coaching. What he may be doing, however, is echoing the terms of an earlier debate. Such echoes are not uncommon in literature. The aristocratic successors of Nestor who first found themselves outclassed by men carefully schooled to make the best of their strength and speed might be expected to have inveighed against the vulgarity of this deliberate preparation; and their sense of outrage transmuted itself with time into a value judgment traditional to their class. The essential for our purposes is that behind the Pindaric outpouring we sense the same change which we know from other sources—the coming of systematic education.

[8] H. A. Harris, *Greek Athletes and Athletics,* London, 1964, pp. 66 and 164. The *pancration* was a single event which combined the actions of boxing and wrestling, except that participants were not allowed to bind leather thongs around their fingers (a general practice in boxing) and were not allowed to hit with the fist clenched. On the other hand, tricks like crushing the fingers were permitted, and the struggle went on until one of the antagonists admitted defeat.

Neither in athletics, nor in music and dance could specialized coaching have been enough. The girls who sang for Alcman had, we may presume, some prior knowledge of music. It is unlikely that he taught them everything from first principles; and it is equally unlikely that trainers for the great games would have had much success if their charges had always come to them straight from the plough. The more advanced training we hear about presupposes the "music" and "gymnastic" which Aristophanes and his contemporaries regarded as the core of their city's traditional schooling.

It is the final stage of this development which remains conjectural. We do not hear of the so-called "old education" in Athens before the end of the sixth century, by which time "music" appears to have included reading, at least the reading of Homer. But the slight oddity of this arrangement which thus classed together singing and the dull business of learning one's alphabet, makes one think that the second of these activities may have been a later addition which had to find a place in an existing curriculum. In that case the musical half of education may at an earlier period have been confined to choral song and dance and the playing of instruments; and it is plausible to suppose that this earlier period went back to the seventh century in view of what we hear about that century's musical and athletic activities.

In short, the evidence at our disposal, which is admittedly meager, suggests that the practice of providing systematic instruction for the young did not develop until the seventh century and then did so simultaneously in aristocratic circles and in the new citizen societies; and so we must reject the hypothesis that the upbringing of children in the emergent city-states was profoundly influenced by an earlier aristocratic tradition of training. The primitive schooling that served as the basis for later forms of Greek education was closely linked to the growth of civic consciousness in a formerly underprivileged class which had struggled and in many cases was still struggling for its political and economic rights.[9]

If we are to use the term elites to describe functional groups with

---

[9] Informal education seems to have had an even more definitely civic character. We are told that boys accompanied their fathers to the law courts so that they could listen to the debates and learn to argue by example.

a high status in their society, we can say that the aristocracy of the Dark Age was simultaneously a political, economic, military, and even intellectual elite. It was quite simply a ruling class superior to the masses in a number of decisive ways. The new citizen bodies of the Archaic Age, on the other hand, had a certain political status in so far as they possessed rights and power denied to non-citizens, and their richer members (probably less than half of the total),[10] who served as hoplites, had a measure of economic and military superiority. But it is plain that neither the citizens nor the non-citizens had the high status which would legitimately allow us to describe them as elites. Even in the fifth century—two hundred years after the period we are immediately considering—political and military power, social distinction and wealth remained to a very great extent the perquisites of the aristocracy; and the institutions which drew their strength from an ideal of civic unity were maintained in opposition to the real governing elites. At the time the first schools were founded, the ordinary citizen regarded himself as one of the common people, and these schools were the products of a popular tradition.

The real history of Greek education begins, however, with the collapse of the system we have been considering, which was transformed as a result of social and political change. But here the story becomes more complicated. This change did not take the same form everywhere, so that Sparta and Athens now require separate examination.

The foundation of Sparta is supposed to go back to the tenth century, and the pacification which welded the Laconian tribes into a single strong unit seems to have occurred around 800 B.C. Certain Spartan institutions, such as the division of the land into lots, one of which was assigned to each full citizen for the duration of his life, seem to have existed as far back as the eighth century, so that the emergence there of some kind of citizen state must be regarded as being of very early date. But that golden age during which Laconia shared and indeed led the development of the rest

[10] A. H. M. Jones, *Athenian Democracy*, Oxford, 1957, pp. 80-81, estimates the hoplite class as forming 40 percent of the total in the fourth century.

of Hellas, when she produced poets, musicians, Olympic winners, and vase painters of merit, and when foreign imports of luxury goods were common, tailed off during the first half of the sixth century. Following upon the Messenian revolt and perhaps in consequence of it, Sparta underwent a revolution which left her the rigid militaristic state that Xenophon knew; and the new order brought a new education in its train.

The reforms which set Sparta apart from the rest of Greece had their origins in her strength and initial success as a city-state. Unified at an unusually early stage, she appears to have evolved institutions which guaranteed her citizens economic equality in sufficient measure to prevent that factionalism which elsewhere set rich and poor at each other's throats. Her civic pride was great, her army efficient, and inevitably she was lured into a career of conquest. Messenia had been the richest prize of her victories; and then with the Messenian revolt of the seventh century it came home to her that this prize would not be easy to hold. In every Greek state, the citizen body was an elite living among slaves and unenfranchised aliens. But generally it formed a substantial portion, if not the majority, of the total population. Sparta was peculiar in possessing a subject race, the original inhabitants whom the Dorian invaders had reduced to serfdom. The Spartans had been outnumbered right from the start by the unprivileged around them and each fresh conquest had made this situation worse. It was the existence of the Laconian helots that made the holding of Messenia such a formidable task.

Moreover, land was almost the only source of wealth in the Archaic Age, and most of the land in Laconia and Messenia had been divided up among the Spartans, so that the helots were not only more numerous, they were also in a much worse position than the unenfranchised of other cities. A foreigner living in Athens could amass a large fortune. No helot could hope to do so. The only way the helots could improve their lot was by overturning the Spartan state; and this produced a most dangerous situation. With the coming of the sixth century, the Spartans faced a simple choice. They had either to surrender their conquests or to keep their citizen army on a permanent war footing; and some of their leaders had the organizing power to make the second and obvious choice effective.

Our knowledge of Spartan education is bedeviled by the existence of a popular legend. Sparta was powerful. Its institutions were peculiar, and it did not welcome strangers. Sparta lent itself therefore to the manufacture of tales calculated to emphasize its differences from the norm; and as the Spartans had no literature, our information about them comes necessarily from the outsiders among whom these exaggerated stories circulated. The ritual floggings, the feats of endurance, the public strippings of respectable girls, the sharing of wives, the stories about systematic instruction in theft and murder may each conceal some kernel of truth, but they bear the stamp of the universal human desire to find in the unknown the obverse of the known. The truth was certainly less colorful.

We are told rather more about the broad organization of Spartan training than about its actual content. The training period lasted thirteen years, from age seven to twenty, each annual stage being given a special name;[11] and there were also three broader divisions corresponding roughly to boyhood, adolescence, and youth. Each age group was divided into troops under the command of a senior, a young man who had completed his training and who was responsible (at least in part) for their instruction and discipline. The troops were then further subdivided into small units—sets of six according to one late authority, the lexicographer Hesychius—with one of the boys acting as leader.[12] The parallels with the modern scout movement are obvious.

This framework was plainly intended to serve the needs of pre-military training; but there are some indications that the system was superimposed on a more orthodox system of schooling. We hear of musical and athletic contests in which boys took part from their

[11] The names are arbitrary and their exact connotation remains uncertain. H. I. Marrou, op. cit. p. 20, provides one interpretation. H. Michell, *Sparta*, Cambridge, Eng., 1952, pp. 166-74, gives another that is radically different.
[12] Three names survive for these divisions— ἴλαι, ἀγέλαι, βοῦαι. I have followed Marrou in assuming that the first two are interchangeable; but there may have been a troop of intermediate size between the smallest and largest.

tenth year onwards.[13] Taken in conjunction with Plutarch's enthusiastic description of Spartan singing and the dances and athletic displays which marked such festivals as the Gymnopaidiae,[14] this fact clearly suggests the survival of the old musical and gymnastic education. Reading and writing were also taught, though not beyond the limits set by practical need.[15] If it is correct, as has been suggested by several authorities,[16] that boys did not leave home until their twelfth year, then the picture which emerges for the initial stage of Spartan education is that of a normal sixth-century school course supplemented by a vigorous form of scout training; and it seems likely that this was a schooling in which girls took part as well as boys.

It was at the next stage of life that the harsh discipline which we associate with Sparta came into its own. The youths lived in barracks, ate sparingly, went barefoot, wore only one garment and slept on beds of reeds which they collected themselves. We hear of exercises plainly intended to promote toughness, as when a group went into the mountains to live on what it could find, and we hear of boys handling arms and performing simple military maneuvers.[17] But it is evident that this Spartan training was concerned not so much with instruction, as with accustoming the boys to a certain way of life.

Great hardihood, simple habits, and a profound respect for the traditions, the opinions, the standards of the community were the fruits of their education; and of these the last two were as important as the first. The citizens formed an elite, but an elite of an unusual sort whose supremacy had not a variety of separate supports, but

[13] Michell, op. cit. pp. 174-5; Woodward, *Annual of the British School at Athens* XV, 48.

[14] Plutarch, *Instituta Laconica* 238 A & B in *Moralia*, III, ed. by F. C. Babbitt, London, 1931, pp. 236-8; on the Gymnopaidiae, Bölte, *Rheinisches Museum für Philologie*, lxxviii, 1929, 124ff., and Wade-Gery, *Classical Quarterly*, 1949, xliii, p. 79.

[15] Plutarch, op. cit. 237A. The statement of Isocrates (*Panathenaicus* 209) that the Spartans were illiterate is a manifest exaggeration.

[16] Initially Fustel de Coulanges (*Nouvelles recherches sur quelques problèmes d'histoire*, Paris, 1891, p. 75), but Marrou, op. cit. p. 20, takes the same view.

[17] Xenophon, *Resp. Lac.*, 2.

just a single one, the ability to field a supremely efficient hoplite
army. The possessors of military power have a problem to solve if
they are to establish themselves as a ruling class. Such power cannot hold its ground alone in any normally constituted society; and
military men must cultivate other skills—intellectual, administrative,
economic—or they must ally themselves with those who have influence in these fields. If they do not wish to do this, they have only
one alternative. They must create a new form of society in which
nothing counts but the power of arms. And that was the Spartan
solution. The influence of ideas was easy to suppress. All they
needed to do was to keep intellectual education at a low level. The
need for administrative skill did not arise: except for a brief period
at the end of the Peloponnesian War, the Spartan state operated in
a small way within a restricted traditional framework. The problems set by economic growth proved, however, more difficult to
manage. And it was here that education played a major part.

Greed, the remorseless amassing of private wealth, was to bring
about Sparta's ruin, but for a long time it was held in check. The
Spartan system of land tenure seems to have provided for a measure of regular redistribution. But more important than any legal
procedure was the fact that the national cult of simplicity and the
practice of communal feeding kept individual expenditure down
to an unimpressive norm. The Spartan way of life excluded that
parade of consumption by which economic power proves its superiority; and this held good not only for the Spartans, but also for
the subject races who shared their country. If there were rich men
among the *perioeci,*[18] they could not outshine their masters by
building vast palaces or collecting works of art. That the Spartan
education and the Spartan social order were closely interlinked is
an obvious fact; but it is equally obvious that the social order was

---

[18] The *perioeci* (Greek, περίοικοι—"dwellers around") constituted an inter-
termediate class between the Spartan citizens and the helots. Tradition
represented them as the original Achaian inhabitants of Laconia but some
at least were Dorians. They lived in their own settlements and enjoyed civil
but not political liberties. They seem to have accepted the social values of
their masters, and while they were exempt from the military training imposed on the Spartans, were compelled to provide auxiliary troops for the
Spartan army.

one which could exist only in a small, largely agricultural, slave state. Plato's attempt to make it the basis of a universally applicable pattern was to lead him into a quagmire of uncertainties.

In Athens we have a society of a very different type. There the outside interests, the economic inequalities which threatened to disrupt the original unity of the city-state had been accepted: and we find a long-drawn struggle for power rather than an established ruling class.

The Athenian Constitution was extravagantly democratic. The power of making decisions of public import rested with the *ecclesia,* an assembly of all the citizens with forty regular sessions a year and a quorum of 5,000. We know admittedly that the *ecclesia's* agenda was prepared by the *boule* or Council of 500, but this council does not seem to have taken advantage of its position as a steering committee to exercise a marked policy-making influence.[19] Its members were chosen by lot, and no man could serve more than two years during his lifetime so that it was not well fitted to develop a corporate policy. We know also that day to day government was in the hands of the 350 magistrates. But they could be deposed by the *ecclesia.* Many, moreover, were chosen by lot. Of those who were elected, the majority served an annual term. Where a man served longer—four years seems to have been the maximum—he could not hold the same post again. It was also common practice to share an office among several men. The ten generals, for example, all had the same formal authority. To exercise power over a longer period as Pericles or Lycurgus did[20] a man had to maintain his influence over the *ecclesia.*

Our meager evidence does not enable us to trace the foundations on which the influence of a Pericles or a Demosthenes rested. Family connections were important, especially in the fifth century.

19 A. H. M. Jones, *Athenian Democracy,* op. cit. pp. 105-8.
20 Pericles held the office of general without interruption for thirteen years (443-430). Lycurgus the orator is supposed to have managed the finances of Athens for twelve years (338-326). For four years he was actually treasurer of the revenues, a quadrennial office which he could not hold again. He then continued to act first through his son and then through a complaisant nominee for a further two terms. But such cases were rare.

Oratorical skill counted and so did a reputation for competence. Fourth-century politicians made their fortunes as advocates of particular interests; and there was an openly accepted network of what we should now call bribery. Demosthenes drew a tidy income from the Athenian and foreign backers for whose advantage he worked, and it is a fair assumption that money was also made available to him to buy the support of associates.

Alongside the amateurs thrown up by the operation of the lot, Athenian public life presents us with men who made their careers in politics and government. But they did not form a cohesive group aware of a common interest and it would be wrong to describe them as a ruling elite.

It is hard to know on all accounts how far we are justified in talking about elites with reference to ancient Athens. The aristocrats certainly cherished their superiority of birth and wealth and co-operated at times in its defense. The rich similarly showed some awareness of the fact that the owners of large fortunes ought to stand together if they were to avoid crippling taxation; and the intellectuals were proud of the education which divided them from the uninformed populace. All these groups have some claim to be described as elites; but in all of them the centrifugal forces of private interest were stronger than the common bond which held their members together; and we shall find this to have been particularly true in the case of the intellectuals. The literate and fluent were the natural leaders in the struggle for power and they struggled ruthlessly one against the other.

We see, therefore, two features of interest for our inquiry arising out of the peculiarities of the Athenian constitution. Deliberately designed to prevent an untroubled enjoyment of authority, the constitution encouraged an excessive competitiveness, the result of excessive mobility among the holders of power, and so militated against the formation of lasting groups representative of broad interests. The Athenian elites did not have the chance to develop that self-awareness and unity which comes from political action. And if all the elites were weak, the intellectual elite was further weakened, as we shall see, by the enticements of a mirage. Since the huge citizen assembly would allow itself to be persuaded only by men who could state their case in terms all could understand, the Athenians came to believe that eloquence and the ability to formulate broad policies were the essential requisites of the art of government. They were eager to develop political wisdom; but their experience led them to seek this wisdom where it could not be found.

In formal education, the music and the gymnastic of the sixth century had been, as we saw earlier, a preparation for communal activities and served a civic feeling still permeated by memories of revolutionary struggle. Then with the generation that preceded Marathon this pattern began to break up; and we see its transformation, slow at first, then increasingly rapid, into a pursuit of intellectual advantages and a dream of power. It was, however, a pursuit typical of an open or relatively open society, competitive not aristocratic.

At some point which cannot be later than the tyranny of Hippias (527-510), reading and writing were introduced into the Athenian curriculum.[21] Homer was the text which the teachers naturally used; and the values of the *Iliad* and *Odyssey* gained an even firmer hold on the popular mind than they had before.[22] The argument that Athenian education was fundamentally aristocratic has always rested on this circumstance. The Homeric ethic extolled individual excellence—"always be the best and keep ahead of the rest."[23] Its characteristics—courage, hunger for praise, fear of insult, some moral insensitivity over choices of means—have been too often and too brilliantly described to require discussion here.[24] It certainly provided material to support the growth of an aristocratic outlook. But the theory that Homer's influence was wholly on the side of aristocratic individualism needs nevertheless to be handled with care. Glory in the Homeric world was not earned in a vacuum. The hero's quest for personal superiority was conducted within a framework constituted by the rights and claims of others; and a school-

[21] The story of Aristides and the peasant shows that by the second decade of the fifth century illiteracy was confined to backward country districts.
[22] Homer may have been used in schools before reading came to be regularly taught; but this is a point about which evidence is wholly lacking.
[23] *Iliad,* vi, 208, and again xi, 784.
[24] One of the earliest and best descriptions is in J. Burckhardt, *Griechische Kulturgeschichte.* The most elaborate formulation is in W. Jaeger, *Paideia,* I.

38

boy reading his Homer would learn as much about the requirements of communal living as about the supreme worth of individual
pre-eminence.

Homer did at most point the way. The real change came with
the advent of the Sophists. In later times, the word Sophist was
used to describe anyone who taught rhetoric or philosophy. We
shall limit its use to the first outstanding group of these teachers
who flourished in the half-century after 460. They had different
specialties. Gorgias, for example, seems to have been mainly concerned with rhetoric, Protagoras with politics. Hippias of Elis was
a man of encyclopaedic learning who had scientific interests. In
some ways, however, their activities followed similar lines; and it
is here that we find the key to their importance. They all offered
intellectual instruction going beyond what could be learnt at school.
With all of them, this instruction was supposed to have a practical
aim, holding out a promise of mastery over men and the universe.
And finally, they all worked for pay, which meant that only youths
with rich fathers could afford their lessons.

They were immensely successful. The age was hungry for instruction at several widely different levels. To begin with, there
was the cult of rhetoric. Once popular assemblies had acquired real
power, the ability to make a persuasive speech had become a
valuable asset. The Sophists, whatever their other interests, all devoted a good deal of attention to the art of persuasion, and as the
subject was a new one whose rules had not been codified before,
they did have something to offer their pupils. But to regard rhetoric
as the sole cause of the Sophists' success would be to take too narrow a view. The hope of learning to speak well was the practical
advantage which excused wider and more utopian expectations.
The fifth century is known for the emergence of a new type of
thinking which rested on the assumption that the workings of the
universe could be explained by invoking uniformities in the shape
of general laws. This approach had produced some remarkable
advances in mathematics and science, and the fame of the Hippo-
cratic school at Cos demonstrated that it could be applied with success in the medical field. The origins of Greek rationalism, its roots
in the habits of thought of the Archaic Age, have yet to be traced.

But it is plain that by the middle of the fifth century, the young and intellectually curious in the major cities were afire with hope. Youths like the Hippocrates who in Plato's dialogue rushes to tell Socrates that Protagoras has arrived were certain that scientific reasoning could provide the answer to all problems, and the Sophists benefited from this enthusiasm. They offered to teach the secrets of statecraft, and in the context of the age, the idea that Protagoras might be able to supply the political equivalent of Anaximander's maps or Pythagoras' theorem was by no means implausible. They also offered to elucidate the secrets of the universe; and here again their contemporaries who remembered the triumphs of the Ionian philosophers cannot be blamed for nursing expectations of a similar success.

We know that the Sophists did not make good their claims. The political and scientific knowledge at their command was too threadbare to form the basis of a discipline or to provide the prospect of any real mastery over man's environment. They disappointed their adherents, and in the end became the target of bitter criticisms. But in spite of that failure, their influence was to prove decisive. As certainly as if they had been lawgivers with the authority of Solon or Lycurgus, they settled the main lines along which men's educational aspirations were to be satisfied, not only for their own generation, but for centuries to come. The aspirations in question were not determinate. Amounting to little more than a wish to control an increasingly complex and subtle world, they could have furnished the motive force for any one of half a hundred possible systems of education. It was the enterprise of the Sophists which provided the outlines of the system that was to gain acceptance. They were the pioneers who established Rhetoric, Philosophy, and Statecraft as the only valid fields of educational effort.

The schools which were to give the Sophistic program its lasting form did not come into being until the fourth century, when models were provided for them by those two commanding figures, Isocrates and Plato. But before that time a development occurred which merits notice. The Sophists had tackled the problems of philosophy and political science from a utilitarian standpoint. They had hankered after knowledge which could be used for the betterment of

man's lot; and when they failed, the realization that their failure
had been inevitable, brought with it a twofold revolt against their
aims and methods. Practical men whose interest had anyway been
primarily in what the Sophists had to offer by way of rhetorical
teaching came to feel that Rhetoric was perhaps best learned alone,
that there was no reason to integrate it, as the Sophists had done,
into a general education. And in the last decades of the fifth century, a number of self-styled experts claiming to give useful instruction in the arts of argument certainly found pupils enough to keep
the wolf from the door. From the standards set by Protagoras and
Gorgias this was a descent into an unimaginative utilitarianism.
We find it, however, matched with its opposite. Led by Socrates, a
new generation of philosophers shifted their attention to a field
which, unlike the fields the Sophists had tried to explore, seemed
to lie firmly within their competence. They took moral questions
as the objects of their inquiries and sought in this context for valid
generalizations using what we now call inductive reasoning.[25] This
was a new departure of great importance. The Socratics were manifestly more accurate in their thinking, more certain of their conclusions than the Sophists had been; but they worked at a level
which was substantially remote from daily life, and philosophy
took with them a decisive step in the direction of the theoretical
and the abstract.[26]

The cheap-Jack rhetoricians and the Socratics had moved away
from the Sophistic position in opposite directions; and what had
been lost in the process was precisely that element of general education which the Sophists had been concerned to offer, and which
after all was an element of some immediate value. Protagoras had
wanted to train statesmen; and statesmen—or at any rate intelligent,
public-spirited citizens—were greatly in demand.

This much was clear to thinking men on both sides of the fence,
among whom two were outstanding. Plato had made a name for
himself as a distinguished exponent of the Socratic credo. Isocrates

---

[25] Aristotle, *Metaphysics A,* 987 b1.
[26] Socrates was well aware of this, but believed that if a man thought
straight, he would act justly and well. The political records of some of his
pupils suggest, however, that he was oversimplifying.

had been a speech-writer of eminence. Their reputations were safe; and when they opened their schools (Isocrates in 393, Plato six years later), they felt free to experiment.

There was no question of returning to the old haphazard, encyclopaedic learning. Isocrates was a professional rhetorician. The instruction he could offer was bound to be concerned in the main with rhetoric. Plato was the nearest the age had to a professional philosopher; and he was committed (in a general way at least) to the Socratic pattern of intellectual inquiry. They were not men who could abandon their specialties. All they could do was to advance from their respective positions, widening the scope of their teaching to include some knowledge of public affairs.

Two of Isocrates' surviving speeches are directly concerned with his educational aims. The *Oration against the Sophists* was a manifesto written to advertise his school at the time it opened.[27] The *Antidosis* was a justification of his career produced in extreme old age. In these he makes it clear how he intended to outbid his fellow rhetoricians who did no more than look to a cheap forensic success. It was his intention to teach his pupils to speak well on great topics, and he claimed that by doing so they would learn to act in a statesmanlike way.

This program sounds promising, and on the strength of it, Isocrates has been regarded as a champion of liberal studies. But what we can discover about his methods prompts a less favorable judgment. The instruction he gave on rhetoric followed the lines laid down by Gorgias: theoretical precepts, then exercises where the pupil composed speeches on set topics learning to imitate his master's style. This was standard practice and does not in itself justify Isocrates' claim to impart an education of a higher sort. Statesmen —and for that matter orators who want to give sound advice on questions of high policy—need to be trained for the job; and it is relevant to ask what sort of training Isocrates provided in this particular field. The *Antidosis* contains a forthright condemnation of philosophers who analyse and discuss ethical or political problems,

---

[27] Isocrates' terminology may be misleading here. The "Sophists" he was attacking were not the great figures of the fifth century, but his rivals, contemporary teachers of a rule-of-thumb rhetoric.

such discussion being harmful to sound principles. We may assume
from this that the instruction given in the author's school laid down
standards of value rather than explored political issues; and a study
of his speeches confirms this belief. He wrote on important subjects.
The *Panegyricus* discusses the unity of Hellas. The *Nicocles* and
its companion piece deal with the problems facing a king. The
Areopagiticus features a critique of democracy. But Isocrates has
scant respect for accuracy. He omits inconvenient facts. He exag-
gerates when it suits his purpose. He does not so much arrive at
his conclusions from a consideration of his data as use his data to
support a prejudged case. It is impossible to imagine him framing
a course which would lead to a real understanding of politics.

Isocrates' teaching emerges on closer scrutiny as the very nega-
tion of enlightment. His work is as rich in platitudes as an extem-
pore sermon and with less excuse. The banality, we find, is inten-
tional. It springs from his method, that method which he considered
an adequate substitute for scientific inquiry. The orator, he tells us,
should relate his subject at every turn to what is most seemly and
edifying;[28] and if we take his practice as a guide to his meaning,
we find that public opinion provides his only criterion of seemli-
ness and edification. He is constantly invoking values that his
readers would automatically approve, so that all his thought is held
tight in the strait-jacket of convention. He discusses grand topics;
but he continues to pursue the fetish of a crude persuasiveness. He
is in the last analysis nothing but an old man eloquent.

Plato opened his school, the Academy, six years after Isocrates
began his career as an educator; and with the Academy we move
right away from the claptrap of the rhetorical convention, but only
to find that Plato like Isocrates was limited by the claims of his
specialty.

The exact nature of his educational achievement is difficult to
assess. Possessing a permanent site and at least a nucleus of long-
term students, offering a course of study which had some claim to
be systematic, the Academy undoubtedly represented a notable
advance on the informal teaching that had been the rule earlier.

---

[28] Isocrates, *Antidosis*, Sec. 277 in *Works*, II, ed. by G. Norlin, London,
1952, p. 338.

But again we must ask the same question that we asked in the case of Isocrates. What was actually taught?

Plato has left us two educational blueprints whose relation to each other remains obscure. It is plain however, that neither the upbringing of the philosopher-kings in the *Republic,* nor that of the citizens in the *Laws,* will help us much when we try to estimate what kind of training the Academy offered. A philosopher will arrive at very different conclusions when he is working out the implications of a hypothesis and when he is faced with the restrictions of a real-life situation. Plato did not have his pupils from the age of six to the age of thirty, nor could they have been like the chosen scholars of the *Republic,* all persons of commanding intellect. His young men came to him in adolescence after a conventional schooling of music and gymnastic, knowing how to read and write, knowing perhaps a little arithmetic, familiar with a few poets and in some cases trained in the elements of rhetoric. We do not know how long they stayed, but not many can have pursued their studies regularly after entering upon the responsibilities of adulthood. What he hoped to achieve with them cannot have come anywhere near the ideal he cherished.

A few facts, however, can be established with reasonable certainty. The members of the Academy saw themselves as superior to utilitarian aims. They formed not so much a school as a brotherhood dedicated to the service of the Muses, and their activities were conducted in that atmosphere of fervent enthusiasm which we normally associate with religious enterprises. Their whole approach to learning disposed them to look beyond practical success. The techniques of argument they were taught were presumably those Plato used in his dialogues—the Socratic search for universal definitions, the hypothetical method, collection and division—and the final goal of their philosophizing was manifestly the search for Truth, a glimpse however partial of the Idea of the Good. Both the techniques and the goal involved a movement away from everyday concerns. "The further we ascend from particulars to what Aristotle regarded as abstractions, the greater for Plato the reality."[29]

[29] J. E. Raven, *Plato's Thought in the Making,* Cambridge, Eng., 1965, p. 230.

Another study likely to have played a major part in the Academy course was mathematics. The five related subjects of arithmetic, geometry, stereometry, astronomy, and harmonics are presented in the *Republic* as the means which "draw the mind away from the material and mutable objects of opinion towards immaterial and constant realities."[30] They constitute the preliminary studies to the method of dialectics; and Plato must have felt the need for them in his own instruction. He certainly needed some method of raising young and relatively ill-educated aspirants to the intellectual level where they would be capable of comprehending his philosophy. But we must realize that these mathematical studies which in our own day are so closely concerned with an understanding of the material world were valued by him exclusively as roads to abstraction, and he insisted that they should be taught in such a way as to eliminate their relation to sense experience.

Although Plato hoped to make his mark as an adviser of statesmen, and although several of his pupils are listed by Plutarch as having taken an active part in public life,[31] the education he gave at the Academy appears to have been too theoretical to be of direct use in the solution of political problems, a circumstance which may serve to explain both his own disappointments in Sicily and the divergent policies of those who came under his influence.[32]

The educational developments of the fourth century may therefore be summed up as follows. Isocrates and Plato had the same goal in view. They both aimed to produce an elite which would rule well and advance man's understanding of the universe. They both failed: Isocrates by reason of the limitations placed on his thinking by rhetoric, Plato because the gap between his theories and current problems was too great to be bridged. But this failure did not prevent their setting a stamp on ancient education which was to prove ineffaceable.

The schools of rhetoric in the centuries following the death of

[30] Ibid. p. 178.
[31] Plutarch, *Adversus Colotem* 1126 A in *Moralia,* xiv, ed. by F. C. Babbitt, London, 1967.
[32] It is difficult to see what Dion of Syracuse and his assassin, Callipus, or Clearchus of Heraclea and his democratic opponent, Chion, had in common as a result of their Platonic education.

Isocrates were never to rise above the standard he set. At their best they passed on a hotchpotch of political precepts and cultural ideals without any attempt at criticism or systematization. At their worst, they sank to that narrow utilitarian level from which Isocrates had tried to raise them. Niceties of style and techniques for organizing the presentation of a legal case preoccupied their teachers until, at the end of the second century B.C., the interest the Romans took in rhetoric led them back to the study of the Attic orators. Men like Antonius and Cicero respected Greece because of her past; and so the Greeks who taught them found it convenient to make the age Athenian greatness the focus of their teaching. Isocrates came into his own again. The rhetorical discipline which had proved insufficient as an instrument of political education, was admirably suited for the task of transmitting a traditional culture. And that was the task which under the Roman Empire the schools of rhetoric eventually made their own.

If the rhetoricians stayed under the shadow of Isocrates, the philosophers for their part failed to advance very far beyond the limits sketched out by Plato. They continued with few exceptions to reject the world of experience and what were regarded as the "practical arts." But among these exceptions was one thinker of great importance about whom something must be said. Aristotle, though educated in the Academy, was averse to indulgence in long discussions.[33] He preferred the careful observation of facts; and when he opened his own school in 335 or soon after, he directed his students' attention to the systematization of scientific knowledge. The vast corpus of his work is evidence of the multiplicity of his interests and the value which his teaching might have had. Eighteen centuries later, modern science was to begin its advance from the basis provided by such remnants of Aristotle's learning as had managed to survive; and so a certain interest must attach to the question why the advance was not made earlier as a direct continuation of his researches.

Aristotle in the Lyceum realized the dream of the fifth-century Sophists. He created a school where the whole of contemporary

[33] Aristotle, *De Generatione et Corruptione* 316 A, in *On Sophistical Refutations,* etc., tr. by E. S. Forster, London, p. 176.

knowledge—politics and rhetoric as well as natural science—could be efficiently studied. It was a school which might legitimately have become the nucleus of an intellectual revolution, if not in the first generation, then with time and the gradual growth of expertise. The fact that it did not do so, the fact that the Aristotelians never again produced anything so great as Aristotle's own work, was due to a number of circumstances some of which we can distinguish. Aristotle was born too late. The kind of knowledge he had to impart would have been useful for solving the problems of a city-state; and that is by no means surprising since he systematized the discoveries of men who had lived in just such states. But by his death, the world had expanded and the problems of Athens could no longer be solved within the confines of the *polis*. The hope of exercising control vanished and with it went its natural concomitant, interest in the sort of knowledge which would make control possible. Also, Aristotle had been encyclopaedic in his approach. His achievement had been to lay the foundation for a possible future progress. The tricky task of choosing the sectors in which this progress could most usefully occur fell to his successors and proved beyond their capacity. Theophrastus and Strato were scholars rather than thinkers, given to compiling rather than experimenting. Under their aegis, the Lyceum came gradually into step with the other schools which had stemmed from Socrates, so that in the end it was speculation and not observation which dominated the teaching of philosophy.

The social influence of these various institutions is not easy to estimate. As far as numbers go, the rhetorical schools were probably the most important. Rhetoric was an easier subject than philosophy. It also had some claim to be useful, and though we have no firm evidence, it is impossible to avoid the impression that there was a substantial number of rhetoricians around. What we can infer with rather more certainty, however, is that the pupils in the schools represented only a small fraction of even the citizen body. When military training was made compulsory after Charonea, some 500 young men presented themselves in each annual age-group. Now Isocrates during his long career had only one hundred pupils, many of whom were not Athenians. It would be reasonable, therefore, to estimate his annual intake as no more than two; and his was a singularly successful school. We should have to assume that there were at least twenty-five rhetoricians teaching in Athens to arrive at an annual total of fifty students; and if we added to these the numbers attending the less popular philosophy schools, we should still be short of a hundred. It seems reasonable to suppose that less than one in five of the citizen body received a higher education.

This minority constituted the intellectual elite, or at any rate, the major part of that elite. The stamp of the rhetorical and philosophical schools can be traced in the literary output of the Hellenistic and Roman Age with a monotonous precision. And their limitations became the characteristic limitations of the Greek mind during its later history. Only the mathematicians and the medical men showed a measure of intellectual independence, pursuing their specialties in a relative isolation.

Since they dominated the field of intellectual endeavor, the schools were bound to have some influence outside that field. During the fifth and fourth centuries, while the city-states and their assemblies possessed some measure of independent power, many of those who attained political eminence did so by virtue of their skill in oratory, to which training usually contributed. The thinking of an Aeschines, a Demosthenes, a Demetrius of Phalerum carried the hallmark of the rhetorical schools. As for the philosophers, they, on their side, had, as we have seen, a deliberate program for producing expert advisers whom they hoped to see flourishing as so many Father Josephs in the courts of contemporary princes. Moreover, we find powerful men, like Euagoras of Cyprus or Philip of Macedon entrusting their sons, who had a hereditary place in the political elite, to some well-known teacher who would give them the best of what conventional education had to offer. But in spite of these intimate connections, the schools seem to have had little influence on the conduct of public affairs. Their efforts to turn their pupils into a political elite proved ineffective.

To some extent, this failure was due to the fact that in the Greek city-states outside of Sparta the distribution of power had a more complicated pattern than men realized. The leaders who were in the public eye did not make all the decisions that mattered. A city's life was guided not by a single elite, but by a group of elites—military, economic, administrative, political, intellectual—which overlapped, but remained essentially separate; and the educators who concentrated their attention on the political leadership limited the range of their influence within a compass that was too narrow to count.

This was bad enough, but the decisive factor making the schools ineffective was probably the unfruitfulness of their teaching. As has been already noted, neither the traditional wisdom peddled by the rhetoricians, nor the theoretical analysis of the philosophers, could contribute at all usefully to the solution of contemporary problems. Demosthenes' blindness to political realities and the tragic fate of King Agis demonstrate in different ways the fatal shortcomings of the educated approach. Except for the fact that it guaranteed literacy and certain habits of industry and ordered thought, education impeded rather than helped its possessors in the world of affairs, and its influence is therefore difficult to assess. But one cannot be in doubt about its unimportance.

Greek education began as an effort to provide the skills and the communal loyalties necessary for the survival of the city-state. Its restricted objects served a democratic purpose. That purpose lasted, however, only so long as the feeling of unity engendered by the struggle for civic rights remained a dominant force. In Sparta successful conquest enabled the original citizen body to establish itself as an elite; and the training of the young was intensified so as to promote a higher degree of military skill and a keener loyalty than before. It was intensified but also transformed, for its main purpose (which it fulfilled admirably) was to ensure the permanence of the Spartan way of life, that simplicity of tastes and that respect for the opinion of one's equals which were the foundations of the Spartan order. Considered in relation to the elite it was intended to create, Spartan education worked well. But the fact that this elite could exist only in a small, economically and technologically backward state diminished the value of its educational achievement for the larger world of democratic Greece. In that world, the original shoulder-to-shoulder citizenry of the first hoplite armies broke up under the pressure of new and diverse interests. Group competed with group, individual with individual. Athens had its elites, men whose word carried weight in the different departments of social activity and who joined in the pursuit of common interests. There were political groupings, economic alliances, philosophical schools. There were also other groups which brought together men of influence from several fields. In such a society the maintenance of a high level of efficiency would have required first of all the provision of advanced training for those who wanted it in a number of specialties. The further problem of how the several groups could be brought together to form one elite from the individually eminent was of secondary importance. The public good did not depend on its solution. And yet it was this secondary problem that the Athenian educators made the focus of their attention. They remained blind to the fact that the continued existence of their world turned upon the effective exercise of many skills; they overvalued the politician's arts and underestimated the growing consequence of administrative, economic, and technical achievement. They clung to the idea of a single group modeled on the aristocracies of the Archaic Age and saw government as a matter of principles and persuasion. If you had the right general aims, you would take the correct decision, and all you had to do then was to win adequate support.

Ancient Greece failed to solve the problems presented by the education of an elite in a developing society; and the records of its experiments and speculations—Xenophon's and Plutarch's accounts of Sparta, the Cyprian speeches of Isocrates, Plato's *Republic* and *Laws*—have confused rather than helped the efforts of later ages. They have certainly encouraged men to ask the wrong questions.

VERNON J. PARRY

Elite Elements in the Ottoman Empire

A SHORT GLOSSARY OF TURKISH WORDS

birun	The Outside Service of the imperial palace
chıqma	The procedure of selection and advancement used the Inside and Outside Services of the imperial palace
devshirme	The tribute of children raised for the service of the Sultan
enderun-i hümayun	The Inside Service of the imperial palace
ghilman *ghulam*, sing.	"Men of the Sultan"
ich-oghlanları *ich-oghlanı*, sing.	"Men of the Sultan" (*ghilman*) under training in the schools of the imperial palace
Sharia	The sacred law of Islam, based mainly on the Koran
ulama *alim*, sing.	Persons learned in the sacred law of Islam

Note

The letter *ı* (without a dot) has no precise equivalent in English. An approximation to it is the sound of the "a" in "imperial."

The Ottoman state came into being about 1300 A.D. It was brought to an end with the abolition of the Sultanate in November 1922 and the proclamation of a Turkish Republic in October 1923. At the time of its greatest splendor, during the fifteenth-seventeenth centuries, the Ottoman Empire extended from the Crimea to the Sudan, from Iraq to Bosnia, from the Caucasus to the Maghrib. It embraced within its confines numerous races, numerous creeds, languages, and traditions. A state of such long duration, so vast in size and so complex in character, had not one, but a number of elites prominent at various phases of its evolution and in diverse regions under its control. To inquire therefore what was the origin and what the nature of the dominant elite in the Ottoman Empire is to encounter at once the need for a more precise definition of the objective in view.

It was neither race nor language, but religious allegiance which determined the status of the group and of the individual within Muslim society. The *Sharia,* the sacred law of Islam, clearly stated that the *ahl al-kitab,* peoples recognized in the Koran as possessors of a book of scripture, should be allowed to follow their own religious faith, continuing as non-Muslims to live under their own religious law subject to their acceptance of a status inferior to that of the Muslims who had conquered them. This meant, in short, the status of *dhimmi* or protected subject, which involved the payment of higher rates of taxation and of a poll-tax not levied from the Muslims. To communities of this kind, for example, the Greek Orthodox Christians and the Jews, was given the name of *millet.* The ecclesiastical dignitaries and the wealthier classes formed within each *millet* an elite endowed with autonomous control over communal affairs.

The Muslims also constituted a *millet*—a *millet,* however, which wielded supreme power in the state. Of the Muslims subject to the Ottoman Sultan, the large proportion residing in Egypt, Syria, and Iraq—lands conquered in the time of Selim I (1512-20) and of Süleyman (1520-66)—requires no more than a brief mention here: the elite elements located among them followed their own lines of evolution. Much more relevant to our present purpose are the Muslims subsumed under the twofold designation of Ottoman and Turk.

Of the word Turk it will suffice to observe that in the golden age of the Empire it denoted above all the rude peasant population, Turkish-speaking, which lived in Asia Minor.[1] To call a member of the dominant elite a Turk would have been in fact to insult him. The word "Ottoman" is not of ethnic but of dynastic significance. It derives from the Arabic personal name *Uthman,* which among the Turks of Asia Minor became *Osman,* the name of the prince (d. 1326) who is regarded as the founder of the Ottoman state. The word *Osman* gave, in Turkish, the form *Osmanlı* (or Otto-man). To belong to the elite which controlled the Empire meant to be an *Osmanlı* raised and molded in the *adat-i othmaniyye,* the Ottoman manner of life: that is, to be an orthodox or *Sunni* Muslim, to serve the Sultan and the state, and to observe the distinctive behavior, language, and culture recognized as Ottoman.

Osmanlı is, however, a term susceptible of a wide interpretation. It can be taken to embrace a number of elite elements distinguishable by location in time, racial origin, or function within the Empire. One or two illustrations will be of value here.

The dynamic force which brought the Ottoman state into being was the idea of *jihad*—war on behalf of the Muslim faith against the infidel. To make *jihad* meant to make *ghaza*[2] from the lands under Muslim rule into the lands as yet unreduced to Muslim obedience. The growth of the Ottoman state can be regarded as the gradual movement, from the fourteen to the sixteenth centuries, of the Muslim frontier from Asia Minor north-westward through the Balkans to the Danube line. The frontier was pushed forward by Muslim warriors, *ghazis,* men whose purpose and mode of life was raiding and plundering. Among the border warriors, above all in the earlier phases of rapid advance and consolidation, there were great families of *ghazi* origin. The lords of the frontier marches—the *uj begleri*—constituted in fact an elite class of large importance in the first centuries of Ottoman rule, but of diminished

---

[1] To the nomadic tribes of Asia Minor and the adjacent lands was given the name Türkmen or Turcomans.

[2] The sense of *ghaza* is found in the Italian word *razzia*—raid or plundering —which derives from it.

weight thereafter, when the central government asserted over them a more effective measure of control.

At various times a number of racial elements rose to especial prominence in the Empire. Bosnia fell to the Ottomans in 1463-64. Much of the local population now went over to Islam, abandoning their old Bogomil allegiance and becoming, under their own lords, the *ghazis* par excellence of the northern frontier. Albania, too, at a later time, in the seventeenth and eighteenth centuries, had a role of high importance: the Muslims of Albania yielded perhaps the best soldiers then to be found in the armies of the Sultan.

A brief mention should also be made of the "feudal" horsemen located in most, but not all of the provinces of the Empire. These men, known as *sipahis,* came to war at the call of the central government, holding in return for this service fiefs, the revenues from which enabled them to function as efficient warriors. Each *sipahi* brought with him on campaign one or more mounted soldiers (*jebeli*) maintained at his own expense. The *sipahi* did not own the lands which constituted his fief. He had the right to the usufruct only: that is, he received various dues in cash or in kind from the peasants who lived on the soil. On the death of a *sipahi* one of his sons, and sometimes more than one, would in normal circumstances be granted a fief. Enrollment within the "feudal" class was not, however, restricted to members of old, established *sipahi* families. Muslim volunteers distinguished for valor in the field, *jebeli* soldiers of long and meritorious service, personnel from the household of the Sultan—all might be recruited into the ranks of the *sipahis*. Here then was a distinctive element—a permanent force of occupation, as it were, in the provinces of the empire—which had, within its appropriate sphere, the status of an elite.

To include under the word *Osmanlı,* however, elements so diverse in character and origin as the *uj begleri,* the local populations of Bosnia and Albania and, in addition, the "feudal" *sipahis* is to extend the term to, and perhaps beyond, the limit of reasonable interpretation. A more restricted and, at the same time, more cogent procedure would be to equate the designation Osmanlı with the government of the empire—and above all, with the régime at the center.

THE CENTRAL GOVERNMENT

The personnel associated with government acted within three main areas of broad functions—religion and law; war and statecraft; and the bureaucratic services: financial, administrative, and secretarial.

Of these categories the first one needs no long examination here. The fundamental law of the Empire was the *Sharia.* This law recognized no distinction between church and state. Indeed, the state, the Sultan and his government, existed only to defend the Muslims from external threat and internal disorder and to foster on earth conditions under which every man might be able to live the life of a good Muslim. The *Sharia* was of divine origin and therefore difficult to adjust to new circumstances. A slow and continuing adjustment was in fact achieved through the interpretative labor of the jurisconsults, through the use of analogical reasoning and through the consensus of opinion gradually emergent among men learned in the law—but not through the will of the Sultan. A Sultan had no right to alter the sacred law at his own behest. He was, however, empowered to issue regulations applicable to matters or to areas of action undefined in the *Sharia,* for instance, within the field of administrative law.

To the men learned in the *Sharia* was given the name of *ulama* (singular, *alim,* one who has *ilm* or learning). The *ulama* received their education in the religious colleges to be found all over the Empire, devoting long years to theological, scholastic, and legal studies: dogmatics, exegesis, rhetoric, jurisprudence, and the like. Aspirants to the highest offices in the judicial system rose through an elaborate *cursus honorum* and served, as scholars and teachers, in the religious colleges of the great cities, chiefly in Istanbul. As the guardians and exponents of a sacred law all-embracing in character, the *ulama* wielded a strong influence over the routine of government and over affairs of state. As practicing judges they were greatly involved in the administration of the Empire during its golden age, and as jurisconsults they were often summoned to give formal verdicts on points of law unresolved in the *Sharia* or to sanction the policies of the central régime, including matters of peace and war. Among the *ulama* can be discerned veritable "dynasties," long-established families dedicated to the religious and legal career and entrusted from generation to generation with high office in the Empire. Here, in fact, was another elite element and of the most durable kind, an elite perforce recruited—and the point needs some emphasis here—from among the Muslim-born subjects of the Sultan.

With the *ulama* thus set in perspective, there remain for consideration the categories of war and statecraft and bureaucratic service. The men of these two categories exemplified in themselves and to the highest degree the prestige, the pride, and the privilege of a dominant elite. They formed the Sultan's household, which was much more than an organization serving the domestic needs of the monarch or the ceremonial needs of a court. It included men engaged in these services, but it also embraced the numerous personnel of the great offices and departments of the central régime and, in addition, of the higher ranks in the provincial administration. To the household, moreover, belonged the armed forces at the center—the Janissaries, the six mounted regiments of the Sultan, and the various specialist corps, for instance, artillerists and engineers.

A "SLAVE" ELITE

The personnel of the household had in general the status of *ghulam* —a term which, although having the lexicographical meaning of slave, is better construed here as servant or "man of the Sultan," since it did not bear the pejorative sense implicit in the English term "slave."[3] The *ghulam* system, or slave household, was old in the world of Islam. It had existed in the time of the Abbasid Caliphate (750-1258) at Baghdad, the center of imperial rule, and in the autonomous régimes which made their appearance during the decline of the Caliphate—for example, in the ninth and tenth centuries, the dynasties of the Saffarids and Samanids in Persia or of the Tulunids and Ikhshidids in Egypt. The system continued to evolve and flourish from the eleventh through the thirteenth cen-

---

[3] The word *qul* is also used to designate the status of personnel belonging to the imperial household.

turies, when the Seljuq Turks dominated Persia and Iraq and when
the Fatimid and Ayyubid dynasties controlled Egypt and Syria. To
the Ayyubids there succeeded a classic example of a slave régime—
the Mamluks, recruited at first from the non-Muslim Turks dwell-
ing in the steppe lands north of the Black Sea, and later from the
Christian *Cherkes* (Circassians) located in the Caucasus. It was
not until 1517 that the Mamluk Sultanate came to an end with the
Ottoman conquest of Syria and Egypt. The *ghulam* system of the
Ottomans was therefore but a late example of an institution long
established in the Muslim world.

It was from the Seljuq Sultanate of Rum in Asia Minor that the
Ottomans acquired the principles and practice of a *ghulam* organization. There is evidence that even in the time of the first Ottoman
princes, Osman (d. 1326) and Orkhan (1326-62), slaves were
being trained for the service of the state. A further development
occurred under Murad I (1362-89). To a Muslim prince engaged
in *jihad* the *Sharia* accorded the right to take one-fifth of the
plunder that his warriors gained in war. Murad I, on the advice of
the *ulama,* began to exact this tribute, or *penjik,* from the warriors,
demanding of them one fifth of the captives acquired in warfare
against the non-Muslim lands. From slaves thus assembled the
famous corps of the Janissaries was formed.[4] Bayezid I (1389-
1403) or perhaps his father Murad I introduced also the *devshirme,* a tribute of children levied at intervals from among the
Christian subjects of the Ottoman state. Often, during the age of
rapid expansion in the Balkans after the capture of Gallipoli in
1354, the Sultans took into their service young men drawn from
the local aristocracies in the subjugated lands; indeed, it is possible
that here, in this practice, the *devshirme* itself had its origin. At
this time, in general, the Sultan's *ghilman*[5] received appointments
only in the armed forces; the great executive offices were reserved
to Muslim-born Turks of the religious and legal class (the *ulama*).[6]
The *ghulam* system was elaborated still further in the reign of

[4] I.e., in Turkish, *Yenicheri;* plural, *Yenicheriler,* the new troops.
[5] Plural of *ghulam.*
[6] A notable example is the house of Jandarlızade, several members of
which, in the fourteenth and fifteenth centuries, attained to the highest office
of all, the Grand Vizierate.

Mehemmed II (1451-81) who insured that almost all the high appointments of state, bureaucratic as well as military, should go to the *ghilman*.[7] It was to become the normal rule under Süleyman (1520-66), Selim II (1566-74), and Murad III (1574-95) that the executive power should be assigned to men of *ghulam* status.

The slave household offered manifold advantages. It did much, during the fourteenth and fifteenth centuries, to establish and maintain the control of the central government over the powerful *uj begleri,* the Muslim lords of the *ghazi* frontier in Europe. At the same time it acted as a counterpoise to the *sipahis,* the numerous "feudal" horsemen in the provinces. *Ghilman,* not *sipahis,* held the highest appointments in provincial administration.[8]

A slave household was thus regarded as the indispensable prerequisite, the essential instrument for the exercise of power. Nor was such a household limited to the Sultan alone. Each governor of a province, for example, and each governor-general had his own establishment of *ghilman* whose number was laid down in the imperial regulations according to the rank and emoluments of the office that the master held. The high dignitaries, indeed, often maintained far more *ghilman* than the regulations demanded of them. Even the "feudal" horsemen or *sipahi* had small households of *ghulam* status, the members of which—*jebeli* mounted warriors and personal attendants—varied in number with the annual yield of the fief. It was possible for slaves trained in the service of the great officials to receive a small fief and thus enter the class of the "feudal" *sipahis*. The *ghilman* of a high official who was executed fell to the Sultan and might be taken into his palace service. At the center and in the provinces, therefore, throughout the war machine and the administration of the Ottoman state, the *ghulam* system flourished as a powerful instrument of cohesion and control.

The exact status in law of the *ghulam* is still under debate.

---

[7] It should be re-emphasized here that to the Muslim-born subjects of the Sultan, and pre-eminently to the *ulama,* was reserved control of the legal, religious, and educational institutions of the Empire.

[8] E.g., as governor (*beg*) of a province (*sanjaq*)—*sanjaq begi;* or as governor-general (*beglerbegi, "beg* of *begs,"* "lord of lords") set over a number of *sanjaqs*.

Murad II (1421-51), in his will dating from the year 1446, made arrangements to manumit some of his *ghilman*. The will would seem to indicate that the *ghulam* household was not held to be public and state property but the Sultan's personal possession. It is significant, too, that the *ghilman* are described here as *abd*, a term meaning slave in a sense unqualified and absolute. Manumission, therefore—although rarely granted, it seems—might change the status of the *ghulam*. A more frequent source of change, however, was the *chıqma* or "passing out" from the Imperial household. The *ghilman* transferred from the palace to appointments elsewhere did in fact obtain an increased freedom of action—such as the right to marry and to possess slaves of their own. This elevation might be connected with the *Sharia* doctrine of *idhn*, which allowed a master to bestow on his slave various rights—among them the power to act in his name. It is also possible that the selection and promotion system modified the relation between master and slave into a bond akin to the relation between patron and client. The Sultan, nevertheless, would retain over the *ghilman* ample means of control, whatever their precise legal situation. Such a control accrued to him indeed, not only because he owned the *ghilman* as slaves in the absolute sense, but because he was after all the Sultan of the Ottoman state.

SELECTION AND ADVANCEMENT

The members of the Sultan's household came from several sources. One source was the tribute mentioned above, the *penjik:* a fifth of the captives taken in land campaigns against the non-Muslim world or else in the raids of Muslim corsairs on the waters and along the shores of the Mediterranean Sea. Great dignitaries prominent in the affairs of the Empire also maintained retinues of slaves trained in their own households—and sometimes gave to the Sultan as a gift the choicest of the slaves. Most of the war captives passed from the soldiers to the slave markets in the great cities, where, at need, the superintendents of the imperial domain would purchase slaves for the service of the Sultan.

To these modes of recruitment—capture, gift, and purchase—

must be added the *devshirme* or tribute of children. At intervals of three or four years, and more often, if necessary, officials came from the central régime to the areas where the *devshirme* was to be levied. There is conflicting evidence about the proportion of children taken from the total number available at a given place and moment. One child to forty households would seem to have been the normal rate, at least from the time of Mehemmed II (1451-81), but this figure was no doubt exceeded if the demand for recruits happened to be urgent. The officials empowered to exact the *devshirme* summoned to their presence the local notables in a village and the heads of families, ordering them to make available for inspection the children of appropriate age—ten to fourteen years was perhaps the most favored age grouping, though youths a little younger or a little older might also be chosen. Once selected, the child tribute was sent to Istanbul, there to join slaves acquired through other channels of recruitment.

To the children of the *devshirme,* as to the youths obtained elsewhere, induction into the Muslim faith was now imminent and indeed unavoidable. Their conversion to Islam was not a matter of mere force alone. The pressure of a new environment, the example of other recruits, and the prospect of advancement in the future would all contribute to render the transition, once made, a more acceptable experience than it might have been. Nonetheless, it is difficult to reconcile an institution like the *devshirme* with the principles of the *Sharia,* the sacred law of Islam. The tribute children came from a population which had the status of "protected subject" and were therefore invested with the right, under the *Sharia,* to observe in full their own religion. How the Ottomans justified the conversion enforced on the children is uncertain. One Ottoman historian, Idris Bitlisi, sought to argue that the fact of conquest had reduced the infidels (the Christian subjects) to a condition of bondage and subjection to the Sultan: to take their children into the Ottoman service was lawful and would strengthen Islam spiritually, by adding converts to the Muslim faith, and materially, by providing new servants for the Muslim state. A modern historian, Professor Paul Wittek, has also brought forward a possible justification of the *devshirme* in legal terms. Orthodox or Sunni

Islam recognized as valid four schools of law interpreting the *Sharia*. Of the four schools one, the *Shafii* school made a distinction between the *ahl al-kitab* or the people with a book (of scripture) who had held their faith since before the death of the Prophet Muhammad, and the people who had embraced it after his demise. The *Shafii* school of law allowed to the second of these two categories only a restricted status as *ahl al-kitab*. This restriction was envisaged in such a fashion as to expose to the risk of enforced conversion most of the Christians in the Balkan world, since the Bulgarians, the Serbs, and the Albanians had been brought into the Christian faith long after the death of Muhammad. The exact nature of the *apologia,* religious and legal, advanced in justification of the *devshirme* must remain a matter of conjecture, but it is well known that the tribute of children was exacted above all from the Balkans and in particular from the areas with a population of Slavonic or Albanian descent; indeed, among the Janissaries (recruited from the *devshirme* and from captives taken in war) the dominant language, during the golden age of the Empire, was Slavonic. At first limited perhaps to the Slavs and the Albanians, the child tribute was later extended to include the Greeks both in the Balkan lands and in Asia Minor. There is some reason to believe that Asia Minor felt the weight of the *devshirme* at least from the reign of Mehemmed II (1451-81), since the Greek and, in the course of time, the Armenian, and even the Laze elements were subjected to the tribute. The Jews, members of a protected religion, remained exempt from the *devshirme*.

The application of the *devshirme* and also of the *penjik* (the fifth of the war captives set aside for the Sultan) involved perforce a degree of initial selection, and the factor of choice was operative also in the case of recruits acquired through gift or purchase. At Istanbul the children, whatever their provenance, came before officials of the imperial household who, under the direction of the Agha[9] of the Gate, the chief of the white eunuchs in the palace service, carried out a further selection, the Sultan himself at times being present on this occasion. The recruits who, insofar as the long experience of the judges could discern, offered the best prom-

[9] *Agha* has the sense of "officer" of high rank, "master."

ise of high intelligence and of physical perfection went into the *Enderun-i Hümayun,* the Inside Service of the palace system. Their immediate assignment would be to the schools maintained for the education of new *ghilman* at Istanbul in the palaces of Ghalata-Sarayı and Ibrahim Pasha and also at Edirne (Adrianople) and Manisa. The schools, well advanced under Murad II (1421-51), had achieved in the time of his son Mehemmed (1451-81) their characteristic, though not their full, development. To the *ghulam* under training in a palace school was given the designation of *ich-oghlanı* (plural: *ich-oghlanları:* "young men of the inside service").

The *ich-oghlanları* received the first phases of their education over a period of from two to as much as eight years in the four palaces mentioned above. There now occurred the selection known as *chıqma* (or "passing-out"), the best of the young *ghilman* moving forward into the palace where the Sultan himself lived—the New Palace which Mehemmed II built at Istanbul.[10] The *ghilman* thus chosen for promotion entered into the Great Chamber or the Small Chamber of the palace. No exact estimate can be given for the total number of *ich-oghlanları* in the two chambers: the Great Chamber had perhaps four hundred or somewhat less and the Small Chamber between two and three hundred *ghilman* in the sixteenth and seventeenth centuries.

Above the Great and Small Chambers there were, at first, three chambers of higher eminence all dedicated to the personal service of the Sultan and ranked in ascending order of precedence as the Private Larder, the Private Purse, and the Private Chamber (Khass Oda). To the three chambers of superior status a fourth was added in the reign of Ahmed I (1603-17) or perhaps a little later—the Chamber of the Imperial Campaign, charged at the time of its formation with the care of the Sultan's clothes when he went to war. This chamber stood below the Private Larder in rank.[11]

---

[10] I.e., The Yeni Saray, later called Topqapi Sarayi.
[11] The various chambers are to be envisaged as palace schools for the training of the *ghilman* (see below), but also as departments within the household of the Sultan. A *ghulam* promoted to the higher chambers was brought into the *intimate* and *personal* service of his august master. Such advancement and such personal service was a mark, not of derogation, but of great honor.

The *ghilman,* having been educated for about four years in the Great or Small Chamber, went through yet another selection or *chıqma.* The most able among them now moved forward to the higher chambers of personal service mentioned above. Of these favored *ghilman* the best, if their conduct was meritorious, might expect advancement to the highest chamber of all, the *Khass Oda* or Private Chamber.

The selection process or *chıqma* occurred at intervals which varied from two to eight years. *Chıqma* involved, within each chamber, the promotion of chosen individuals from the status of *ajemi* or junior to the status of *eski* or senior member. It also meant the transfer of *ghilman* with senior rank from the chambers of lower to the chambers of higher precedence where, of course, a junior status awaited them. The four higher chambers each had twelve members of senior rank. All promotions and transfers of the *ghilman* came about through the granting of an imperial rescript in response to a proposal emanating from the head of the white eunuchs or from his nearest subordinate, who was in charge of the Private Chamber.

Advancement to the Private Chamber—comprising forty members since the time of Selim I (1512-20)—would bring the *ghulam* into close contact with the Sultan. A senior (*eski*) of this chamber might be appointed to one of several offices embraced within it. He might have the care of the Sultan's weapons, or his footwear, of his outer clothing, or his turbans, or of the keys controlling the routine affairs of the Private Chamber. To the *ghilman* who held these appointments was accorded the rank of *agha.*

The household of the Sultan, in addition to the *Enderun-i Hümayun* or Inside Service, included also the *Birun* or Outside Service, that is, the governmental apparatus and the armed forces constituting the central régime of the empire. Among the great dignitaries of the Outside Service can be numbered the Agha of the Janissaries, the Standard Bearer, the Chief of the Gate-Keepers, the Master of the Horse, the *aghas* of the mounted regiments of the imperial household, the Chief of the Artillerists, and the Chief of the Armorers. To most of the high officials in the *Birun* was given the right to ride close to the Sultan—hence, their designation as

"Aghas of the Imperial Stirrup." The "Outside Service" embraced also a number of special corps, including the *Müteferriqalar,* a select guard attendant on the Sultan.

As for the *Enderun,* so too for the *Birun,* the essential inflow of slaves was assured through the *devshirme* and the *penjik,* and through gift and purchase. No more than a limited proportion of the children arriving at Istanbul found admittance to the Inside Service. Most of the recruits would in fact be sent to Muslim estates located either in Asia Minor or in the Balkans, there to pass some years adapting to Muslim life, to Turkish customs and language, and especially to a process of physical hardening. Of the recruits thus seasoned through discipline and labor some, on their recall to Istanbul for service in the Birun, might enter the corps of *Bostanjıs,* which acted as a kind of police.[12] Most of them, however, were enrolled in the Janissaries as novices destined to receive a rigorous training in the practice of war.

There was, in addition, a flow of slaves from the Inside Service to the Outside Service. The *ghilman* assigned to the palace schools of first instance at Istanbul, Edirne, and Manisa, yet not chosen subsequently for admission to the Great and Small Chambers in the Sultan's palace, might be drafted into the four lowest in status among the six mounted regiments of the central régime. Of the *ghilman* in the Great and Small Chambers the *eski,* or senior members, would be raised, at an appropriate *chıqma,* to the superior chambers; their fellow *ghilman* not of senior rank often went into the two highest of the six mounted regiments. Again, in the superior chambers, the *ghilman* not selected for the Private Chamber (the highest promotion of all) would be transferred to the Outside Service, for example, to the Sultan's select guard, the *Müteferriqalar.* At the level of the Private Chamber, there was a further selecting-out to high positions within the Outside Service. Senior members were sent out to command the regiments or corps of the Outside Service, or to serve in the administration of the provinces as *sanjaq begi*—governor of a province.

There was also a movement of *ghilman* to high rank from the

---

12 A special corps of guards serving within the palace and its precincts. The word *Bostanji* means in fact "gardener."

Birun or Outside Service itself. The Aghas of the Imperial Stirrup might be advanced to the office of *sanjaq begi* or even *beglerbegi*—governor-general over a group of provinces. To the personnel of somewhat lower status in the Outside Service, for example the *Müteferriqalar* and the men of the mounted regiments, the regular selection process sometimes brought assignment to a large fief in the provinces; on the *ghilman* of still more modest rank, like the Janissaries of long and distinguished service, it might confer a small fief as their reward.

At each level, therefore, the *chıqma* caused a movement of personnel—within the Inside Service itself, from the Inside to the Outside Service and from both into the provincial world of the governors and the "feudal" horsemen (*sipahis*). Such movement was not restricted to functions and offices which, like most of the examples given above, had to do with war and administration. The *ghilman* within the chambers of the Inside Service found freedom and encouragement to develop particular inclinations and capacities. Young men ill-endowed for the military and executive career, but gifted in arithmetic, in language, literature, and related studies, would be allowed to follow their true vocation in the bureaucratic sectors of government—secretarial, administrative, and financial.

The *ich-oghlanları* who attained to the highest chambers of the Inside Service had before them, if all went well, the chance of a splendid future.[13] Two typical examples will illustrate. Ayas Pasha, of Albanian descent, born near Valona, was recruited through the *devshirme* in the reign of Bayezid II (1481-1512). He left the *Enderun* with the rank of *agha* and in 1514 commanded the Janissaries at the battle of Chaldiran against the forces of Ishmail, the Safawid Shah of Persia. Also as Agha of the Janissaries he served throughout the campaigns of conquest in Syria and Egypt (1516-

---

[13] The appointments granted to the men of the Inside and the Outside Service—for example, as governor of a province (*sanjaq begi*)—were *not* hereditary. In general, during the golden era of the Empire, when the *ghulam* institution had attained its "classic" form, the children of a *ghulam* were absorbed into the broad mass of the Muslim-born subjects of the Sultan—being themselves of Muslim birth and free, whereas their father, although converted to Islam, would have been of non-Muslim origin and of *ghulam*, or slave, status.

17). Ayas Pasha now became *beglerbegi,* or governor-general, of Anadolu and, after helping to crush a revolt in Syria (1520-21), was made *beglerbegi* of Damascus. He fought at the siege of Rhodes (1522) as *beglerbegi* of Rumeli and, rising to the rank of third and then of second vizier,[14] served thereafter in the campaigns of Mohács (1526), Vienna (1529), Güns (1532), and Iraq (1534-35). Ayas Pasha became Grand Vizier in March 1536, retaining that office, the highest in the Empire, until his death in July 1539. Of the events occurring in these years the most notable were the war against Venice (1537-40), the Moldavian campaign (1538), and the expedition of Süleyman Pasha, the governor of Egypt, against Diu in western India (1538-39).

Also of great distinction was the career of Chighalazade Sinan Pasha, born in the Genoese house of Cicala, captured at sea in 1561 or perhaps a little earlier, and then carried as a slave to Istanbul. Becoming now a *ghulam* in the Inside Service, he rose to senior status within the highest chamber of all, the Private Chamber. His marriages, in 1573 and in 1576, to the great-grand-daughters of Sultan Süleyman (1520-66) assured him of continued advancement. He was Agha of the Janissaries from 1575 to 1578 and thereafter saw much active service in the long Ottoman-Persian War of 1578-1590. As *beglerbegi* of Van he fought well in the campaign of 1585 against Tabriz and as *beglerbegi* of Baghdad, during the last years of the war, brought under Ottoman control Nihawand and Hamadan in western Persia. Sinan Pasha, after a short interval as *beglerbegi* of Erzurum, became in 1591 High Admiral of the Ottoman fleet, holding that office until 1595. He was now made third vizier and, during the Hungarian campaign of 1596, shared in the capture of Egri (Erlau). At the battle of Mezö-Keresztes, fought in October, 1596, soon after the siege of Egri, Sinan Pasha helped to change a near defeat into a great success for the Ottomans. He was now made Grand Vizier but retained the appointment only for little more than a month (October-December,

---

[14] The rank of vizier was given to great officials of long service and experience in war and administration. It entitled them to a seat in the Council of State (*Diwan*), which controlled the great affairs of the empire. The Grand Vizier, first in status among the viziers, was responsible, under the Sultan, for the government of the Empire.

1596). After a term of service as *beglerbegi* of Damascus, he became in May, 1599 High Admiral for the second time. Sinan Pasha, commanding the Ottoman forces in a new war against Persia, met with small success in the campaign of 1605 and died in the course of a difficult retreat.

TRAINING AND EDUCATION

Of the schools in the *Enderun* which trained men like Ayas Pasha and Sinan Pasha, the general surveillance was entrusted to the chief of the white eunuchs and his subordinates. These eunuchs maintained a strict control over the young *ghilman,* supervising all their actions, recording in detail the progress of their studies, and sleeping among them in the dormitories. Discipline was prompt and severe—for example, beating with a thin lash on the soles of the feet—but care was taken to keep it within bounds: corporal punishment was not to be given more than once a day to the same *ghulam*. The *ich-oghlanları* received instruction from special teachers, from members of the *ulama* (men learned in the sacred law), and from noted scholars who arrived at set times to give lessons. Some of the abler students also acted as tutors to the younger and less experienced pupils. The number of students at each level of the educational system was not large—and it diminished at each ascending level, until, at the summit of the whole structure, the *Khass Oda* or Private Chamber contained no more than forty *ich-oghlanarı*. It was not difficult, therefore, for the officials in charge of the various chambers and for the teachers and the *ulama* who gave instruction in them to gain a detailed knowledge of the intelligence, the aptitudes, the physical endowment, in short the strength and weakness of each student. They would also have acute insight into the personal qualities which distinguished each student—his resolution, self-discipline and initiative, for example, or his lack of such desirable attributes. At each *chıqma* full account was made of these abstract and moral qualities as well as of more concrete standards of judgment such as the degree of progress made in a particular course of studies or training. No doubt the fallibilities of human nature rendered the process of continuous assessment less than perfect, but the long series of able soldiers, statesmen, and administrators sent out of the *enderun* in the golden age of the Empire affords striking evidence of the steadfast care devoted to the pursuit and, in no small measure, the attainment in practice of an exalted ideal.

To pass through the schools of the Inside Service from the lowest to the highest degree was a long and arduous affair, so that a member of the Private Chamber might be twenty-five years old or more when he received at the time of *chıqma* an appointment elsewhere in the service of the Sultan. The education given in the schools was designed, in the measure that individual aptitudes made possible, to transform the child recruit into a loyal Muslim, a servant of the state skilled in war and administration, and a gentleman versed in the mores and culture of the Osmanli. Moreover, the range of that education was wide, since it embraced religious studies, liberal arts, training both physical and vocational, and also military skills.

The *ghilman* learned first to read, speak, and write Ottoman Turkish; in addition, to become familiar with the Koran and with the principles of the Muslim faith. Attention was directed to grammar and syntax, and to literature, not only in Turkish, but also in Arabic and Persian. A program of this kind had ample justification —linguistic, in that Ottoman itself was an amalgam of Turkish, Arabic, and Persian, and cultural, in that Arabic and Persian constituted, as it were, the classical humanities of the Ottoman world. Arabic was the language of the Koran and of the sacred law. Persian served as a medium of polite intercourse among the Ottomans. An acquaintance with these languages, even if limited, was held to be desirable in men who might be called to high office. The *ich-oghlanları* devoted some of their time to mathematics and to geography and history. There was instruction, too, in the scripts used for Ottoman Turkish and also in the composition of official documents and letters. The program sought, in fact, to develop aptitudes serviceable no less in the bureaucratic career than in the fields of war and politics. The level of attainment reached in the schools varied, of course, from one *ghulam* to another: for example, the Ayas Pasha already mentioned, appears as a man unpolished and even illiterate, and the Lutfi Pasha who followed him as Grand Vizier, as an accomplished man, the author of a chronicle and of the *Asafname,* a percipient monograph analyzing the duties of a good vizier.

Attention was given in the schools of the Inside Service to physical training, horsemanship, and the use of arms. No effort was spared to bring the student to physical perfection through exercises and the use of weights, through wrestling, and the like. The game of *jerid*—a kind of mock warfare fought between mounted *ghilman* hurling darts or javelins—did much to transform the students into skilled horsemen. Also included in the program was expert tuition in the arts of the bow, the lance, and the sword.

The *ich-oghlanlari* had to learn, in addition, the duties which fell to them as attendants in the personal service of the Sultan: for example, the men of the Private Chamber took care of the imperial wardrobe and accouterments. Of each *ghulam* it was demanded, moreover, that he master a special vocation; that is, acquire a particular skill such as making arrows and quivers, repairing guns, leather-work, or miniature-painting. This practice was one that even the Sultans observed: Mehemmed II is said to have been a gardener and Süleyman a goldsmith.

The *ghulam* was a slave of the Sultan, brought into a close, indeed intimate, contact with his lord. To his master he looked for maintenance and clothing; from him he received a stipend measured according to the rank that he had won. He spent in the Enderun some of the formative years of his life—cut off from the world outside the palace, exposed to a severe discipline, and subject to a system intended to make him, in thought and deed, a "man of the Sultan." Loyal and prompt obedience to the will of his lord was inculcated in him through all the long time of learning. The education bestowed on him excelled in its range, its duration, and its thoroughness. Care was taken to discern the *ghulam* of talent, to assess and foster his abilities, and to insure that, when his training was complete, he would be directed to a form of service where he might best advance the interests of the Ottoman state.

THE DECLINE OF THE SYSTEM

The *ghulam* institution, as it existed in the fifteenth and sixteenth centuries, began to change under the influence of factors operative even before the death of Sultan Süleyman in 1566. Major wars to the east against Persia (1578-90) and to the west against Austria (1593-1606) imposed on the Ottomans the need to increase the armed forces of the central régime. Warfare in the harsh terrain and climate of Armenia, Azerbayjan, and the Caucasus meant a high rate of casualties. The attempt, moreover, to subjugate and hold these wide regions demanded the establishment of numerous forts and garrisons. It was a policy which could be carried out effectively, not by horsemen, but only by a rapid enlargement of the infantry (the Janissaries) and the technical corps belonging to the household of the Sultan. On the Danube line and in the adjacent lands the Christians had erected a system of defenses often manned with some of the best professional troops in Europe. A war against Austria, therefore, meant for the Ottomans an arduous assault expensive in both men and equipment. The river valleys of Hungary witnessed a bitter conflict of sieges where once again the need was for infantry and specialized troops rather than for cavalry. With so high a loss of life, the normal methods of recruiting into the household of the Sultan—the *devshirme,* capture in war, gift, and purchase—became inadequate to meet the demands of the new situation. Entrance into the ranks of the *ghilman* had been limited to slaves, non-Muslim and non-Turkish in origin—the Muslim and Turkish subjects of the Empire remained in general excluded from the system. The altered circumstances of war blurred and broke down this line of demarcation. Muslims of Turkish descent began now to be recruited for service as "men of the Sultan"—recruited above all, under the pressures of changing warfare, into the armed forces of the imperial household, and notably into the corps of Janissaries. Of these Muslim elements, a large proportion entered as grown men fit for war. They were very different from the young slaves who had been captured in battle or acquired through purchase, divorced from their former milieu and then endowed with a profound awareness of their special relationship to the Sultan and of their privileged status compared with other subjects. One of the main principles underlying the *ghulam* system as a whole— its exclusiveness—was now seriously impaired. The institution would indeed survive, but with an esprit de corps, a sense of discipline, and a degree of efficiency much diminished from the excellence characteristic of the golden age in the fifteenth and sixteenth centuries.[15]

A further change, also unfavorable, occurred at this time. The Empire was passing through a prolonged crisis, economic and social in character. This crisis, visible above all in Asia Minor, where it led to spasmodic and bitter rebellion, arose from several causes. Amongst the causes was a rise in population with consequent pressure on the means of subsistence, and harsh fiscal policies (e.g., debasement of the coinage) undertaken by a government desperate to meet the enormous cost both of an enlarged personnel and of a difficult and generally unrewarding warfare. One result of the crisis was a notable increase in the size of the retinues attendant on high dignitaries in the provinces. Men not of the *ghulam* system became soldiers in their service. Some of them rose to important office in the administration and in the armed forces of the provincial régimes. A change of this kind signified the abandonment of yet another principle vital to the slave institution of the golden era—the principle that the Sultan should, in general, delegate power to act in his name to no one save his own *ghilman*.

The character of the elite elements controlling the Empire was modified still further in the seventeenth and eighteenth centuries. Most of the great executive offices had been assigned thus far to "men of the Sultan" trained for war and politics. Now, at the center and in the provinces, above all after 1700, these appointments began to pass into the hands of men raised in the bureaus of state

---

[15] During this age children of the *ghilman,* being born of Muslim fathers, did not themselves attain the status of *ghilman.* With the introduction of Muslim-born elements into the *ghulam* system, above all, after the death of Süleyman the Magnificent in 1566, instances of a son succeeding his father in high office are not difficult to find. The most notable example is perhaps the Grand Vizier Mehemmed Köprülü (1656-61), who was able to ensure that, on his own death, his son Ahmed should assume the Grand Vizierate, an appointment that he was to hold (1661-76) with even greater distinction than his father. Under the circumstances prevailing in the seventeenth and eighteenth centuries such factors as the personal alliances of the high dignitaries and the marriage connections existing among them often had a decisive influence in the transmission of power within the central régime and the provinces of the Empire.

dealing with financial, administrative, and secretarial affairs. These officials molded in the bureaucratic traditions of the central régime were closely allied with another class now rising to prominence—the Greek merchant elite of Istanbul known as the Phanariots. This elite, often educated in Italian universities, and familiar with the languages and customs of the Christian world through their cosmopolitan contacts in trade and finance, served the Ottomans—until 1792 without permanent embassies abroad—as interpreters and diplomats competent to act on behalf of the Sultan in negotiations with the states of Europe; and indeed, the resourcefulness of the skilled diplomat was essential to an empire henceforth exposed to reiterated and severe defeat in war against Austria and Russia.

The provinces, too, saw the emergence of local elites, as the power of the central government went into decline. After the conquest of Egypt in 1517, the Ottomans had taken over, as a kind of militia, large elements from among the troops of the preceding Mamluk régime. There now arose within this militia, during the seventeenth and eighteenth centuries, a class of *begs* or "grandees," each trained in the *mamluk,* that is, *ghulam* household of an earlier *beg* and in turn training *mamluks* or *ghilman* in his own establishment. This class, mainly though not wholly of Circassian origin, was able to acquire almost complete control over the administration of Egypt. A *ghulam* institution also dominated the affairs of Iraq in the years 1704-1831. Its personnel consisted of *mamluks* obtained in large measure from Georgia. The household was the creation of two *beglerbegis* of Baghdad—Hasan Pasha (1704-23) and his son Ahmad Pasha (1723-34, 1736-47). After the death of Ahmad in 1747 the government of Baghdad was vested, until 1831, in a succession of *mamluks* drawn from this slave institution. The gradual emergence of local elites can be exemplified also in other regions of the Empire. Much of Asia Minor came under the domination of the Derebeys ("lords of the valleys"), while in the Balkans, especially along the lower Danube, groups of notables called *a'yan* gained control of the provincial administration. The movement towards radical reform of the empire along European lines, which began in the reign of Selim III (1789-1807) and gathered momentum under Mahmud II (1808-39), brought to an end, however, some of these autonomies and the elites identified with them. It brought, too, a series of measures which meant the death of the old order. These measures included the suppression of the Janissaries in 1826 and the reform of the palace system from 1831 to 1833.

The slave institution was at its meridian in the reign of Sultan Süleyman (1520-66)—a reign which the later Ottomans regarded as an age of unexampled splendor. It is a truism that no government has ever rested on merit alone. And yet on rare occasions there has been, though short-lived and precarious, some approximation to the ideal. Such was no doubt the view of Ogier Ghiselin de Busbecq, the ambassador at Istanbul during the years 1554-62, of the Hapsburg Archduke Ferdinand of Austria—and it is perhaps to Busbecq that the last word should be given here. He believed that the Ottomans, having discovered a man of high talent, rejoiced greatly as at the finding of a precious thing (*"tanquam adepti rem preciosam"*) and spared no labor or effort to foster his abilities, above all if they saw in him an aptitude for war.[16] As he recalled the ceremonial audience at Amasia, where he was presented to Süleyman for the first time, Busbecq was moved to write a tribute still more eloquent and memorable:

> . . . There was not in all that great assembly a single man who owed his position to aught save his valor and his merit. No distinction is attached to birth among the Turks; the deference to be paid to a man is measured by the position he holds in the public service. There is no fighting for precedence; a man's place is marked out by the duties he discharges. In making his appointments the Sultan pays no regard to any pretensions on the score of wealth or rank, nor does he take into consideration recommendations or popularity; he considers each case on its own merits, and examines carefully into the character, ability, and disposition of the man whose promotion is in question. It is by merit that men rise in the service, a system which insures that posts should only be assigned to the competent. Each man

---

[16] *De Acie Contra Turcam Instruenda Consilium*, 157: ". . . Habent enim hoc omnino Turcae, ut hominem nacti egregium, tanquam adepti rem preciosam, vehementer gaudeant, neque in eo excolendo quicquam laboris aut studij praetermittant: praesertim si ad rem militarem idoneum esse cognoverint . . ."

in Turkey carries in his own hand his ancestry and his position in life, which he may make or mar as he will. Those who receive the highest offices from the Sultan are for the most part the sons of shepherds or herdsmen, and so far from being ashamed of their parentage, they actually glory in it and consider it a matter of boasting that they owe nothing to the accident of birth; for they do not believe that high qualities are either natural or hereditary, nor do they think that they can be handed down from father to son, but that they are partly the gift of God, and partly the result of good training, great industry, and unwearied zeal. . . .[17]

A BIBLIOGRAPHICAL NOTE:

C. T. Forster and F. H. B. Daniell, *The Life and Letters of Ogier Ghiselin de Busbecq*, London 1881, I, 154 (cf. E. S. Forster, *The Turkish Letters of Ogier Ghiselin de Busbecq*, Oxford, 1927, 59-60); *Itinera Constantinopolitanum et Amasianum ab Augerio Gislenio Busbequij . . . Eiusdem De Acie contra Turcam instruenda Consilium*, Antwerpiae 1581, 157; A. H. Lybyer, *The Government of the Ottoman Empire in the Time of Suleiman the Magnificent*, Cambridge, Mass., 1913; B. Miller, *The Palace School of Muhammad the Conqueror*, Cambridge, Mass., 1941; J. A. B. Palmer, "The Origin of the Janissaries," in *Bulletin of the John Rylands Library*, xxxv/2, 1953, 448-81; P. Wittek, "Devshirme and Sharī'a," in *Bulletin of the School of Oriental and African Studies*, xvii/2, 1955, 271-8; S. Vryonis, "Isidore Glabas and the Turkish Devshirme," in *Speculum*, xxxi, 1956, 433-43; S. Vryonis, Seljuk Gulams and Ottoman Devshirmes," in *Der Islam*, xli, 1965, 224-52; V. L. Ménage, "Sidelights on the devshirme from Idrīs and Sa'duddīn," in *Bulletin of the School of Oriental and African Studies*, xviii/1, 1956, 181-3; V. L. Ménage, "Some Notes on the Devshirme," in *Bulletin of the School of Oriental and African Studies*, xxix/1, 1966, 64-78; B. D. Papoulia, *Ursprung und Wesen der "Knabenlese" im osmanischen Reich* (Südosteuropäische Arbeiten, 59), München 1963; *Encyclopaedia of Islam*, 2nd ed., s.v. Ghulam.

---

[17] *The Life and Letters of Ogier Ghiselin de Busbecq*, ed. by C. T. Forster and F. H. B. Daniell, I, 154.

The *Grandes Ecoles*

The French educational system has been mainly influenced by two conceptions: one emphasizes the link between elite formation and State efficiency; the other, the use of education to transcend the incompatibility between an elite structure and the democratic postulate of equality. The two outlooks originate from different historical traditions and reflect conflicting interpretations of the relationship between the state and society. The Revolution of 1789 transformed the rigid structure of the absolutist state and endeavored to introduce co-ordinated changes in society by promoting social mobility through an open school system. The main priority of this policy was to ensure equality of access to instruction, envisaged as a guarantee of citizenship and a key to individual promotion. This insistence on designing the system around the individual led to a complementary neglect of the national role of education as a source of trained specialists, whose number and competence would be geared to social needs defined by and for the state.

While this republican ideal subsequently became embodied in the primary school of the nineteenth century, secondary and higher education acquired the imprint of the imperial régime. Napoleon's attempt to endow France with trained cadres was inspired both by his concern for the efficiency of the state machinery and by his wish to institutionalize elite recruitment. The egalitarian postulate of the Revolution became supplanted as the objective of education and increasingly subordinated to the service of the state. In this concep-

tion, the formation of elites was indispensable on grounds of efficiency and justified by reference to the use of merit as a selection
device. The competitive examination, or *concours,* reflected both
approaches, being democratic as a means of selection and elitist as
a method of classification. Indeed the *concours* was a prerequisite for entry into specialized higher education and, as a terminal
examination, served to rank in order the successful candidates.
Therefore, while merit provided the standard for initial admission,
ultimately it also provided the basis of a hierarchy, reflected by subsequent employment at various levels of the state services.

The *grandes écoles,* establishments of higher learning devised
under the Republic and developed under the Empire, provided an
enduring model for the reconciliation of the two historical traditions. Throughout the nineteenth century the two sets of priorities
co-existed within these schools, since both entrance requirements
and placement of graduates could serve either end. While the continuity of such institutions may appear to reflect a continuity in educational philosophy, their adaptability conceals a diversity of political inspirations.

The history of French education illustrates how a planned system
of general instruction for the average citizen postulates the co-exist-
ence of specialized training for selected individuals. While this co-
existence is a common enough characteristic, the usual sequence
appears to have been reversed. The provision of education for privileged groups or for specific functions generally precedes the extension of popular instruction. In the case of France, this trend was
dramatically accelerated by the initial phases of the Revolution and
seemed to be then reversed. By formally abolishing outdated institutions and discarding contemporary traditions, the legislators of
the new Republic undertook to design their own system of universal
education. Within this system, the requirements of specialization
resulted inevitably in differentiation, reintroducing thereby a hierarchy of qualifications and a plurality of programs. This evolution
complied with the republican postulate of state efficiency but challenged the revolutionary ideal of social equality. The fundamental

contradiction between the establishment and the maintenance of a democracy was thus brought into the open.

The new educational system of the First Republic was clearly intended to depart from the traditions, the institutions, and the methods of the monarchical régime. Traditionally entrusted to religious orders, teaching had been imparted in *collèges* until the Revolution, and the methods applied there reflected the values which permeated all the institutions of the *ancien régime*.[1] Although various types of *collèges* existed in the eighteenth century, they all imitated to some extent the model set by Jesuits and Oratorians. This pattern was fairly rigid, insofar as it aimed at a homogeneous quality of student, which it attained by standardizing both subject matters and teaching methods.[2] In the curriculum, Latin and classical studies predominated, while the instruction emphasized discipline and uncritical acceptance. As a result, the system fostered a strong awareness of social position and a respect for hierarchy exhibited in submission to authority, as well as disregard of lower-class people. It was also integrated with the prevailing ethos in the approach to religion, based on an increasingly formal observance of set practices. Racine wrote to his son, " . . . one cannot be a gentleman without paying all one's debts to God"[3]—as if religion were an insurance policy. In spite of the social and religious conformism implied by this conception of the *honnête homme,* it should

---

[1] *Collèges* were establishments of secondary education, mainly though not exclusively, run by religious orders, and in particular by Jesuits and Oratorians. The curricula were classical in orientation, and the organization reflected the hierarchical structure of the particular order. See H. C. Barnard, *The French Tradition in Education,* Cambridge, Eng., 1922, pp. 144 f.

[2] See F. Vial, *Trois siècles d'histoire de l'enseignement secondaire,* Paris, 1936, p. 45: "La méthode d'autorité requise dans l'enseignement de la religion, s'étend et s'impose par contagion à toutes les autres matières." (The authoritarian method required to teach religion spreads to all other subject matters and affects them by a process of contamination.) Ibid. p. 48: "Il n'y a pas de choix possible entre diverses combinaisons de matières. Une seule route à sens unique est ouverte à toutes les intelligences. l'homogénéité qui est le résultat visé est en même temps la condition de ce résultat." (There can be no choice between various combinations of subject matters. All minds must follow a single one-way road. Homogeneity is both the aim sought and the condition of this result.)

[3] *Lettres à son fils,* quoted by Régine Pernoud, *Histoire de la bourgeoisie en France,* II: "Les Temps Modernes," Paris, 1962, p. 51.

be acknowledged that its intellectual foundations were cemented in the classical culture reinterpreted since the Renaissance.[4] This rationalistic humanism, for all its philosophical and literary merits, entailed an aversion to applied knowledge, technical skill, and manual occupations. A trend towards exaggerated abstraction increasingly led to a divorce between the content of the education given and the types of issues the educated had to face.

The dislike of a practical approach to concrete problems did not preclude in any way a theoretical formulation of global solutions. The general systems propounded throughout the eighteenth century all reflected the same disregard for temporal and spatial variations in the pattern of societies and in the aspirations of individuals. This concern for an abstract Man, and the optimistic belief in the practicability of over-all schemes, was handed down by the philosophers whose works inspired the Revolution to the legislators who attempted to consolidate it.

The transition from purely theoretical philosophy à la Rousseau to the submission of plans for a republican educational system can be found in the works of Condorcet. His report, presented to the Legislative Assembly in 1792, was one of many successive blueprints[5] and was neither adopted nor in fact discussed. However, it influenced not only his contemporaries, but the educational reforms of the July Monarchy and the Third Republic. Its impact stemmed from an internal consistency, due to the comprehensive theory of democratic education on which it was based. It reflected also the receptiveness of French reformers to the attractions of intellectual constructions. The cornerstone of Condorcet's philosophy was the general concept of Man as a rational being, who could therefore be

---

[4] See R. Pernoud, *Histoire de la bourgeoisie . . .* , op. cit. pp. 34 f., on the model of the *honnête homme* and on the classical education which shaped it.
[5] See J. Leif and G. Rustin, *Histoire des institutions scolaires,* Paris, 1954, pp. 101 f., on the twenty-five plans of educational organization drawn up between 1791 and 1799. The main programs were those of Talleyrand (1791), Condorcet (1792), Lanthénas (1792), Sieyès and Daunou (1793), Lepelettier de Saint Fargeau (1793), Romme (1793), and Bouquier—which provided a basis for the decree of the twenty-ninth Frimaire Year II (19 December 1793) on compulsory and free state education. See also F. Levasseur, *Histoire des classes ouvrières et de l'industrie en France de 1798 à 1870,* 2 vol., 2nd ed., Paris, 1903, pp. 73 f. and 90 f.

considered in isolation from cultural antecedents, historical vicissitudes, and environmental pressures.[6] The existence of rights, natural since they were both derived from and founded upon a universal
human nature equated with reason, was not only to be respected by
the state, but also protected by its positive intervention. This went
beyond the postulates of Rousseau, since, by abolishing inequalities
in society in order to protect "natural" rights, the state creates these
very rights. In other words, to destroy educational inequality requires the establishment of state schools, open to all, and filtering by
aptitude from grade to grade. While the definition of freedom postulates enlightenment, that of equality entails not only the provision
of basic primary instruction for all, but the organization of professional training for the development of individual potentialities. The
definition of personal fulfillment as a natural right led to a paradoxi-
cal postulate. A pyramidical structure of education was seen as the
implementation of egalitarianism. Although the provision of higher
education was also related to the need for increasing enlightenment
and the belief in scientific progress, its main theoretical foundation
was the interpretation of equality as equality of opportunity.

THE EMPIRE

Whereas the early republicans sought to embody in the educational
system the duty of the state towards the citizen, the imperial heirs
of the revolutionary tradition founded educational institutions on
citizens' obligations to the state. This definition of citizenship as a
commitment rather than a right was in no way alien to the spirit of
republican France, since it could be traced to Jacobin policy, dic-
tated by considerations of national necessity rather than enlightened
idealism. Liberty may have provided a source of inspiration, but
as a subject of instruction it soon appeared aimless. While practical
and financial considerations prompted many Napoleonic reforms,[7]
they were not the main determinant of the reorganization which
formed the basis of the French educational system. Without break-

[6] See F. Vial, *Condorcet et l'éducation démocratique,* Paris, n.d., pp. 13 f.
[7] G. Weill, *Histoire de l'enseignement secondaire en France, 1802-1920,*
Paris, 1921.

ing away from the revolutionary tradition, the imperial régime was primarily concerned with insuring continuity, if only to consolidate the achievements of the Republic. This could only be guaranteed by the institutional stability and the administrative efficiency derived from the selection and solidarity of new elites. The disappearance of the old aristocratic ruling class, and the obvious inability of temporary rulers and military leaders to establish themselves, left a vacuum and made it possible to redefine the form and functions of leadership. The definition was imposed from above and shaped both by the imperial régime's need for efficient administration,[8] and by the Emperor's idealization of the Roman state.

Napoleon's own legitimation was a success and this endowed the whole régime with a pragmatic approach, in spite of a readiness to use the outward symbols of divine right monarchy and aristocratic elite. Pragmatism rejected the revolutionary ideology implicit in the philosophy of natural rights but took over the notion of individual fulfillment as a justification for a hierarchy based on merit. The elements of "conservative freedom"[9] and constructive equality abstracted from this philosophy were linked with the criteria of efficient selection. Indeed the fulfillment of individual potentialities was not only the right of the citizen, but his duty towards the state. The recognition of merit led to the acceptance of a meritocracy. The premium on efficiency accounted both for the formation of a new administrative elite and for the concern with the training of future replacements. Expediency took precedence over theoretical justifications that went beyond mere efficiency.

AFTER NAPOLEON

As a source of administrative stability, the system outlived the Napoleonic framework for which it had been designed. The very survival, throughout the nineteenth and indeed the twentieth centuries, of the *Université Impériale*'s main institutions, and even its characteristics, has been both the cause and the effect of this con-

[8] See G. Ferrero, *Militarism* (translated from the Italian), London, 1902, p. 194.
[9] That is, freedom to achieve mobility by merit—an approximate definition.

tinuity.[10] The very nature of the education dispensed meant that a group was trained on the principle that education should provide for the needs of the state. Successive generations shared the ideal imparted by this type of training.[11] They ensured the preservation of educational standards that legitimized and protected their position. Loyalty to the state and enlightened self-interest coincided.

The juxtaposition of military discipline and idealistic rationalism which permeated the educational system revealed the double parentage of imperial prestige and late-eighteenth-century tradition. The fall of Napoleon caused a sharp decline in the army's position and power, strengthening the identification of the Civil Service with the state, and restoring its civilian character. The same transformation occurred within the educational system, though without affecting the intellectualism of curricula and method inherited from the pre-Revolution period. Cartesian philosophy, classical literature, the study of antiquity, and an increasing, but always theoretical, interest in the sciences dominated—to the exclusion of modern languages and cultures and of applied arts and techniques. This type of in-

[10] See R. Pernoud, *Histoire de la bourgeoisie* . . . , op. cit. p. 393: "Il n'est pas besoin d'insister sur les différences profondes entre l'Université d'Ancien Régime et l'Université impériale; à plus forte raison sur les caractères fondamentalement opposés qui distinguent l'Université médiévale de cette Université nouvelle; entre l'Université autonome, corps libre dont les membres s'administrent par eux-mêmes, et l'université—organisme d'Etat, instrument du pouvoir, organisé et payé par lui." (There is no need to insist on the deep differences between the University of the Ancien Régime and the imperial University; even less so on the fundamentally opposed characteristics which distinguish the mediaeval University from this new University: between the autonomous university, a free body whose members are self-governing, and the State-run university, an instrument of the public powers, who organize and subsidize it.)

[11] See L. Liard, *L'Enseignement supérieur en France 1789-1889*, Paris, p. 69: ". . . D'où nécessité pour l'Etat d'avoir une doctrine, et non seulement de l'avoir, mais de la formuler, et de considérer l'enseignement comme garantie de sa propre stabilité. Instruire est secondaire; le principal est de former, et de former d'après le modèle qui convient à l'Etat et que, par suite, il a le droit et le devoir d'arrêter et d'imposer." (Hence, the state needs a doctrine and it needs not only to have one but to formulate it, and to use the educational system as a guarantee of its own stability. To instruct is secondary; the main thing is to train, and to train according to the pattern which suits the state, and which it is therefore entitled and even bound to define and to impose.)

struction was remote from practical issues, and secondary education, culminating in the *baccalauréat* degree,[12] could guarantee admission to higher studies, but was not an effective preparation for careers. Impracticality, however, was no obstacle to prestige. Indeed prestige was derived from, and therefore equated with, status rather than social utility. The symbolic value of secondary education resulted from the separation between the secondary[13] and primary schools—a separation which reflected and perpetuated the deep division between the bourgeoisie and "the people."[14] Thanks to this estrangement, the Catholic Church regained its former role in popular education under the Empire and retained it under the auspices of social conservatism, in spite of the recurring attacks of political "laicism."[15]

In its anxiety to differentiate itself, the bourgeoisie emphasized all differences separating it from the people. Educational differences were obvious without being wholly invidious. They appeared to reward individual attainment, whereas in fact they confirmed family position. They protected and strengthened existing positions rather than stimulated individual mobility. The content of education accentuated this attitude. Its emphasis on non-applicable subject matters oriented it towards prestige rather than efficiency.

There was, therefore, an obvious disjunction between the needs and requirements of the Civil Service—needs shared by industry and trade—and the purely formal qualifications dispensed. Tariff policies confirmed this imbalance in the private sector; the protectionist pol-

---

[12] See E. Goblot, *La Barrière et le niveau. Etude sociologique de la bourgeoisie française moderne,* Paris, 1930, p. 127.

[13] See F. Vial, *Trois siècles . . . ,* op. cit. about the Napoleonic lycée, combining the monasticism of the ancient *collèges* with militarism, "établi sur le type d'une dictature politique et militaire" (established on the pattern of a political and military dictatorship—p. 181), which endured from 1802 to 1865.

[14] By Third Estate was meant all those who did not belong to either nobility (First Estate) or clergy (Second Estate). Therefore it was a broad category including the bourgeoisie, which came to be known as the Third Estate, and the people, which were never recognized as a Fourth—a point made by early socialists.

[15] See e.g. R. Escarpit, *Ecole laïque, école du peuple,* Paris, 1961, pp. 107 ff. and B. Mégrine, *La question scolaire en France,* Paris, 1960, p. 34.

icies[16] prevailing in the nineteenth and the first half of the twentieth century sheltered the less competitive concerns. Added to customs barriers, state subsidies constituted a disincentive to organizational efficiency, thereby reducing the premium on technically trained personnel. In public administration, decision-making was concentrated among the top echelons, in accordance with the military model initially adopted, its strict hierarchy, and its dislike for delegation. The concentration of authority among the higher grade officials implied that they accepted responsibility for subordinates whose proficiency was limited and who could not therefore be held fully accountable. For many, a civil service career represented a guarantee of security[17] rather than an avenue of mobility. For a few, it constituted a complete dedication to the service of the state.

This conception paralleled closely the *ancien régime* tradition of service to the dynasty. Under the Bourbons, administrative centralization favored the establishment of an administrative elite.[18] It was by design, in order to weaken the nobility and increase the personal authority of the monarch, that Louis XIV surrounded himself with *grands commis* of bourgeois descent.[19]

> . . . I believed that it was not in my interest to seek men of more eminent station because . . . it was important that the public should know, from the rank of these whom I chose to serve me, that I had no intention of sharing my power with them . . . that they themselves, conscious of what they were, should conceive no higher aspirations than those which I chose to permit.[20]

[16] See F. Goguel, *Le Régime politique français,* Paris, 1955, p. 11.

[17] See R. de Jouvenel, *La République des camarades,* Paris, 1914, p. 131: "L'Etat ne demande à ceux qu'il emploie ni intelligence, ni compétence, ni vertus, ni talents. Il leur demande d'avoir des droits acquis." (The state does not expect from its employees either intelligence, or competence, or virtues, or talents. It only expects them to have acquired rights.)

[18] See F. L. Ford, *Robe and Sword. The Regrouping of the French Aristocracy after Louis XIV,* Cambridge, Mass., 1953.

[19] *Grands commis* was the traditional name given to the individual advisers of the kings of France, who, apart from being consulted on policy, also supervised its execution and were therefore heads of the emerging administrative services. By extension this name applied to the high civil servants of the Republic in the nineteenth century.

[20] *Mémoires de Louis XIV,* ed. by C. Dreyss, Paris, 1860.

But it was under that "reign of vile bourgeoisie," as Saint-Simon was to call it, that a judicial nobility of the robe began to crystallize. This evolution from a former position of responsibility without privilege to aspiration for privilege without responsibility deprived the sovereign of competent advisers and the Third Estate[21] of powerful representatives. Following the coalition of robe and sword, the eighteenth century witnessed an aristocratic reaction; and the defense of privileges, whether inherited or bought, precipitated the fall of the monarchy. But the principle of a centralized administrative structure survived and its application was intensified,[22] thereby maintaining the need for a body of administrators.

Unlike their predecessors of the *ancien régime,* the *grands commis de la République* achieved their position by virtue of formally tested merit (rather than inherited rank or purchase), justified it by proved competence (rather than royal favor), and maintained it throughout—or because of—the vicissitudes of an unstable political life. Those elements of systematic selection, operational efficiency, and guaranteed continuity add up to the concept of career. Independence from the political pressures implied a separation from the rulers as well as the ruled, which could amount to isolation. This led unavoidably to an esprit de corps, reinforced by common background and shared training. At the same time, mistrust of oligarchies, inherent in democracy, but felt under all régimes because of their instability, meant that neither heredity nor wealth provided an adequate means of legitimation.[23] The only alternative hallowed by the revolutionary theory of a natural right to the development of individual aptitudes, consisted in basing recruitment on objective standards of intellectual attainment. Specialized higher education

---

[21] See J. H. Meisel, *The Myth of the Ruling Class,* Ann Arbor, Mich., 1958, p. 97: "The great revolution was precipitated by a double class defection: the old feudal class deserting their king, the new feudal class deserting its bourgeois basis."

[22] See A. de Tocqueville, *De la démocratie en France,* Paris, 1849.

[23] See A. Thibaudet, *La République des professeurs,* Paris, 1927, p. 236: "A l'égard des aristocraties de naissance et de fortune, le devoir démocratique est simple: défiance, surveillance, contrôle." . . . (The democratic duty towards aristocracies of birth and wealth is simple: distrust, watchfulness, control.)

was aimed at producing candidates of appropriate caliber; the whole educational system stressed the supremacy of the intellect.

The French ideal of the "intelligent man" attempted to reconcile contradictory imperatives. Democratic selection had to co-exist with a highly organized state hierarchy; the liberalism of an individualist but enlightened society was challenged by an aristocratic tradition, more directly self-centered. Not unlike that of the English gentleman,[24] this ideal illustrated national codes of behavior, systems of values, and sets of prejudices, with the distorting accuracy of stereotypes and caricatures. It could be traced to its ancestor, the *honnête homme* of the *ancien régime,* whose Cartesian inheritance was both prestigious and limiting. It could be preached as a revolutionary dogma of personal fulfillment, or justified as an expedient means of maximizing social efficiency. Like most tenets of French republican ideology, it was the product of a historical evolution predating 1789 and of a compromise between conflicting postrevolutionary influences. Thus, the intellectualism permeating the educational system, attacked by opponents of the régime in the nineteenth century[25] and deplored by supporters of modernization in the twentieth,[26] did not only reflect a neo-Kantian, republican ethic. Maurras's criticism of an arid classicism and cult of state authority could equally well have been aimed at the *collèges* of monarchical France. In fact, the whole educational history of the nineteenth century has been summed up as the struggle between this tradition, reincarnated in the *lycée,*[27] and that of the short-lived *écoles centrales,* intended to implement revolutionary paedagogical ideas.[28]

---

[24] See M. F. Hignette, "The Primacy of the Rational in French Secondary Education," in *The World Yearbook of Education,* 1958.

[25] See M. Curtis, *Three against the Third Republic, Sorel, Barrès, and Maurras,* Princeton, N.J., 1959, pp. 165-72.

[26] See M. Crozier, "Le Citoyen" in "Esprit," February 1961.

[27] A type of secondary school.

[28] See A. Cournot, *Des Institutions d'instruction publique en France,* Paris, 1864, p. 271 ff. Established by the law of the third Brumaire Year IV, the *écoles centrales* were intended to teach predominantly mathematics, modern languages, and civics. Teaching methods, inspired by Condorcet, were to emphasize individual aptitudes and freedom of choice; see S. F. Lacroix, *Essai sur l'enseignement en général et sur celui des mathématiques en particulier.* About their abolition in 1802, cf. F. Vial, *Trois Siècles . . . ,*" op. cit. p. 166: "Les écoles centrales n'avaient à offrir que le péril d'une liberté complète sans l'attrait d'une règle morale. . . ."

The durable nature of the intellectual tradition and the continuity between academic establishments under different régimes account for the "social and educational stability"[29] which characterized and shaped republican France. Secondary education successfully endowed the bourgeoisie with social prestige and supplied higher establishments with trained recruits. Primary education perpetuated the nationalist and secularist aspects of the republican creed, succeeding as a source of patriotism even while it failed as a real training for citizenship. It provided the people with an opportunity for social promotion by a "creaming" process rather than with a preparation for working life. It thereby gave witness to the ideal of *embourgeoisement,* prevalent under the Third Republic, which underestimated technical training and "learning to think with one's hands."[30] The separation between the primary and the secondary "cycles," which were not closely inter-related exemplified the contradiction between the social bias and the political ethos of the régime.[31] Intellectual merit had to secure occupational promotion and increased income before it could qualify for the consecration of the *baccalauréat* and claim its full rewards—as a rule, in the following generation. In short, secondary schooling favored a middle-class outlook and required economic resources.

ECOLE POLYTECHNIQUE AND ECOLE NORMALE SUPERIEURE

Higher education originally reflected Napoleon's distrust of the *idéologues,* and the priority given to training for concrete roles in the state machinery. The imperial university was mainly concerned with the network of *lycées,* whereas above the secondary level it was deemed enough to assert the principle of centralization, and state

[29] See C. Morazé, *Les Français et la Republique,* Paris, 1956, p. 103, on "stabilité socioscolaire."
[30] Denis de Rougemont's expression, quoted by G. Friedmann, *Où va le Travail Humain?,* Paris, 1959, 13th ed.—see pp. 272 ff. about technical education.
[31] See R. Dumaine, "La démocratisation de l'enseignement: Assession à la culture et sélection des élites," *Semaines sociales de France* (45E session, Versailles, 1948); *L'enseignement, problème social,* Lyons, 1958, pp. 231 ff.

monopoly[32] was asserted but not fully implemented. Within this rigid framework, the establishments created during the Revolution[33] in lieu of the twenty-two universities of the *ancien régime,* officially suppressed in 1793, were reorganized or resurrected. As an example of reorganization, the Ecole Polytechnique, instituted by the revolutionary Convention[34] and faithful to its revolutionary origins throughout the first half of the nineteenth century,[35] was granted military status. It was no longer subject to the Minister for the Interior and its internal regulations were modeled on the army, thereby providing a unique corps of uniformed and disciplined mathematicians and scientists trained to serve the state. The school's emphasis on the service of the state remains predominant,[36] al-

[32] On the ease with which this monopoly could be used to serve monarchic ideas under the Restoration, as it had served Napoleon, see S. d'Irsay, *Histoire des universités françaises et étrangères des origines jusqu'à nos jours,* Paris, 1933, II, 231. The first relaxation in this rigidly centralized system occurred only in 1896.

[33] Revolutionary creations included: the Museum (for chemistry, biology, minerology and geology), the Conservatoire des arts et métiers, the Ecole des traveaux publics (future Polytechnique), the Bureau des longitudes, the Ecole des langues orientales and the Ecole normale. See J. Leif and G. Rustin, *Histoire des institutions . . . ,* loc. cit.

[34] Created as Ecole Centrale des Travaux Publics on the twenty-first Pluviôse Year II (11 March 1794), it was renamed Ecole Polytechnique in 1795. This name, intended to emphasize the need for a broad approach removed from the prevailing academism, was used colloquially before it became official. The school was first considered as preparatory prior to specialized training. Conditions of entry were "a good behavior, attachment to republican principles" and a knowledge of mathematics (see M. d'Ocagne, *Les Grandes Ecoles de France,* Paris, 1873, p. 92). After three years of study, students were given posts as military or civil engineers according to their aptitudes.

[35] The *Polytechniciens* showed republican leanings under the Empire and the Restoration, and some of them participated actively in the July Revolution. On the difference of recruitment between Polytechnique, which attracted the urban bourgeoisie, and Saint-Cyr, where rural milieux predominated, see P. Chalmin, *L'Officier français de 1815 à 1870,* Paris, 1957, pp. 150 ff.

[36] Cf. General B. Cazelles in *L'Ecole Polytechnique en 1962,* Paris, 1963: "On ne peut être un polytechnicien valable que si l'on se sent capable, intellectuellement et moralement, de servir l'Etat, comme civil ou comme militaire, même si l'on se destine à une carrière privée." (One cannot be a *polytechnicien* of value unless one feels intellectually and morally able to serve the State, as a civilian or as a soldier, even if one aims at a career in the private sector.)

though it is now understood that not all former *polytechniciens* will devote themselves to the civil service and that only a few will opt for a military career.

A re-creation occurred when the Ecole Normale, which the Convention intended to be the apex of a pyramid of teacher-training institutions and which survived for only three months,[37] was set up again by imperial decree.[38] Napoleon considered it his own "creation, a necessary creation;"[39] he either overlooked the previous episode or considered he had radically altered the initial design by reversing the original balance between the sciences and the literary disciplines. Under the Republic, the most eminent scientists had been willing to learn how to teach, whereas teachers of literary subjects had been men of much lesser accomplishments.[40] The refounded school emphasized the study of Latin and French literature —in accordance with the Emperor's belief in the formative virtue of the classics. The reading of great works was not only advocated as a training for the mind, but as a disincentive to revolutionary thinking, since their aesthetic merits were inseparable from a conservative philosophy. Napoleon put it very frankly:

> Above all, let us give some sound and strong reading material to the youth of the régime. Corneille, Boussuet, those are the masters it needs. That is great, sublime, and at the same time regular,

[37] Created by decree of the ninth Brumaire Year III (30 October 1794) as Ecole Normale de Paris, in order to train teachers for the departmental teacher training colleges (*écoles normales*). This decree, known as "décret Lakanal" after its instigator, was superseded by the Law of the third Brumaire Year IV (25 October 1795) or "loi Daunou," which instituted a three-layer educational system: primary schools in the "cantons," *écoles centrales* in the "départments," and *grandes écoles* at the national level. The system remained largely at the blueprint stage, since parts of it were never implemented and others did not endure. On the failure of the Ecole Normale de Paris, due mostly to the uneven quality of the teaching and the uneven level of the audience, see J. Fayet, *Le Révolution Française et la science* (1789-1795), Paris, 1960, pp. 342 ff.

[38] See *Ecole Normale, règlements, programmes et rapports,* Paris, 1837, for the school's statute of 30 March 1810.

[39] See Villemain, *Souvenirs,* Paris, 1856 (reprint of an article first published in *Revue des Deux Mondes,* 15 April 1852).

[40] See E. Herriot, *Normale,* Paris, 1932, pp. 20 ff., on the imperfections of the literary courses in the initial school. On the quality of science teaching, see J. Michelet, *Le peuple,* 4th ed., Paris, 1866, pp. 283 ff.

peaceful, subordinated. Those do not make revolutions; they do not inspire any. On the sails of obedience, they enter into the established order of their time; they strengthen it, they embellish it.[41]

Whether the study of *lettres* within this definition was the best method for training "respectful civil servants" is certainly debatable.[42] But it did prove a very effective means of strengthening the humanistic bias in secondary education, conceived as a preliminary to higher education and imparted by *professeurs agrégés* whom the Ecole Normale had imbued with a sense of superiority over their scientific colleagues.[43] Therefore, the trend was continued from generation to generation and is only being reversed very slowly, within the whole educational system, under the pressure of economic needs and of an "intellectual revisionism" which is beginning to affect the *normaliens* themselves.

[41] Translated by Michalina Vaughan from Villemain, *Souvenirs,* loc. cit., quoting Napoleon: "Avant tout, mettons la jeunesse du régime à de saines et fortes lectures. Corneille, Bossuet, voilà les maîtres qu'il lui faut. Cela est grand, sublime, et en même temps régulier, paisible, subordonné. Ah! ceux-là ne font pas de révolutions; ils n'en inspirent pas. Ils entrent à pleines voiles d'obéissance dans l'ordre établi de leur temps; ils le fortifient, ils le décorent."

[42] Cf. A. François-Poncet's introduction to A. Peyrefitte, *Rue d'Ulm,* Paris, 1946: "L'Ecole Normale Supérieure devait fabriquer des fonctionnaires respectueux. Elle en fabrique. Elle en fabrique même d'irrespectueux. Fidèle à son origine révolutionnaire, elle a toujours, été un foyer d'esprit critique. . . . Aussi lui est-il arrivé d'être punie, et même fermée, à plusieurs reprises." (The Ecole Normale was to turn out respectful civil servants. It does turn out some. It even turns out some disrespectful civil servants. Faithful to its revolutionary origin, it has always been a center of *esprit critique.* . . . Therefore it has been penalized, and even closed, on several occasions.)

[43] Cf. G. Pompidou's introduction to A. Peyrefitte, *Rue d'Ulm, chroniques de la vie normalienne,* rev. ed., Paris, 1963: "Quand un normalien littéraire tutoie un scientifique et n'hésite pas à lui adresser la parole en public sur un ton d'affectueuse sollicitude, ne vous méprenez pas: il n'y a là que la manifestation de son esprit social. Ainsi le descendant des croisés, quand il a été bien élevé, parle de pair à compagnon avec la noblesse d'Empire." (When a literary *normalien* says "tu" to a scientist and addresses him affectionately in public make no mistake: he is just being socially minded. Similarly a well-bred descendant of the Crusaders will speak to the imperial nobility on equal terms.)

The two main *grandes écoles* embody the revolutionaries' belief in perfectibility through education, in the alliance between science and liberty, and in the coincidence of individual intellectual fulfillment with the service of the state. They witness to the farsightedness of their designs, though not necessarily to the durability of their achievements. Institutionally, they can both be traced to the imperial period of reforms, or re-formations. They have both been designed, or redesigned, to supply highly trained civil servants, selected according to the most exacting intellectual criteria and molded by a military or a monastic discipline[44]—the quality of recruitment being a guarantee of competence and the organization of the studies a test of dependability. In fact, students sometimes perceived an underlying contradiction between intellectual independence and political conformism, both emphasized in their education. The result, periodically, was an outburst of criticism within the schools, and anti-government activities by the students. Graduates of the schools have, later in their career, reconciled or even equated loyalty to the state with a disapproval of existing governments. Such a state of mind has often been experienced by high-ranking civil servants in times of political instability or under ephemeral cabinets. But the lack of a strong executive was not foreseen in the Napoleonic blueprint for a docile civil service. The failure to obtain unlimited obedience has to be measured against unqualified success in securing an intellectual level which heightened the prestige of the administrative cadres, compensating both for the inferior quality of lower grades[45] and for the impermanence of political rulers.

The maintenance of this high quality has been guaranteed by a system of recruitment maximizing competition and resulting in a preselection of candidates, who are graded at entry and not just admitted into the school. This device of the competitive examina-

[44] The severity of the internal regulations applied at Normale was quasi-military during the nineteenth century. It was increased under the Second Empire by ministerial instructions. See J. Thomas, *Sainte-Beuve et l'Ecole Normale, 1834-67,* Paris, 1936.

[45] For a comparison between the French and the British approach to the training of medium rank civil servants, see B. Chapman, *The Profession of Government,* London, 1959, p. 93. See also G. Tixier, *La Formation des cadres supérieurs de l'Etat en Grande-Bretagne et en France,* Paris, 1948.

tion, or *concours,* insures that only the very best applicants will be retained[46] and that the criteria used in assessing them will be objective, insofar as they have been standardized. Democratic as a means of selection, since it rules out patronage and rewards only proved ability, the *concours* could also be advocated on grounds of efficiency, because it tests the kind of knowledge and, more conclusively, the form of mind which provides a favorable basis and a suitable ground for the education given by the school. In this sense, success is a consecration, the recognition of an intrinsic aptitude, increased by and verified through acquired knowledge, but transcending this knowledge. Its elitist implications, therefore, go beyond the obvious effects of classifying by merit. The system perpetuates a group adhering to a basic definition of merit and committed to the defense of shared criteria—a stronger and subtler bond than common values can provide.

Both Polytechnique and Normale illustrate this role of the *concours* as a means of admission into intellectual milieux whose habits of thought are imparted for life, and into educational establishments leading up to a variety of careers, not all of them in the civil service.[47] Moreover, Polytechnique constantly grades by merit throughout the two years of the course, since the final ranking (*classement de sortie*) depends on the results of six-monthly examinations and determines the choice of a given career.[48] In other words, the most

---

[46] In the case of Polytechnique, the average figures per year are 300 successful candidates out of 1800 who have been preparing for the *concours* since the *baccalauréat*. The preparation lasts two to three years. See *L'Ecole Polytechnique,* op. cit. p. 5.

[47] The main outlets for *polytechniciens* are *grands corps techniques de l'Etat* (state control over industry, management of state monopolies, central posts of economic and technical services), the armed forces (to a lesser degree than in the past), research (in the state laboratories of the National Center for Scientific Research—CNRS, under the provisions of "décret Suquet" of 24 August 1939) and industry (mining, oil, textile, etc.). Outside the field of education (and that of research, explicitly added by the new Statute of 2 October 1962), *Normaliens* are currently found in journalism, diplomacy, politics, finance, and the literary professions.

[48] See M. d'Ocagne, *Les Grandes Ecoles* . . . , op. cit. p. 105: "Le classement de sortie a une importance capitale, puisqu'il détermine le choix de la carrière." (The final ranking is extremely important, since it determines the choice of a career.)

successful students obtain a privileged career position, but privilege is linked with proved intellectual eminence.

Both Polytechnique and Normale, although their creation was intended to supply the country's needs in trained specialists, have evolved towards a very broad intellectual formation. The scientific culture given to the *polytechniciens* is based on extensive study of mathematics and physical sciences, but completed by an "initiation" into other subjects relevant to understanding the modern world. It is intended as a "general training for thought and action."[49] Insofar as *normaliens* read for university degrees (*licence ès lettres* or *licence ès sciences* during their first year and *agrégation* during their third and last year at the school), they share in the general instruction given by the Sorbonne.[50] But, within the school itself, the second year is a period of unrestrained freedom of study[51] and, throughout the course, intellectual curiosity is never subordinated to a narrow view of the future teachers' responsibilities.[52] Individual development predominates over teacher training.

[49] According to *L'Ecole Polytechnique,* op. cit. the program covers, apart from scientific subjects (algebra, higher and analytic geometry, mechanics, and physics, theory of general and physical chemistry, applied sciences), one foreign language (English, German, or Russian), elements of economics and of social sciences, lectures on history, literature, architecture, and artistic design. There is an extensive program of athletic and military training.

[50] The reform of 1903, which changed the name of Ecole Normale Supérieure into Ecole Normale, strengthened existing links between the school and the University of Paris, without depriving it of its administrative and budgetary autonomy.

[51] See R. Rolland, *Mémoires et fragments de journal,* Paris, 1956, pp. 47-8: "Trois ans de jeux austères et enivrants de l'esprit . . . Mais la seconde, quel paradis! On était libre de penser tout ce qu'on veut." (Three years of austere and intoxicating intellectual games . . . But the second, what heaven! One was free to think as one wished.)

[52] See E. Bersot (former director of Normale), *Etudes et discours,* Paris, 1879 (quoted by A. Peyrefitte, *Rue d'Ulm* rev. ed., op. cit. p. 200): "Education de luxe, éducation absurde, si nos jeunes gens, une fois professeurs, ont l'intention de reverser à leurs élèves tout ce qu'ils ont appris; éducation sensée, s'il est vrai qu'on ne sait pas assez si l'on ne sait que ce que l'on enseigne, et qu'après avoir bien travaillé pour ses élèves, il n'est pas interdit de travailler pour soi." (Luxury education, absurd education, if our young men, when they become teachers, intend to inflict on their pupils all that they have learned; sensible education, if it is true that one does not know enough when one knows only what one teaches, and that, after having worked well for one's pupils, one is allowed to work for oneself.)

Both Polytechnique and Normale give students an active role and much initiative, by contrast with traditional French education imparted ex cathedra and absorbed in comparatively passive fashion. Normale pioneered the method of group discussion, called *conférence,* later adopted in Germany under the name of "seminar."[53] This technique, introduced by the statute of 1810 as an alternative to dogmatic teaching, fostered intellectual liveliness and freedom of thought. Moreover, the group has played an important role not only as a learning, but as a "living" unit, perpetuating elaborate rituals and vocabularies devised by previous generations of students. It would be vain to analyze the prestige of either school without taking into account the solidarity generated by years of communal living in an atmosphere imbued with traditions. The importance of this collective memory and this common language as a link between age groups (*promotions*) deserves to be stressed; it is unusual in France, where boarding schools are the exception rather than the rule. The originality of approach for which both schools are famous,[54] and the strong sense of mutual help which *polytechniciens* are alleged to possess, are reinforced by the outer signs of an esprit de corps, at times akin to "esprit de caste."[55]

[53] See N. Fustel de Coulanges (Normalien and former director of Normale), "L'Ecole Normale" in *Séances et travaux de l'Académie des Sciences morales et politiques,* Paris, 1884, XXI, p. 836 f.

[54] There are many definitions of *esprit polytechnicien* or of what the school (known as X) stands for and many attempts at defining *esprit normalien* (or the spirit of the Rue d'Ulm) or even at ascertaining if it really exists. For an attempted parallel, see A. François-Poncet's speech in *Bulletin de la Société des Amis de l'Ecole Normale,* Paris, February, 1951. Attacks on the schools range from Balzac's *Curé de Village* to Flaubert's *Education Sentimentale* and from Zola's *Une Campagne* to Péguy and Martin du Gard. From Sainte-Beuve to Giraudoux, many have written in praise of Normale. Polytechnique has understandably offered less inspiration to writers, but its yearbook provides invaluable information on the role of its former pupils in the civil service and in industry alike. On Polytechnique and the army, see General Serrigny, "Formation des élites militaires" in *Revue de Paris,* 1 December 1929.

[55] See R. Aron, *L'Age des empires et l'avenir de la France,* Paris, 1945, p. 190.

THE NETWORK OF *Grandes Ecoles*

Polytechnique and Normale are set apart from other schools by their historical role, the prestige and breadth of their education, and the variety as well as the eminence of the posts they supply. Nevertheless, other *grandes écoles* have similar characteristics. Their founding dates show when it was officially recognized that a given activity required special training and a given field needed advanced study. Thus, the institution of the Ecole des Chartes under the Restoration coincided with the rediscovery of mediaeval history and art[56] and that of the Ecole Centrale with the beginnings of industrialization as well as with the growth of Saint-Simon's technological philosophy.[57] Likewise, the reorganization of a military school at Saint-Cyr[58] under the Empire evidenced a concern for institutionalizing the recruitment and training of officers. Conditions of entry and curricula varied necessarily from school to school, but they reflected planned attempts to standardize the criteria by which merit was assessed: hence, the predominance of the *concours*. They also represented a broad view of the background, be it artistic, scientific, or (less frequently) technical, required to qualify for a varied selection of posts. Military schools were by definition more strictly limited, but civilian schools did not lead to employment in the civil service alone. Furthermore, bonds of fellowship formed in the years of study, and the special understanding of administration acquired during the course, were considered a useful basis for collaboration between the public and private sectors.

During the nineteenth century, the expanding network of *grandes écoles* compensated in many respects for the deficiencies of a

[56] Founded in 1821, the Ecole des Chartes was refounded in 1829. Cf. R. Pernoud, *Histoire de la France . . .* , op. cit. p. 486.

[57] See M. d'Ocagne, *Les Grandes Ecoles . . .* , op. cit. p. 178: "C'est là que doivent se former les grands industriels, les directeurs des grandes usines, tandis que l'Ecole Polytechnique conservera la mission d'alimenter de sujets capables tous les services publics de l'Etat." (It is there that great industrialists, heads of great factories are to be trained, whereas the Ecole Polytechnique will retain the task of supplying all state services with competent persons.)

[58] See V. Pellegrin, *Histoire de Saint-Cyr,* Paris [no date printed] and G. Castelan, *Histoire de l'armée,* Paris, 1948.

university system which lacked political as well as intellectual independence. Because it had proved so successful in the special domains to which it had been applied, it offered a pattern to be considered especially by those who attributed the defeat of 1870 to the inadequacies of the French educational system[59] and to the lack of trained administrative and political leaders. General education for specialists could also be used to give a special education to generalists. Optimism about the accuracy of the emerging social sciences allied itself to a confidence in the efficiency of education. The first was typical of the age; the second was inherited from the previous century. Since there was no doubt about the diagnosis, a crisis in French leadership, the remedy seemed obvious.[60] The elitist aspect of this new "scientism" led to an interpenetration between the spheres of politics and public administration, tantamount to a confusion between the roles of political leader and high-ranking civil servant. This imprecision, characteristic of the Right's political thought and derived from its emphasis on "competence" as opposed to representativeness, presided over the foundation of the Ecole des Sciences Morales et Politiques in 1872.

Unlike other *grandes écoles,* the new school was a private institution. Its founder, Emile Boutmy, had been a follower of Saint-Simon and shared his confidence in the rule of trained administrators (*gouvernement des capacités*). The purpose was to train civil servants who could assume the direction of the main administrative services, to form diplomats, financiers, politicians "and, if possible, statesmen," and to ensure that France would have "mechanics, technicians, experts in politics."[61] Therefore, the school was chiefly

---

59 See E. Renan, *Réforme intellectuelle et morale de la France,* Paris, 1871.
60 See T. Jouffroy, *Mélanges philosophiques,* 1866, p. 139; "Economistes, administrateurs, légistes, nous avons de tout cele en abondance; de ces hommes-là, on en forme en France à la douzaine; nous en avons des fabriques, comme de médecins; mais d'hommes politiques, mais d'hommes d'Etat, nous n'en avons point, et, à la manière dont vont nos affaires, on s'en aperçoit." (Economists, administrators, lawyers, we have all those in numbers; such men are trained in France by the dozen; we have factories turning them out, just like physicians; but we have no politicians, no statesmen and the way in which our business is conducted makes it obvious.)
61 See A. Leroy-Beaulieu's speech in memory of Boutmy (quoted by R. Pernoud, *"Histoire de la bourgeoisie* . . . , op. cit. p. 594-5): "Il fallait . . . à l'Etat des serviteurs aptes à en conduire tous les grands services; il fallait

intended to train for the *grands corps de l'Etat,* the main administrative bodies of the Napoleonic state. Until the Third Republic, appointments to these posts had been discretionary; in an attempt to
"depoliticize" the civil service, recruitment by *concours* had been
introduced and the concept of an administrative career strengthened. The number of *concours* held to fill a variety of posts reflected
the increase of state services in metropolitan France and in the col-
onies,[62] and satisfied the aspiration for security and status which
prompted applicants.[63] But the main *concours,* corresponding to
vacancies in the great central administrative bodies, and therefore
leading up to positions of eminence rather than quiescence, were
almost monopolized by the Ecole des Sciences Politiques."[64]

---

dresser pour la France nouvelle des administrateurs, des financiers, des
diplomates, des politiques et, si possible, lui élever des hommes d'Etat. . . .
Ces mécaniciens, ces techniciens, ces spécialistes politiques, [Boutmy]
résolut de les donner à la France." (The state needed civil servants capable
of conducting all its great services; it was necessary to train administrators,
financiers, diplomats, politicians, and, if possible, statesmen for new France.
. . . Those mechanics, those technicians, those specialists in politics
[Boutmy] resolved to give them to France.)

[62] Two hundred *concours* a year were held in 1935 and about seventy were
still left in 1945. See B. Chapman, *The Profession of Government,* op. cit.
p. 81.

[63] See D. Halévy, *La République des comités* (*Essai d'histoire contemporaine*) (*1895-1934*), Paris, 1934, pp. 41-2: "Le goût de la fonction d'Etat
est une des caractéristiques des familles françaises. . . . Les deux formes
françaises de la propriété, c'étaient la terre et l'office, qui s'appelle au-
jourd'hui l'emploi, la fonction." (A taste for the civil service is one of the
characteristics of French families. . . . The two French forms of property
were land and office, which is now called post, function [in the civil
service].)

[64] See pamphlet issued by the Ecole des Sciences politiques in 1940, quoted
by R. Pernoud, *Histoire de la bourgeoisie* . . . , op. cit. p. 595: "Au cours
des trente-sept dernières années, sur 120 candidats reçus au Conseil d'Etat,
116 sortent de l'Ecole; sur 218 candidats reçus à l'Inspection des Finances,
209 sortent de l'Ecole; sur 94 candidats reçus à la Cour des Comptes, 83
sortent de l'Ecole; sur 284 candidats reçus dans la diplomatie, 249 sortent
de l'Ecole." (During the last thirty-seven years, out of 120 candidates admitted to the Council of State, 116 came from the school; out of 218 admitted to Inspection des Finances, 209 came from the school; out of 94
candidates admitted to the Cour des Comptes, 83 came from the school; out
of 284 candidates admitted to the diplomatic service, 249 came from the
school.)

The programs of the *concours* of admission to the Conseil d'Etat, Cour des Comptes, and Inspection des Finances,[65] as well as to the diplomatic career, emphasized "general culture," a balanced judgment, clarity of thought, rather than precise knowledge. Elegance of style in written essays and fluency of expression during oral examinations were considered important indications of a candidate's aptitude.[66] These criteria could be compared to the British concern with "character" in the recruitment of leaders, and the presumption that required intellectual traits could be developed in the Ecole des Sciences Politiques parallels the reputation of the older English universities. The similarity should not be overemphasized since the over-all structure of both countries' educational systems differed so widely. But it uncovers a similar equation between a certain definition of "culture" as a basis for leadership and a pattern of thought and behavior characterizing a limited social group. The French definition of "culture" was more concerned with purely intellectual elements—and, accordingly, the school in which the relevant education was given did not resort to the boarding system. But its recruitment ensured that students originated from a narrowly circumscribed milieu and shared therefore a similar background as well as the same training.

Until the Second World War, administrative cadres recruited by *concours* came almost exclusively from the Ecole des Sciences Poli-

---

[65] Conseil d'Etat is the supreme administrative court and central consultative body to the French government. Cour des Comptes is the administrative body auditing public accounts and possessing judicial powers in this field. Inspection des Finances is the highest category of financial comptrollers, who are frequently seconded to the most important administrative posts. On the role of Conseil d'Etat and other *grands corps de l'Etat,* see G. Langrod, *Some problems of Administration in France Today,* San Juan, Puerto Rico, 1961.

[66] See "Le Conseil d'Etat, la Cour des Comptes, l'Inspection Générale des Finances," collection Sillages, No. 11, p. 57: "Les jurys s'attachent moins aux titres des candidats qu'à leur valeur réele. Ils apprécient moins l'abondance des diplômes que l'équilibre du jugement, l'étendue et la profondeur de la culture, la clarté de l'intelligence et du raisonnement telle qu'elle ressort du style et de l'exposé oral." (Boards are less interested in the candidates' titles than in their real value. They appreciate the number of diplomas less than a balanced judgment, the extent and depth of culture, the clarity of thought, and reasoning evidenced by style and oral examination.)

tiques; and the period has been described as the era of the Parisian bourgeoisie. Indeed, the clientele of the school was limited not only socially, but geographically, not only by the comparatively high fees, but also by the inconvenience of its location in Paris and by the exclusiveness of its atmosphere.[67] Links between conservative society and university circles had been weakened by the anti-clerical reaction and the anti-intellectual counterreaction polarized by the Dreyfus Affair.[68] The position of the Ecole des Sciences Politiques outside the state educational network increased its appeal.

Exclusiveness was accentuated by the economic principles on which the civil service career was based. These had the indirect result of limiting recruitment to a certain level of income. The initial requirement of a private income as a guarantee of financial independence was abandoned at the beginning of the twentieth century. But the low level of salaries for those who entered the main administrative bodies crystallized further a socially "eligible," economically self-sufficient, and intellectually inbred group.[69] The higher administrative posts were filled by virtual co-optation, and the *concours* served to classify aptitude by rank rather than detect it.

Close links between the public and the private sectors resulted from the fact that high-ranking civil servants tended to belong to the milieu from which the top level of business management was also recruited. The inadequacy of official salaries confirmed this trend, both by discouraging impecunious outsiders from competing for government posts and by furthering the practice of a "second career" in business after retirement or resignation from the administration. The *polytechniciens'* qualifications were particularly suited to the requirements of industry, and their connections were valued as much as their competence. Similar transfers occurred from all branches of the civil service into corresponding private posts, for instance from the directorates of the Ministry of Finance into bank-

---

[67] See P. Lalumière, "L'Inspection générale des finances de 1919 à 1956" (unpublished thesis, Law Faculty), Paris, 1956, pp. 52 ff.
[68] See L. Bodin and J. Touchard, "Définitions, statistiques et problèmes" in *Revue Française de Science Politique,* (issue on) *"Les Intellectuels dans la société française contemporaine,"* IX, No. 4, December, 1959.
[69] See F. Piétri, *Le Financier,* Paris, 1931, pp. 179 ff.

ing.[70] This entwining of two theoretically separate spheres, facilitated by similarity of social and intellectual background, furthered ties of solidarity existing between individuals. In such a context, the *grandes écoles* assured the cohesion of an elite by establishing interpersonal relations and strengthening the bonds between successive generations.[71]

The history of the Third Republic was characterized by an increasingly close connection at decision-making-levels between public administration and private enterprise,[72] and by an almost complete identification between administrative cadres and a Parisian bourgeois elite. Both trends became particularly marked between the world wars. They were denounced by the political Left[73] and viewed with distrust by the public as additional evidence that "two hundred families" ruled the country. Nevertheless, the type of training given to future civil servants and their screening through the system of *concours* retained a high prestige. This was understandable since the whole educational system propagated respect for intellectual brilliance and the Left's creed recognized differences in intellectual aptitude as the only valid basis for a hierarchy.[74] While the ideal of *grandes écoles* remained acceptable even to those who advocated a reorganization of the educational system, the tradition of *grands corps de l'Etat* or main administrative services did not repel those who envisaged a reform of the state machinery.

ECOLE NATIONALE D'ADMINISTRATION

After the liberation in 1944, structural reforms appeared both necessary and possible. As a result of the Vichy régime, most state institutions were discredited, and vested interests had been tempo-

---

[70] See E. Beau de Loménie, *Les Responsabilités des dynasties bourgeoises*, Vol. III, Paris, 1954.

[71] See C. Chavanon, "L'Administration dans la société française," in *Aspects de la société française*, A. Siegfried, ed., Paris, 1954.

[72] See A. Siegfried, *De la Troisième à la Quatrième République*, Paris, 1956, p. 246.

[73] Cf. A. Hamon and XY2, *Maîtres de la France*, Vol. II, Paris, 1937, as an example of a violent leftist attack on the recruitment of high-ranking civil servants.

[74] See A. Thibaudet, *La République des professeurs*, op. cit. pp. 237 ff.

rarily silenced. Significantly the democratizing and modernizing of the civil service were initiated by the creation of a new *grande école,* the Ecole Nationale d'Administration, intended to destroy the previous geographic and social monopoly, but nevertheless organized according to a familiar pattern.[75] Admission to the school was to be by *concours,* but there was an innovation which consisted in having parallel avenues of entry, corresponding to two different types of candidates. Category A was to include young men and women who had received an education up to *licence* level or taken a diploma from one of the twelve institutes of political studies, to be set up in the main towns under the auspices of the local universities. This new network was clearly designed to abolish the former supremacy of Paris. It included the former Ecole des Science Politiques, no longer private, but reorganized as a state foundation under the name of Institut d'Etudes Politiques, and endowed with a measure of autonomy in spite of its formal connection with Paris University. The intention was to attract candidates from the provinces and to give them an equally sound preparation for the *concours.*

There was also an attempt to encourage applicants who had graduated in subjects other than political science, and to avoid the "intellectual nepotism," as well as the geographical and social isolationism, of the previous period. It is with all those considerations in mind that Category B was created and a special *concours* devised for mature applicants with five years' experience of the civil service and without any academic qualifications. This innovation facilitated promotion within the civil service, so that merit would no longer be impeded by the lack of formal qualifications at the outset. It also increased efficiency by drawing on competent civil servants who had not hitherto been used to best advantage. This was an answer to former criticisms of *grandes écoles,* which pointed out their exaggerated emphasis on purely intellectual values, their disregard for practical experience, their tendency to turn out "brilliant young men rather than men."[76]

While there were two separate channels of admission, there was

---

[75] See B. Chapman, *The Profession of Government,* op. cit. pp. 88 f.
[76] See R. Aron, *L'Age des empires,* op. cit. p. 190.

to be only one *concours de sortie*.[77] This replaced the multiple *concours,* held before the Second World War, by administrative bodies to fill vacancies in their midst. The new system, reminiscent of the Polytechnique pattern, gave the successful candidates a choice between posts in *grands corps de l'Etat* or in the prefectoral corps according to their rank.[78] The connection between scale of performance and hierarchy of posts was maintained, but centralized testing was expected to prove more democratic and less subjective than was the virtual co-optation prevailing in the Inspection des Finances[79] as well as other state organs to a lesser extent. The purpose of the reform was to restore the dual character of the *concours* as a device for selection and for classification; the former aspect had been almost superseded by the social pre-selection effected in the Ecole des Sciences Politiques. This aim could not be reached unless the curriculum of the course was altered, either by the adoption of a more practical bias, or by an attempt to redefine "general culture" in less socially exclusive terms.[80] As a compromise, the program of the Ecole Nationale d'Administration was to include a period of training in an administrative post (*stage*) and to cover a range of subjects intended to bring out skills other than purely verbal.[81]

---

[77] To be distinguished from *concours d'entrée* comprising the two forms of entrance examination, one for university graduates, the other for serving officials. *Concours de sortie,* a single final competitive examination after two and a half years of study at the E.N.A., is taken by all candidates.

[78] Prefects are the representatives of the central government in the (provincial) *départements.* See B. Chapman, *The Prefects and Provincial France,* London, 1955.

[79] See F. Piétri, *Le Financier,* op. cit. p. 79.

[80] See C. Brindillac, "Les Hauts Fonctionnaires," in *Esprit,* June, 1953.

[81] The course at the Ecole Nationale d'Administration (E.N.A.) covers two years. During the first year, the *stage* is a period of service under a senior administrator, intended to broaden the student's knowledge, to give him a practical experience of administrative procedure and to enable him to prepare a short thesis on a subject of local interest. The second year is a period of study in four major sections: General Administration, Financial and Economic, Social Administration, and Foreign Affairs. General courses common to all or several sections deal with problems of national interest or provide an introduction to the topics covered in one division for the students of the others. Each division offers specialized courses and seminars, the teaching being undertaken by higher civil servants, university teachers, and persons with special experience in a given field. See E.N.A., *Recruitment and Training for the Higher Civil Servants in France,* Paris, 1956.

Since the new school was designed primarily to democratize the civil service, it is by this standard that it must be largely judged. It does seem to have widened the basis of recruitment, for a high proportion of its students have been sons of low-ranking civil servants.[82] The previous position of the high bourgeoisie has clearly been challenged by the middle and lower strata of the bourgeoisie. But the working class is still under-represented, and there has been no transformation in the values equated with "culture." Rather such values tend to be assimilated by those who have not already acquired them by virtue of the appropriate background. The Instituts d'Etudes Politiques facilitated this transition. If one considers only Category A and disregards the experienced civil servants, the number of upper-class students exceeds that of candidates to the *concours d'entrée* belonging to the same social sphere—a fact which is surely significant. No less characteristic is the steady drift from the civil service into private business. In pre-war days, it could be interpreted as a confirmation of existing ties within an almost closed milieu. The pattern is no longer so simple, since new links are being established which cannot be explained by a common social background. Possible interpretations could include the establishment of connections during the period of studies and of state employment. But personal relations facilitate the transfer; they do not cause it. As in the case of *polytechniciens*—who initiated this exodus into the private sector and coined the term *pantouflage*[83] to describe it—the prestige surrounding a certain form of training derives both from the competence of those who have received it and from their influence. The comparison implies that the Ecole Nationale d'Administration has acquired a high status within a short time. It suggests also that the *grand école* has proved an extremely adaptable institution: this is confirmed by the proliferation of higher technical training establishments which have claimed the name and followed more or less accurately the organizational pattern associated with it. It shows how a reform can produce valuable unintended results.

[82] See T. Bottomore, "La Mobilité sociale dans le haute administration française" in *Cahiers Internationaux de Sociologie*, XIII, Paris, 1952.
[83] More precisely, *pantouflage* means the practice of resigning from an administrative post to take up lucrative employment in industry or trade.

CONCLUSIONS

The French educational structure in general and the network of *grandes écoles* in particular were devised and maintained to supply the state with competent cadres. The system owed its endurance to the widespread acceptance of a meritocracy justified by merit rather than by mere efficiency. The common background, derived from the universal educational system and implying a general recognition of intellectual values, presided over initial selection and permitted final ranking.

While each school was primarily designed as a training center, an inseparable characteristic of intensive instruction was the promotion of group solidarity, reinforced by continuous contact in active life. The anticipated advantages and substantial satisfactions of belonging to such a group initially attracted ability, but later tended to encourage entrenchment. The selection procedure increasingly became a means of recognition and confirmation, perpetuating an elite, rather than a rational choice of individuals, ensuring the quality of cadres. The interpenetration of existing elites gradually transformed the nature of the claims made to justify the superior position of the administrative class. Efficiency appeared less as an aim than as a by-product, and position less as an achievement than a right. These unintended consequences of institutionalized training never completely invalidated its planned effects. However, they neither reinforced the efficiency of the system nor confirmed its democratic claims. Institutional continuity became an aspect of traditional social stability without ceasing to strengthen and serve the administrative machinery which constituted the Napoleonic state. At present, social change and administrative modernization are making conflicting demands on the educational system. The requirements of increasing democratization, prompting a series of proposed and projected educational reforms, are hard to reconcile with the imperatives of growing specialization. The disruption resulting from either a choice or a compromise would be greater than dissatisfaction with the continuation of tradition.

APPENDIX I—*grandes écoles* IN EXISTENCE IN 1866

I. *Ecoles militaires* (Military Schools)

Artillerie et Génie (Fontainebleau).
Application du corps d'état major.
Application du génie maritime.
Cavalerie (Saumur).
Hydrographie.
Médecine militaire (Paris, Val de Grâce).
(Ecoles de) Médecine navale.
Navale (Brest).
Polytechnique.
Prytanée militaire (La Flèche).
Saint-Cyr (Ecole spéciale militaire de St.-Cyr).

II. *Ecoles civiles* (Civilian Schools)

Académie de France (Rome).
(Ecoles d') Agriculture.
Arts et métiers.
(Ecole d') Athènes.
Beaux Arts.
Centrale (Ecole centrale des arts et manufactures).
(Ecole des) Chartes
(Ecole de) Cluny.
Conservatoire de musique et de déclamation.
(Ecoles de) Droit.
(Ecole pratique des) Hautes Etudes.
Langues Orientales.
(Ecole des) Manufactures de l'Etat.
(Ecoles de) Médecine.
(Ecole des) Mines.
Normale (Ecole Normale Supérieure).
(Ecoles de) Pharmacie.
Ponts et Chaussées.
(Ecoles) vétérinaires.

(compiled from M. d'Ocagne, *Les Grandes Ecoles* . . .)

APPENDIX II—*grandes écoles* IN EXISTENCE IN 1966

I. *Defense nationale* (Defense)

Ecole de l'Air.
Ecole des Elèves Ingénieurs Mécaniciens de la Marine.
Ecole Navale.
Ecole Polytechnique.
Ecoles du Service de Santé de Lyon et de Bordeaux.
Ecole Spéciale Militaire (Coëtquidan).

II. *Ecoles civiles* (Civilian Schools)

1. *Agriculture:* (Agriculture) thirteen *grandes écoles*.

2. *Beaux-Arts* (Arts).
   Ecoles Nationale Supérieure des Beaux-Arts.
   Ecoles Régionales d'Architecture (thirteen).
   Ecole Spéciale d'Architecture.

3. *Commerce* (Commerce)
   Ecole des Hautes Etudes Commerciales.
   Ecole de Haut Enseignement Commercial pour Jeunes Filles.
   Ecoles Supérieures de Commerce (thirteen).
   Ecole Supérieure des Science Economiques et Commerciales de
       l'Institut Catholique de Paris.
   Ecole National d'Assurances.
   Institut de Sciences Financières et d'Assurances (Lyon).
   Instituts d'Etudes Commerciales (Grenoble, Nancy, and
       Strasbourg).

4. *Droit et Sciences Economiques* (Law and Economics)
   Ecole Nationale d'Administration.
   Institut d'Etudes Politiques.
   Instituts d'Etudes Politiques de province (Strasbourg, Grenoble,
       Lyon, Toulouse, Aix, Bordeaux.)

5. *Enseignement* (Teacher Training)
   Ecoles Normales Supérieures (Rue d'Ulm, Sèvres, Saint-Cloud,
       Fontenay aux Roses).

Ecole Normale Supérieure de l'Enseignement Technique.
Ecoles Normales Nationales d'Apprentissage.
Ecoles Normales Supérieures d'Education Physique et Sportive
(Joinville-le-Pont, Chatenay-Malabry).

6. *Lettres* (Literary Studies)
Ecole Nationale de Bibliothécaires
Ecole Nationale des Langues Orientales Vivantes.
Ecole Nationale des Chartes.
Ecole Supérieure d'Interprétariat et de Traduction.
Institut de Psychologie.
Instituts de Psychologie rattachés aux Facultés de Province (four).

7. *Sciences et Techniques Industrielles* (Science and Technology)

A. *Formation générale:*
Ecole Polytechnique.
Ecole Centrale des Arts et Manufactures.
Ecole Nationale Supérieure des Arts et Métiers.
Conservatoire National des Arts et Métiers.
Ecole Polytechnique féminine.
Ecoles or Instituts de province (Lille, Lyon, Marseilles, Nancy,
Strasbourg, Toulouse—ten in all).

B. *Ecoles spécialisées:*
Bâtiment (three)
Céramique (one)
Chimie (twenty-five)
Electricité, électromécanique, électrotechnique (twenty)
Electronique, radioélectricité, télécommunications (eight)
Sciences Géographiques (one)
Horlogerie et Micromécanique (one)
Industries extractives (four)
Mécanique, métallurgie (six)
Optique (one)
Papeterie (one)
Physique (three)
Textiles et cuirs (seven)
Travaux Publics (three)

(compiled from official publications)

A SELECTIVE LIST OF WORKS
ON FRENCH EDUCATION

Alain,*   *Propos sur l'Education*, Paris, 1938.

H. C. Barnard,   *The French Tradition in Education*, Cambridge, Eng., 1922.

G. Bertier,   *L'Ecole des Roches*, Juvisy, 1935.

F. Clarke,   *Freedom in the Educative Society*, London, 1948.

C. Compayré,   *Histoire des doctrines de l'éducation en France*, Paris, 1904.

F. de Dainville,   *Les Jésuites et l'éducation de la société française*, 2nd vol., Paris, 1940.

L. Decaunes and   *Réformes et projets de réforme de l'enseigne-*
M. L. Cavalier,   *ment français de la Révolution à nos jours*, Paris, 1962.

C. Desmaze,   *L'Université de Paris, 1200-1875*, Paris, 1876.

E. Desmolins,   *L'Education nouvelle*, Paris, 1898.

G. Duveau,   *Les Instituteurs*, Paris, 1958.

R. Escarpit,   *Ecole laïque, école du peuple*, Paris, 1961.

J. Fayet,   *La Révolution français et la science, 1789-95*, Paris, 1960.

J. Floud and others,   *Ecole et société*, Paris, 1959.

W. R. Fraser,   *Education and Society in Modern France*, London, 1963.

M. Glatigny,   *Histoire de l'enseignement en France*, Paris, 1949.

M. F. Hignette,   *The Primacy of the Rational in French Secondary Education*, World Yearbook of Education, 1958.

P. Hunkin,   *Enseignement et politique en France et en Angleterre depuis 1789*, Paris, 1962.

* The pen name of E. Chartier.

S. d'Irsay,	*Histoire des Universités françaises et étrangères des origines jusqu'à nos jours,* Paris, 1933.
J. Leif and G. Rustin,	*Histoire des institutions scolaires,* Paris, 1954.
J. Leif and G. Rustin,	*Pédagogie* *Pedagogie générale par l'étude des doctrines pédagogiques,* Paris, 1959.
L. Liard,	*L'Enseignement supérieur en France, 1789-1889,* Paris.
M. d'Ocagne,	*Les Grandes Ecoles de France,* Paris, 1873.
B. Megrine	*La Question scolaire en France,* Paris, 1960.
Semaines Sociales de France,	*L'Enseignement problème social,* Lyon, 1958.
Université d'Aix-Marseille,	*La Laïcité,* Paris, 1960.
F. Vial,	*Condorcet et l'éducation démocratique* Paris, n.d.
F. Vial,	*Trois siècles d'histoire de l'enseignement secondaire,* Paris, 1936.
G. Weill,	*Histoire de l'enseignement secondaire en France, 1802-1920,* Paris, 1921.

YOSHINORI IDE AND TAKESHI ISHIDA

The Education and Recruitment of Governing Elites in Modern Japan

A SHORT GLOSSARY OF JAPANESE WORDS

hanbatsu Literally means a "clansmen oligarchy," a consolidated group of clansmen drawn from the old fiefs which had played a leading role in overthrowing the ancient "feudal" régime, the Tokugawa Shogunate.

kobun The higher civil service characterized by special methods of recruitment, privileged status, and a strong esprit de corps as elite administrators. Classified into two subcategories, the *chokunin* and the *sonin*. The word *kobun* is an abbreviation of *koto-bunkan*.

chokunin "Imperial appointment": a senior group of higher civil servants appointed personally by the Emperor.

sonin "Imperial approval": a junior group of higher civil servants, appointed through the Emperor's approval on recommendation of a minister.

hannin "Appointment by minister's seal": non-*kobun* civil servants appointed by a minister holding delegated authority.

I. INTRODUCTION

Among Western, especially American, scholars of Japanese history there has recently been a tendency, in re-evaluating rapid Japanese modernization, to emphasize her success. Whether one agrees with this view or not, one can hardly question that the governing elites were responsible for both the advantages and disadvantages of rapid modernization in Japan.

The term "governing elites" may include various categories of national leaders such as politicians, high-ranking bureaucrats, and military leaders. Here, however, we will limit our subject to high-ranking bureaucrats not simply for convenience but rather because their importance was one of the characteristics of Japanese political history. The purpose of this article is to investigate how the Japanese bureaucratic elites were recruited, with some reference to their social and educational backgrounds, and to indicate some basic characteristics of the Japanese prewar bureaucracy.

The Meiji Restoration in 1868 was the beginning of the rapid establishment of a highly centralized government to promote industrialization and to maintain national independence. In the newly emerged centralized government, bureaucrats composed the core of modernizing elites. At the beginning of the modern period the distinction was not clear between higher bureaucrats and political leaders who were in charge of decision making. The political leaders in the early Meiji (roughly the last few decades of the last century) had an antipathy to political parties and were more interested in creating able bureaucrats than in reproducing political leaders. Many influential politicians, such as party leaders, were recruited from among high-ranking bureaucrats. In fact, out of more than forty prime ministers in modern history, roughly one-third were recruited from high-ranking civil bureaucrats.

Imperial prerogatives, which were actually exercised by the bureaucracy, added to the importance of bureaucrats among the governing elite. In 1932 party government came to an end when rightist naval officers assassinated Prime Minister Inukai, who was also the president of the *Seiyukai* party. Thereafter, political parties lost their influence and the role of the bureaucracy became more important. Later two other factors increased the bureaucracy's importance: one was the dissolution of all political parties which were integrated into the Imperial Rule Assistance Association in 1940; and the other was the increased role of the bureaucracy in a planned economy to achieve total war. Special types of bureaucrats called

Shinkanryo ("new bureaucrats") or *Kakushinkanryo* (literally meaning "bureaucrats for innovation") emerged among the middle management of the administration. Generally speaking, they were anti-liberal, anti-parties, nationalistic, pro-military, pro-fascist, and above all in favor of strengthening government control. Despite the radical change caused by the defeat and the occupation, even today approximately one-third of the government party members in the Diet belongs to the category of ex-bureaucrats.

In Meiji Japan, government initiative was seriously needed in order to catch up with Western countries. "To enrich the country and to strengthen the military" was the most emphasized and popular slogan of the early Meiji period. Thus many modern industries were sponsored and then subsidized by the government, heightening the importance of the bureaucracy even within the business world. As the slogan indicates, the military was another influential sector of the society, particularly from the 1930's until the end of the last war. In this essay we shall occasionally refer to the military bureaucracy for comparison with the civil bureaucracy.

A key aspect of the civil bureaucracy was the examination system for higher officials which enabled the bureaucracy to recruit competent people from various social strata. This recruitment provided the society with a high degree of vertical social mobility.

Mention should be made of the historical conditions for introducing the examination system. First, we should note the high rate of school attendance, estimated by Professor Ronald Dore to be between 40 and 50 per cent among boys by the time of the Meiji Restoration. A new system of compulsory education was introduced in 1872, and by 1910 school attendance was 98 per cent. Upon this basis higher education also developed rapidly. A broad background of primary, secondary, and higher education was a prerequisite of the examination system for higher officials: it provided a way of recruiting capable students as candidates.

Another important factor in the recruitment of bureaucrats was the role of national universities whose tuition fees were lower than those of private universities. Although already in the late nineteenth century there were a number of private universities which produced many businessmen, journalists, and politicians, the national universities produced the most. Among Japanese private universities there were no counterparts to Oxford and Cambridge in England. Because of the low tuition in national universities, even boys of rather humble family background, not sons of poor peasants but at least sons of owner farmers, could go to national universities if they were able to pass the examination. Various kinds of scholarships enabled many boys from middle-class families to become bureaucrats via the national universities. People in "old fiefs"[1] were interested in producing competent candidates for higher offices in order to promote the social prestige and political influence of their fiefs. Scholarships were established by local communities to express their communal ties and loyalty to their fiefs. The social mobility mentioned above was responsible for the myth that every imperial subject was equal and that if one worked hard one could become the prime minister. In reality, this was not the case since the system excluded the sons of poor peasants for economic reasons. On the other hand, military schools did not charge tuition, and hence those who could not send their sons to universities could afford to let them attend military schools where, if they were able, they could become military officers, even to the rank of general or admiral. In the early 1930's many young military officers from rural areas, who sympathized with the miserable situation of the poor peasants, became extremely nationalistic. Their ultranationalism resulted from a psychological projection of their resentments against urbanization, which they identified with Westernization.

Another condition for the introduction of the examination system was the legacy of the Tokugawa Shogunate system. As is well known, the Shogunate system was a kind of semi-centralized government. Although each fief had a certain amount of autonomy, there was indeed a central government with limited control over the whole country. Both in the Shogunate government and in the governments of fiefs those who obtained high positions came from prestigious family backgrounds. However, later in the Tokugawa period more importance was placed on ability. This was also the case in schools operated by the Shogunate and by local fief governments.

---

[1] The domains whose leaders had wielded great political influence at the end of the "feudal" Tokugawa régime. See *hanbatsu* in the glossary.

The political crisis caused by direct contact with the West necessitated the recruitment of able persons without considering hereditary criteria. Thus the criterion of achievement was already used under the late Tokugawa régime, which had been a status-oriented feudal system. This was both the cause and the effect of organizational reform in the fiefs and the Shogunate government.

One can compare the semi-centralized government in the Tokugawa period with the traditional Chinese centralized bureaucracy. Both had strong Confucian influences. Indeed, unlike Indian and Western cultures, both Chinese and Japanese cultures were oriented toward this world, due to their common Confucian influence. But in China, the Confucian ethic was the orthodoxy among the *literati* in the civil bureaucracy—a scholar-official class—whereas in Japan, the ethic was borne by warriors who often became bureaucrats but not *literati*. The Chinese *literati* were more interested in memorizing Confucian classics than in promoting practical knowledge, while among the Japanese warriors practical ability was emphasized both in military training and in administration. This emphasis on practicality made Japan the readier to introduce new methods of recruiting able bureaucrats, unhindered by the traditional examination system which survived in China until 1905.

II. CIVIL BUREAUCRACY: THE SYSTEM
FOR HIGHER OFFICIALS

Appearance of the Examination System

In any country the establishment of a modern examination system based upon merit leads to the formation of a rational public administration system. In order to have an effective administrative system meeting the demands of a modern state, Japan had to introduce a civil service examination.

The first attempts to do this came in the late 1880's, when the new Meiji régime, struggling and compromising with various opposed forces, tried to set up a modern framework of government. The Constitution of 1889 was a concentrated expression of these efforts. We should not, however, overlook the fact that the Meiji régime had tried to complete, even in advance of the adoption of the Constitution, a detailed blueprint for the administrative system and had found that one of its key problems was to replace the patronage system by the merit system.

During the first two decades after the Restoration, government officials were recruited largely on a patronage basis from those political sectors which had made the most active contribution to overthrowing the old régime. These were the *hanbatsu*, clansmen drawn from the old fiefs.[2] In 1874, 65 per cent of the *chokunin* (first class) officials and 38 per cent of the *sonin* (second class) officials were reported to represent the political influence of the four leading fiefs. But, with the passage of years, criticism against this practice increased and in 1885 Prime Minister Ito came to insist, in one of the *Five Chapters on Governmental Reorganization,* on the need to introduce the examination method of recruitment. It is interesting to note that he issued this new policy very shortly after he was appointed to head the cabinet which in 1885 replaced "pre-modern" government.

The remaining four of the *Five Chapters* covered the following items: definition of official responsibility, elimination of red tape, reduction of superfluous expenditure, and establishment of official discipline. Based upon these principles, above all the first one, a series of efforts was made to improve the organizational structure of central departments, to draw clearer lines of authority between *chokunin, sonin,* and *hannin* officials, to fix the number of officials, and to clarify the grading system and pay scale of the officials. Then, imperial ordinances such as the *Organization of Administrative Departments Ordinance* were issued in 1886.

The formal shape of the government organization improved remarkably by the adoption of the cabinet system and other new administrative schemes. Nevertheless, these institutional reforms did not necessarily have much effect on public administration until the examination method was introduced in 1887. A political leader commented on this to the cabinet in 1887. He said that the patronage system which had caused the most harm in public administration remained unchanged, and so "government projects were pro-

---

[2] See glossary at the beginning of this chapter.

vided for the office and the office for the men, not the men for the office and the office for the needed projects."

To remedy this situation the "Civil Officials Examination and Internship System" was proposed in 1888. It largely resembled the Prussian model. Recruitment of government personnel was for the first time regulated by law. The "higher examination" and "ordinary examination" were respectively provided for the *sonin* and the *hannin* posts, though the highest *chokunin* posts were still left to be filled by patronage.

The establishment of the higher examination, however, did not necessarily mean that every applicant for the *sonin* posts had to take it. Graduates from the Law Faculty (and Literature Faculty) of the Imperial University (Tokyo University) could be appointed to *sonin* posts without taking the examination. This gave rise to the tradition of the so-called *gakubatsu* (academic clique or university patronage). In addition, some of the *sonin* positions to be occupied by technicians and other professionals were exempted from the examination. So were applicants with a specified career background such as ex-bureaucrats and commissioned and non-commissioned military officers. The appointment of ex-military people helped the Japanese civil bureaucracy to adopt a rather military hierarchical form.

There were several reasons why the *hanbatsu* government tried to make these radical reforms from 1885 to 1887. In the first place, the public which criticized the *hanbatsu* (old fief) bureaucracy and patronage had to be placated. Second, the government could not neglect the increasing ill effects of patronage itself. Third, in order to revise the "unequal treaties" which Japan entered into under the Tokugawa régime, the government had to demonstrate to Western countries its efforts at modernization, including an improvement of the public administration system. And fourth, the government wanted to prepare for the scheduled 1890 opening of the National Diet by establishing, outside the party politics which were anticipated, an authoritative, administrative hierarchy with the Emperor at its head. The *hanbatsu* leaders calculated that the merit system would help to preserve their political domination.

Thus the establishment of a nonpolitical civil bureaucracy was prompted by highly political considerations. "Removal of politics from public administration" needed the Emperor's absolute authority. It is no wonder that the "Civil Official Discipline Ordinance" was issued in 1887 to keep pace with the start of the "Civil Official Examination and Internship System" and lasted without any revision until 1947 when the Meiji Constitution was abolished. It declared in its first article that an official must be loyal to the Emperor and his government. The Meiji Constitution which came two years later confirmed that control of the administration, appointment of the officials, and so on were the Emperor's prerogatives.

Change of the Recruitment System and Development of the Civil Bureaucracy

A prototype of the Japanese civil bureaucracy was thus created. However, it had to be confronted with the increasing influence of the political parties before it could be fully institutionalized.

The influence of the political parties was felt at once after the opening of the National Diet. Dominated by the opposition parties, the Diet demanded that the *hanbatsu* administration reduce government expenditure and reorganize the administration. The administration immediately replaced the "Civil Official Examination and Internship System" with the "Civil Official Appointment System" of 1893. By this replacement, the administration hoped not only to satisfy the Diet's demand for administrative reorganization but also to protect the bureaucracy from party influence. According to the new ordinance, the Imperial University graduates, too, had to take the examination to enter government service. However, this change had only a limited effect, for while ordinary applicants had to take both the preliminary and the final tests, Imperial University graduates were exempted from the first test. The equalization of appointment which public opinion demanded was not established. Furthermore, the top-grade *chokunin* posts were still subject to patronage.

When the first so-called party cabinet was organized by the *Kensei* party in 1898, a number of party members were appointed to *chokunin* posts such as those of vice-minister, bureau chief, and prefectural governor. The *Kensei* party further proposed the re-appointment of all *chokunin* and *sonin* officials. For fear that the *hanbatsu* (old fief) patronage might be replaced by party patronage, the *hanbatsu* cabinet[3] which succeeded the first party cabinet after only four months revised the Civil Officials Appointment Ordinance to reserve most *chokunin* posts for career civil servants. At the same time, in order to define more clearly the legal status of the officials and to strengthen their security, the Cabinet issued two other imperial ordinances: the *Bunkan Bugenrei* (Ordinance for the Security of Civil Officials) and the *Bunkan Chokairei* (Ordinance for the Punishment of Civil Officials). Then, to make it more difficult to amend these ordinances, it was decided in 1900 that all revisions should be subject to the approval of the *Sumitsuin* (Privy Council).

These measures meant that the basic framework of the civil service system had become a formal institution. The civil bureaucracy of Japan was now entrenched. The methods of recruitment were almost completely systematized and most of the key senior posts were allotted to the administrative elites whose members had passed the higher examination. To pass this examination was to obtain access to a privileged group in government and therefore in society.

As the professional civil servants who had passed the higher examination in the early period began to reach the top government posts and to increase in number, entrenched bureaucracy became an independent force and a dominant power in Japanese politics. It could directly cope with the political parties after the decline of the *hanbatsu*. This decline, however, meant the relative rise of political party influence. Therefore, as party government appeared, the bureaucracy had to make necessary compromises with the political parties. Such was the general situation of the so-called *Taisho* Democracy (roughly from the end of the 1910's to the end of the 1920's). During this period, some *chokunin* posts, though not many, were transferred by law from the merit system and became party spoils or rewards. With the increase of partisan influence, this was true even of other regular posts such as prefectural governors.

[3] The cabinet members were all from *hanbatsu* fiefs (see glossary), and the Prime Minister, Aritomo Yamagata, was one of the most influential leaders of the group.

Although they had been covered by the merit system, the political party in power could actually discharge unfriendly officials by making use of a provision in the *Bunkan Bugenrei,* (the security ordinance) which stated that through the judgment of an agency an official could be relieved from duty.

In 1918, there was an important change in the higher examination. Previously, besides the higher examination, there existed an examination for diplomats as well as one for judges and attorneys. In 1918 these three examinations were integrated into the *Koto Shikenrei* (Higher Examination Ordinance). This gave a complete statutory status to the *kobun* system of higher civil service examinations. Among other things, the newly issued Higher Examination Ordinance was designed to prevent Imperial University graduates from becoming judges and attorneys without taking the examination. It was also meant to widen the range of the applicants by exempting all university or college graduates from taking the preliminary test. But we should remember that the examiners were not recruited from among private university professors.

When, as mentioned earlier, the influence of the established political parties decreased due to the appearance of the military authority as a political force, the tide changed again. Bureaucratic elements known as the *Shinkanryo* co-operated with military authority in a regimentation of Japanese society. This produced what has been called a "rebirth of the bureaucracy."[4]

[4] The Shinkanryo ("new bureaucrats") was a political force, composed of relatively young, elite bureaucrats who rapidly increased their influence from the early 1930's, under the pressures of economic depression, social crisis, and political disintegration. It could be regarded as a fellow traveller of the military-fascist power in Japanese politics, although it was not always united. While the "new bureaucrats" of the Home Ministry aimed at integrating the nation and giving social and economic relief by administrative power, the economic bureaucrats who were gathered at the newly established National Planning Authority (1937) intended to mobilize the nation through economic planning. The last type of bureaucrats were often called the *kakushinkanryo,* or "bureaucrats for innovation." Although there were different opinions among the *Shinkanryo* (and the sub-group of *kakushinkanryo*), generally they were in favor of strengthened government control and an increased role for bureaucracy. Even in the postwar period, after Japan's recovery of independence, some of the *Shinkanryo* came back to the political circle as influential leaders. For example, Mr. Nobusuke Kishi, the Prime Minister from 1957 to 1960, was one of the champions of the *Shinkanryo.*

The changing tide could already be seen in the 1932 revision of the *Bunkan Bugenrei,* which was intended to prevent career officials from being relieved from duty against their will.[5] In order to ensure this, a special commission was newly established. Any removal of officials against their will was to be investigated and approved by this commission. From this point on, the civil service became an even more strongly entrenched bureaucracy. For example, in the Home Ministry, the number of changes among higher officials reportedly decreased from over one hundred a year to thirty or so a year. In 1934, measures were even taken to minimize the number of the posts which had legally been treated as political posts.

Finally, in 1941, a group of imperial ordinances regarding the civil service system was revised to meet wartime conditions. One of the major purposes of this general reform was ironically to expand the range of "free appointments" at all ranks so that the government could freely recruit from every possible source a massive number of officials demanded by the war administration. In order to make this possible at the *chokunin* and the *sonin* ranks, the commission set up to investigate dismissals was abolished. When, as a result of the dissolution of political parties, the governmental bureaucracy came to regulate the whole nation, so that the society itself became a highly regimented bureaucracy, there was no longer the necessity to keep government officials as a group legally separated from the rest of society. The *kobun* examination also had to be suspended in 1944, for most university students had been sent to the battlefields or to munitions factories. Each ministry of the national government had to rely upon its own selection procedure to recruit candidates for future high positions.

The Civil Service System and the Kobun *Elites:* Basic *Features*

Although the civil service system of prewar Japan several times underwent major as well as minor changes, its basic structure remained almost unchanged during the whole period. Under the Meiji

---

[5] The term "career officials" is used throughout this chapter to mean professional, long-service bureaucrats.—*Ed.*

Constitution the appointment of civil servants was one of the Emperor's prerogatives, so they had a sense of unlimited service and loyalty to the Emperor, while in their relations with the people they behaved as representatives of the Emperor's absolute authority. This basic characteristic of the civil servants did not change even during the years of party government. Since the legal framework of the civil service system based upon merit was very strict, the political parties' attack on it was in effect limited. Therefore, the political parties chose to preserve and to make use of the established civil service system rather than to break it.

As representatives of the Emperor, the civil servants were given exact ranks indicating their distance from the Emperor. From this there emerged a hierarchical civil service structure, characterized by a clear distinction between the higher and lower ranks. The posts were classified into three categories which we have already seen: 1) *chokunin* (imperial appointment); (2) *sonin* (imperial approval); and (3) *hannin* (minor) ranks. Although, ultimately, appointment to these three ranks was one of the Emperor's prerogatives, the legal procedure needed for appointment varied among the ranks. The appointment to *chokunin* posts depended on an imperial order which carried the Emperor's seal. The appointment to *sonin* posts was, after the Emperor's approval, announced by the Prime Minister. But, in the case of *hannin* posts, the appointment was simply made by the head of the agency concerned. The first two ranks were somewhat apart from the last rank.

Even farther apart from these three groups, there existed the *yatoi,* a nonofficial group. They "sold" their labor to the government under a contract based upon private law, while the *kanri,* the three higher ranks already mentioned, served the Emperor in a special relationship based upon public law. *Yatoi* could not become higher civil servants. Before 1900, the number of *kanri* usually exceeded the number of *yatoi*. But, in 1903, the *yatoi* group (52,000 persons) exceeded for the first time the *kanri* group (48,000 persons), and thereafter this difference continued to grow; there were four *yatoi* to one *kanri* in the 1930's. In this sense, the *kanri* were all "selected people."

There were other differences of status in the civil bureaucracy.

Within the higher rank, *sonin* officials qualified to be promoted to the *chokunin* rank were clearly distinguished from the remaining *sonin* officials. Also, within the group of the *sonin* officials with promotion qualifications, the *bunkan* (general administrator) officials with legal backgrounds were given more privileges than the *gikan* (technicians). And finally, among the *bunkan* group of the *sonin,* graduates from the imperial universities, especially those from the Law Faculty of the Tokyo Imperial University, were informally given the most privileges.

Analyzed in this context, we can conclude that the civil bureaucracy of prewar Japan was a grand pyramid of formally and informally distinguished statuses. At the top of this complex pyramid there were, of course, a few elite-bureaucrats recruited by the *kobun* examination, the majority of whom had received a legal education at the Tokyo Imperial University. The more complicated the status distinctions, the finer the quality of the *kobun* elites. Conversely, the special way of recruiting *kobun* officials was designed to create these very status distinctions within the bureaucracy.

So far, we have been stressing the status aspect of the civil service, but we should keep in mind that the system had another important aspect, namely, the value placed on individual achievement. The procedure for selection and promotion by merit was, of course, an institutional expression of this value. Though the *kobun* examination was the gateway to careers giving elite status, the examination itself was essentially an apparatus to recruit men of ability, not men of status. For this reason, the *kobun* examination was a symbol of the achievement value, and because of this value the civil bureaucracy could play a role as promoter of Japan's modernization.

Nevertheless, achievement was never separated from status. For example, in the case of the *kobun* examination, achievement was an absolute requirement for elite status, and elite status was a major inducement for achievement.

In this connection, mention should be made of the form of appointment. In the case of a *kobun* official, this usually involved both an appointment to a *kan* (official post) and assignment of *shoku* (work). An example was appointment to the clerical *kan* of the

Finance Ministry, coupled with a work assignment as chief of the account section. Since the work of the Finance Ministry's clerical *kan* was not concretely defined and there were a number of clerical *kans* in the Finance Ministry, appointment to the *kan* had to be complemented by assignment of concrete work. (Only in some top posts such as vice-minister, was there no assignment of *shoku* in addition to appointment to *kan*. The two became identical since there was only one such post in the ministry, and hence only one type of work for that post.)[6]

This form of appointment suggests that in the civil servant system, the concept of *kan* was usually separated from that of *shoku*. The concept of *kan* was considerably, though not completely, different from the concept of "function" or "job." Essentially, the concept of *kan* indicated the legal rank of the Emperor's official, while *shoku* represented a concept nearer to "functional." In other words, *kan* was a matter of status, *shoku* more a matter of achievement. In order to work effectively, the civil bureaucracy of prewar Japan required both elements, and it had them until it collapsed.

III. THE PERSONNEL AND THEIR ENVIRONMENT

Social Origin

We must now examine more closely the relationship between *kobun* officials and their environment. This included the social origins of *kobun* bureaucrats, their education and examination, and the post-examination personnel policies governing training, placement, promotion, and so forth.

Because of insufficient data, it is difficult to know what the social origins of *kobun* bureaucrats were. However, it can be said that their social origins were neither narrow nor special. A good family background was undoubtedly an advantage, but not a decisive one. An absolute requirement for becoming a *kobun* bureaucrat was to

[6] A vice-minister is the top civil servant of a ministry, corresponding to Permanent Secretary of a British ministry, or more roughly, Under Secretary of a U.S. federal department, the difference being that the latter is not a career civil servant.—*Ed.*

have ability and this meant an educational background sufficient to pass a prescribed examination. Thus there arose the expression, "birth is much, but education is more." The social origins of *kobun* bureaucrats extended to every family with enough capital to let its sons receive a college education.

This does not necessarily mean that *kobun* bureaucrats came from rich families. There were many parents who, in spite of needy circumstances, strained to send their sons to college with hopes for their sons' future. This pattern of "education fever" was seen especially among those families which had once enjoyed well-being but had later declined, such as the old *samurai*[7] families which had lost their income because of the Meiji Restoration and the landowning families which were affected by the economic and social changes caused by the industrialization of Japan. However, it is also important to remember that there were various scholarships established by private persons, companies, local communities, and the state to help intellectual sons of poor families to ride an "escalator of education" leading to the imperial universities. Thus, "money is much, but brain is more."

The spread of "education fever" greatly contributed to the widened social base of *kobun* bureaucrats—and vice versa. The bureaucrats had been recruited from many geographical areas, diverse occupational backgrounds, and varied social classes.

Geographically, the more populous areas have tended to produce more *kobun* bureaucrats than others.[8] This is as one would expect; indeed, it is usually said that in the early stage of Japanese bureaucracy most elite officials came from rural areas, but in later periods,

[7] *Samurai* literally means "warriors." In the old "feudal" structure, they had the status of a ruling class and enjoyed various privileges such as a family name and the right to wear a sword. For income, they depended on the rice stipend given by their lords.

[8] A survey (roughly covering the past two decades, the early 1940's to 1961) conducted in 1961 by Kiyoaki Tsuji and associates (including Yoshinori Ide) found that the more populated prefectures such as Tokyo, Osaka, and Kyoto, produce more bureaucrats with the rank of section chief and above than do less populated prefectures. Although the interviewees of the survey included a small number of non-*kobun* bureaucrats, the result seems to show a general trend which can be properly applied to *kobun* bureaucrats. At the time of writing, the final report of the study was not yet published.

most came from urban areas. The shift was a natural outcome of industrialization and the consequent increase of population as well as educational opportunities in the towns and cities. But the urban concentration of *kobun* bureaucrats was not very great, even in the case of metropolitan areas like Tokyo and Osaka. This was partly because in urban areas, as a result of diversified value systems, there were many opportunities for capable young people to form professional elites other than bureaucratic elites. Another reason was that capable young people from the countryside and small towns, who thought of a rise in governmental circles as a short-cut to an elite group in society, gathered at the Tokyo Imperial University by way of the "escalators of education" throughout the country.

Occupationally, too, the family backgrounds of *kobun* bureaucrats have covered a very wide range extending from agriculture to industry. According to a recent survey of contemporary civil servants, higher bureaucrats' fathers have included agricultural people as well as small independent businessmen (19%); low-ranking governmental officials (12%); company employees (10%); school teachers (9%); company managers (7%); high-ranking government officials (4%); university professors (2%); military men under the rank of general and admiral (1.7%); general and admiral (1.3%). Although the survey includes non-*kobun* bureaucrats and the various percentages may vary from one period to another, the general result would probably be the same. Assuming that there was a higher percentage of agricultural people in the past, one can hardly conclude that the sons of agricultural fathers dominated *kobun* bureaucracy.

At the same time, as already pointed out, the class background of *kobun* bureaucrats has not been limited to the upper sector of society. The survey showed that the sons of company managers, generals and admirals, senior civil servants, and other high-ranking people comprised but a minority of "elite bureaucrats." The same survey also indicated that most elite bureaucrats judged their fathers' families to be middle class: 22.1 per cent upper middle, 53.1 per cent middle middle, and 18.8 per cent lower middle. Only 5.3 per cent considered them to be upper class, and less than 1 per cent, lower class.

Education and Examination

Although the social background of the *kobun* bureaucrats was diverse, a majority of them shared the common background of education. The survey already mentioned indicates that about 96 per cent of those interviewed were university graduates. Of these 95 per cent were from national as opposed to private universities, and 81 per cent of them came from Tokyo Imperial University. This finding is supported by many others. In the early 1950's, for example, another survey showed that out of 1862 posts of section chief rank or higher in the central ministries and agencies, 80 per cent were occupied by Tokyo University graduates. The percentage alters with the years and with the ministries, but the average percentage figures of Tokyo University graduates among high-ranking bureaucrats is between 70 and 80 per cent. And generally, the higher the official rank, the higher this percentage.

This remarkable pre-eminence of Tokyo University graduates can be ascribed to the historical role of the University as a central organ for elite recruitment. The Imperial University Ordinance which was issued in 1886 defined the role of the Imperial University as an institution to "teach academic knowledge and arts which meet the needs of the state." The previous definition, in the School Ordinance of 1872, had described the University as "an advanced school to teach advanced academic knowledge," so there had clearly been a basic change in the conception of the University. As mentioned earlier, in the latter half of the 1880's there was a series of institutional reforms designed to modernize the Japanese government. A re-definition of the University was part of them. The *hanbatsu* administration, which was trying to build a modern public administration system, attempted to make the Imperial University an educational institute for bureaucratic elites. A historical document prepared by Prime Minister Ito insisted: "Now there is a Military Academy for the Army and a Naval Academy for the Navy . . . , but there seems to be no place to educate public administrators; therefore, the Imperial University should take this responsibility."

It was not an accident that the new Imperial University Ordinance was issued before the establishment of the "Civil Official Examination and Internship System." Approval of Imperial University graduates' privileges in this examination system reflected the character of the Imperial University as a training institute for bureaucratic elites. Since bureaucratic elites required legal knowledge, graduates from the Law Faculty were granted special privileges. In the examination as well as in the university's curriculum, the study of law was emphasized. In fact, from the beginning (and until 1893) it was customary for the president of the University to be the ex-officio Dean of the Law Faculty. After other imperial universities were established, beginning with Kyoto Imperial University in 1897, Tokyo Imperial University had to face rivals in various fields of education and sciences. And yet the basic character and privilege of the Law Faculty of Tokyo Imperial University remained almost the same.

Naturally, many young men of ability gathered at the Tokyo Imperial University. Each prefecture and even each local community competed in establishing an "escalator of education" leading to the top, the Tokyo Imperial University. The historical legacy of old fiefs' schools, which numbered over two hundred and fifty at the end of the Tokugawa period, contributed to this trend. When these educational escalators had been established, Tokyo Imperial University could absorb elite students from every corner of the country to produce a corps of talented people for the state. This function of producing governing elites was performed so effectively that there was strong criticism of the Tokyo Imperial University. The public was indignant that the old *hanbatsu* patronage was being replaced by the new *gakubatsu* ("educational patronage").

The *kobun* examination was inseparably associated with this function of the Tokyo Imperial University. The first civil service examination system of 1888 was designed to exempt Imperial University graduates from the examination. For the three years 1888-90 when the system was in use, there were 152 applicants for the administrators' examination, but only 9 of them passed. Most ministry demands for new personnel were met by accepting Imperial University graduates. In 1893 this exemption for Imperial University graduates was changed to an exemption from a preliminary test only and not from a final test. In 1918, exemption from the preliminary examination was extended to every university graduate. But even so, students of the imperial (national) universities, especially the Tokyo Imperial University, still had the advantage because many of the examiners were the professors from these institutions. In addition, the *kobun* examination was only a qualifying examination. To obtain a real job in any specific ministry, applicants had to take the appointment examination set by the ministry concerned. And at this final place of selection most ministries were usually interested in taking students of Tokyo Imperial University.

Though the subjects for examination varied in different periods, law was always emphasized. In the Civil Official Appointment Ordinance of 1893, the purpose of the higher examination was to "test the applicant's knowledge of theoretical doctrines and the existing legal system as well as his ability for practical application." The 1888 examination system covered six subjects: civil law, commercial law, economy, constitution or public administration, and finance or international law. The examinations were composed of a great number of questions requiring short answers on Western legal systems. The final test of the 1893 examination system covered six required subjects: constitution, criminal law, civil law, administrative law, economics, and international law, and in addition one other subject to be chosen from finance, commercial law, criminal procedure law, and civil procedure law. Since the Meiji Constitution and other laws were already in effect, questions were chosen from Japanese laws, not from Western legal systems.

Criticism mounted against this emphasis on legal knowledge, and the Higher Examination Ordinance of 1918, which had emphasized it, was largely revised in 1929. The number of required subjects also changed from six to four—constitution, administrative law, civil law, and economics—and three subjects instead of one had to be chosen from twenty optional subjects which extended from philosophy to social policy. This revision, however, did not greatly affect the traditional pattern of the *kobun* examination. In 1931, an occupational guidebook commented: "Although many optional subjects were added, there was no change in required subjects. The examination is still entrenched by legal subjects."

The 1941 revision of the *kobun* examination, the last of the pre-war revisions, was aimed at re-emphasizing the importance of legal knowledge by eliminating more than ten subjects from the optional list. Psychology, sociology, political history, social policy, and others disappeared from the list, while Japanese history was added. Still later, under wartime pressures, when the civil service and its selection system was reorganized, the tradition of legal emphasis in the *kobun* examination was adhered to even more clearly.

Personnel Policies After the Examination

In the 1930's, about two thousand applicants took the examination every year. As shown in Table 1, only about one-tenth of them were successful. In addition, even successful applicants were not always guaranteed appointment. Some of them failed to pass the examination required by the ministry they wished to enter. To obtain a job in a desired ministry, an applicant had to have a good academic record at his university as well as good results in the *kobun* examination. These records of achievement were often regarded as the most important criteria for personnel decisions even after appointment.

The *kobun* officials who were admitted through this narrow gate of recruitment were given special treatment as elite bureaucrats in each ministry. At various points, the personnel policies for *kobun*

Table 1: Number of successful applicants in *Kobun* examination

1930	204	1935	265	1940	238
1931	252	1936	194	1941	228
1932	238	1937	144	1942	411
1933	326	1938	197	1943	547
1934	302	1939	214	1944	—*

(*no examination held)

officials were sharply separated from those for *hanin* officials and the non-*kobun* type of *sonin* officials who were promoted from *hanin* rank. And, of *kobun* officials, those who were graduated from the imperial universities were given the highest privileges as officials with "M" careers.[9]

One example of the privileged status of the *kobun* official within the bureaucracy was his salary. Usually, the initial salary of a *kobun* official was 75 yen per month. This was equivalent to the sixth grade of *hannin* rank. After a short period of service (approximately from one year and a half to two years), he was appointed to Grade 7 of *sonin* rank with a salary of the eleventh or tenth grade of pay list No. 1 for *sonin* rank. Although non-*kobun* officials were promoted from *hannin* to *sonin* ranks after long service (more than seventeen years on the average), they were not covered by pay list No. 1. There was a clear line drawn between pay list No. 1 which applied only to *kobun* officials and pay lists Nos. 2 and 3 which applied to non-*kobun* officials. Even under the same category of *sonin* rank, there existed three different pay lists.

One of the established personnel policies for *kobun* officials was rapid promotion. The speed of promotion of "M" career officials was astonishing. There was, of course, a difference of speed among the ministries, but, as indicated in Table 3, an average "M" career official could reach the top grade only after nineteen years and one month. He was able to obtain a *chokunin* post in even fewer years than *hannin* officials (non-*kobun*) spent to reach a *sonin* post. In the case of "K" career officials, namely those officials who graduated from an imperial university but were not appointed by way of the *kobun* examination, speed of promotion was slower, and promotion beyond Grade 3 to a *chokunin* post was very difficult. Such was the case for most technical officials in government. Because of rapid promotion, the length of service of "M" career officials, from examination to retirement, was generally short. The average length of office of "M" bureaucrats was reported to be twenty years and

---

[9] This was part of a lettering system which classified educational background. "A" meant elementary school; "B" an advanced elementary school; "K" an imperial university; "L" a private university plus *kobun* examination; "M" an imperial university plus *kobun* examination.

Table 2: Official ranks and pay lists (1942)

Chokunin officials

Amount of annual salary specified for each official

Chokunin rank: 1 – 2

Pay list for *Sonin* officials

Grade	1	2	3	4	5	6	7	8	9	10	11	12
pay list no. 1	4,050	3,660	3,400	3,050	2,770	2,420	2,150	1,820	1,650	1,470	1,300	1,130
pay list no. 2	3,400	3,050	2,770	2,420	2,150	1,820	1,650	1,470	1,300	1,130	1,050	
pay list no. 3	2,770	2,420	2,150	1,820	1,650	1,470	1,300	1,130	1,050	970.	900	

(An annual salary: yen)

Sonin rank: 3 – 9

Higher official: *Chokunin* rank and *Sonin* rank

Pay list for *Hannin* officials

Grade	1	2	3	4	5	6	7	8	9	10	11
Amount	145	125	110	95	85	75	65	55	50	45	40

(A monthly salary: yen)

Hannin rank: 1 – 4

Table 3: Promotion speed of "M" career officials (in years and months)							
Ministry	From 1st appointment to grade 7	Grade 7 to grade 6	6 to 5	5 to 4	4 to 3	3 to 2	2 to 1
Finance	2.2	1.10	2.4	2.4	2.11	6.5	3.6
Home	1.6	2.1	2.3	2.7	2.9	6.1	2.11
Average of all Ministries	2.1	2.0	2.2	2.4	2.7	5.7	3.1

eleven months, in contrast with "K" technicians' twenty-three years and five months, and "B" officials' thirty-six years and one month.

During this twenty-year period "M" officials were frequently transferred from one office to another within the same ministry. The average number of times "M" bureaucrats changed during their term of office was reported to be about twelve. This suggests that most *kobun* bureaucrats remained at the same post for only a very short period, one year and a half or so. It is also reported that *kobun* officials were more likely to be transferred between different kinds of posts than between similar kinds of posts. These frequent transferences provided an in-service training; they gave to *kobun* bureaucrats the continuous stimuli of fresh tasks, and helped them to develop the broad view and flexibility which were regarded as indispensable requirements for top administrators.

In terms of training one can further say that the whole cluster of policies governing *kobun* officials provided in-service training. Although there was no modern-style training system, the personnel policies for *kobun* officials were primarily designed to give the able men selected by the *kobun* examination a strong sense of belonging to an elite as well as a broad and flexible view. A series of special privileges, granted only to *kobun* officials, served this purpose. At the most basic, everyday level distinctive office furniture—a specially-made table, a green table cloth, a pivot chair—and a dining room reserved for *kobun* officials gave young bureaucrats a sense of their elite status.

In this way, each ministry and agency recruited and trained a group of "M" career administrators, men of strong elite consciousness and great ability. The efficient operation, good or bad, of big government in Japan was made possible by this group.

The system, however, was not without drawbacks. Generally speaking, the promotion of "M" officials had at least five characteristics. (1) Because *chokunin* posts were reserved for them, most "M" officials could be promoted to top administrative posts usually without exception. (2) Promotion without exception meant adoption of the seniority rule as the promotion criterion. (3) As a result of the seniority rule, "M" career administrators' terms of office became quite short. (4) To ensure promotion, the number of "M" career men was usually adjusted to the number of top administrative posts available. And (5) frequent transference of "M" career men was related to speedy promotion. Promotion by seniority would obviously tend to increase status consciousness rather than concern for achievement. The short terms of office could mean that men of ability who had been produced at public expense were discharged from the government before they reached their full potential. (On the other hand, this contributed to the increased importance of *kobun* bureaucrats as a pool of elites for the whole society. Ex-civil servants often became top managers of large industrial concerns, executives of various public organizations and institutions, and key members of political parties.) The close relationship between the number of *kobun* officials and the number of top administrative posts could result in the arbitrary establishment of new posts to meet the number of surplus officials. And when *kobun* officials were transferred so often, there was a danger that they would become nothing but nominal decision makers. Again, this could change the joint emphasis on status and achievement to a sole emphasis on status.

In the last analysis, these qualities of the bureaucratic system produced a unique but irrational and even destructive mentality, as many scholars have pointed out. It can only be briefly mentioned here that the traditional behavior of *kobun* bureaucrats were represented in a most concentrated form by the "new bureaucrats."[10]

10 Or *Shinkanyro*. See p. 117n.

Their wartime appearance, the last stage of the history of the *kobun* official system, was an eruption of the worst features of elitism. The exaggerated elite consciousness of *kobun* bureaucrats who went hand in hand with the military elites contributed substantially to the collapse of Imperial Japan.

IV. POSTWAR YEARS IN RETROSPECT

The defeat and occupation of Japan brought forth a drastic reform in the civil service system as well as a basic change in the political régime. The institutional expressions of this change were the adoption of the new Constitution and the National Civil Service Law of 1947. The new basic principles embodied in these were designed to reorient the civil service from the concept of being the Emperor's servants to the idea of being public servants, and from the emphasis on status to an emphasis on achievement.

Efforts to reorganize the civil service system had already begun in 1945. Only three months after the surrender, the Shidehara cabinet announced its decision on the "Change of the Officials' System." This cabinet decision was intended to make the civil service open and democratic by replacing the *chokunin, sonin,* and *hannin* ranks with a classification of first, second, and third ranks, adopting more general titles such as *jimukan* (clerical official) or *gikan* (technical official), which do not indicate distinct gradations of official rank, and adopting one salary system to replace the previous complex and discriminatory pay schedules. Another purpose of this cabinet decision was to secure more efficient performance in public administration by introducing new ideas and methods such as personnel training and ratings for efficiency. In order to do this, the cabinet decision paid keen attention to the necessity of improving the *kobun examination.* It suggested that the value attached to legal backgrounds should be reduced and the scope of the examination extended.

These reforms were made law in 1946 by a series of imperial ordinances. On paper, they looked drastic; in reality, they were rather moderate. For instance, the qualifications for the newly approved first, second, and third ranks were almost the same as those for the traditional *chokunin, sonin,* and *hannin* ranks. The *kobun* examination itself, after a two-year suspension (1944 and 1945) due to the war, was reopened (1946-1947) and continued to supply young blood to the bureaucracy until the new examination system was established in 1948. (During 1946 and 1947, 362 persons passed the examination, while 327 more persons who had been directly employed by each ministry during its period of suspension came to be regarded as *kobun* officials.)

With the promulgation of the new Constitution based upon the popular sovereignty doctrine, the fundamental principles of the civil service changed. The Constitution defines public officials as the "servants of the whole community" and declares that "the people have the inalienable right to choose their public officials and to dismiss them." In accordance with this principle, new legislation entitled "the National Civil Service Law" was enacted in 1947 to take the place of the old imperial ordinances which had long ruled the civil bureaucracy of Japan. The concept of "officials" appointed by the Emperor, with an unlimited obligation of service to him, has formally disappeared. The complicated network of heterogeneous statuses has been broken and a clear establishment of homogeneous public servants has emerged. The distinction between *kan* ("legal rank") and *shoku* ("work-position") has virtually disappeared, and the emphasis is now on the latter. In other words, efforts are being made to replace the traditional attachment to achievement and status with an emphasis on achievement alone. The method of civil service recruitment has been changed accordingly. In 1948, the Examination for Public Servants of the Sixth Grade (presently, the Examination for Senior Public Servants) replaced the *kobun* examination.

But obstacles to the thrust of these changes still exist. For example, despite the provision for it in the National Civil Service Law, a classification of posts based on job function has not been fully established. Correspondingly the achievement concept still has not permeated the entire bureaucracy; and complete modernization of the recruitment system has yet to be accomplished. Though the *kobun* examination as a legal reality has disappeared, some of its basic features still exist. Among them are an emphasis on legal knowledge and favoritism for Tokyo University graduates. Each ministry and agency is still interested in appointing those who passed the law examination rather than those who passed other topical examinations. And a majority of those who pass the legal examination with good results are students of Tokyo University (formerly, Tokyo Imperial University). In their subsequent careers, those who passed the legal examinations are formally and informally treated as specially qualified senior civil servants. Hence, one may well say that while the institutional framework has changed, there is a remarkable continuity in the recruiting system and ethos of civil bureaucracy. Young administrators with a fresh spirit may be able to remold the old ethos, but it seems likely that the old ethos will stifle the young administrators.

There are several background reasons for this postwar situation. In the first place, the indirect Allied occupation preserved the administrative authority of the civil service. Second, the conservative parties' dependence on the bureaucracy for recruitment of party leaders has contributed to a substantial increase in the power of the bureaucracy. Third, the poor operation of local government and other systems of decentralization has concentrated more power in the central bureaucracy. And finally, there is increasing importance of the bureaucracy's role in the planned, welfare state.

One of the most remarkable facts in modern Japanese history is the lag between the nation's highly rational way of executing policy and the less rational way of making it. The policy-executing function has been efficiently performed by the bureaucracy with a solid core of highly selected elites. Japan's destiny will depend upon how much she can rationalize major decision-making to match the efficiency of the administrative machine.

British Education for an Elite in India (1780-1947)

I. THE HISTORICAL BACKGROUND

The impact of British education on India between 1780 (when Warren Hastings set up a college for Oriental studies in Calcutta) and 1947 (when the British bowed themselves out) cannot be understood without some idea of what transformed the British East India Company from a trading enterprise into a political power and led it to bother with education at all.

The eighteenth century saw the disintegration of the Mughal empire. This began under the Emperor Aurangzeb (1658-1707), a high principled bigot, who exhausted his resources by trying to conquer southern India, and provoked his Hindu subjects (the Muslims being a minority ruling class) to revolt by demolishing "all schools and temples of the infidels," debarring Hindus from high office, and indulging in iconoclasm, sacrilege, economic repression, forced conversion, and restriction of worship.[1]

Aurangzeb left a tottering empire to weak successors. The rebels, of whom the Marathas were the most important, fell apart in principalities carved out by seceding generals, adventurers, and bandits. During a century of devastation, unpaid fighting men roamed the continent, exacting Danegeld. It was as if the Thirty Years War had not only lasted a hundred years but had engulfed all Europe, obliterating the fruits of the Renaissance, by destroying all centers of government, industry, and learning. "The carcase was in a condi-

---

[1] Cf. H. H. Dodwell, *Cambridge Shorter History of India,* Cambridge, Eng., 1934, Ch. XII, passim.

tion to invite the eagles. As for the administration, which cloaked the rapine and pillage and march and counter-march of armies . . . it was a pretence."[2]

The East India Company tried to steer clear of these troubles but became embroiled. In 1757, Robert Clive, with the aid of 450 British troops, 2,500 sepoys, and bribes, put to flight 50,000 troops of Bengal's Mughal viceroy, thus revealing that the empire was a façade. The unforeseen result of Plassey—not even a battle, a skirmish —was to pitchfork the East India Company from a group of foreign merchants, trading by license, into an Indian territorial power.

The laws which the Company, as, first, the representative and then the successor of the Mughal emperor, had to administer were inextricably mixed up with religious dogmas and could only be expounded by Muslim theologians and Brahmin priests. It was the inadequate number of these monopolists which suggested the need for oriental colleges. But Warren Hastings, first Governor of Bengal (1774-1786), was also deeply interested in the civilizaton of the sub-continent. Wishing to govern in harmony with the traditions of the people, he recruited the first of a long series of British scholars to study the ancient literatures and laws of India. The methods of Western scholarship turned the Vedas from a mysterious ritual, sacred monopoly of Brahmans, the meaning of which had been lost,[3] into living works, *available to all,* to be studied and interpreted like Hebrew, Greek, and Latin classics. Until the coming of the British, the history of pre-Mughal India did not exist, the very name of the Emperor Asoka (273-232 B.C.)—whose four lions independent India has taken for her emblem—had been forgotten until a Company engineer, James Prinsep (1799-1840), deciphered the Brahman and Karoshthi alphabets. The translation of Sanskrit literature and philosophy by Sir William Jones (1746-1794), and his successors, electrified the German transcendentalists, Schlegel and Schopenhauer, and through them Coleridge, Carlyle, Emerson, and other leaders of thought in Europe, America, and India.

[2] E. Thompson and G. L. Garratt, *Rise and Fulfilment of British Rule in India,* London, 1935, p. 63.

[3] See H. G. Rawlinson, *Cultural History of India,* New York, 1938, pp. 406 ff.

The administrative reforms of Lord Cornwallis (Governor-general 1786-1793) demoted the Company's trading officials and promoted the first generation of highly salaried British administrators, who proved to be men of character and vision. Such were Thomas Munro, Charles Metcalfe, Mountstuart Elphinstone, and many others. In outlook, they were men of the eighteenth century, the Age of Reason and Enlightenment. Free from the Victorian preoccupation with Utilitarian material progress and Evangelical moral progress, they were compassionate and friendly. There was no Versailles.[4] The first generation of British administrators treated India's defeated ruling classes with the respect due to men who had functions in maintaining the social structure, which the British did not wish to disturb more than they could help.[5] They were, from the first, conscious that British rule in India must induce social changes that would limit its duration or transform its character. Here is an expression of opinion by Elphinstone (Governor of Bombay, 1819-1827), which was but one of similar expressions by Lord Hastings, Thomas Munro, and others:[6]

> I conceive that the administration of all the departments of a great country by a small number of foreign visitors, in a state of isolation produced by a difference of religion, ideas, and manners, which cuts them off from all intimate communion with the people, can never be contemplated as a permanent state of things . . . the progress of education among the natives renders such a scheme impracticable, even if it were otherwise free from

[4] Suggested subject for a Ph.D. thesis: Find evidence for and against the view that the enforced break-up of the Austro-Hungarian Empire, and the deposition of the Hohenzollerns and natural leaders of Germany in 1918, led to Mussolini, Hitler, and World War II. Speculation on the present power and influence of the U.S.S.R., deprived of suzerainty over ex-territories of the Austro-Hungarian Empire, may be included in an appendix.

[5] For the philosophical background of the East India Company's early administrators, see F. L. Lucas, *The Art of Living*, London, 1959, a review of the eighteenth century, in which Lord Jeffrey (1773-1850) is quoted as urging proportion on the fanatical young Carlyle: "Why must you be so dreadfully earnest? You have no *mission* upon earth, whatever you may fancy, half so important as to be innocently happy. . . ."

[6] See P. J. Griffiths, *British Impact on India*, London, 1952, and R. Coupland, *India: A Restatement*, Oxford, 1945, for texts of early British forecasts that education would lead to self-government.

objection . . . it is vain to endeavor to rule them on principles
only suited to a slavish and ignorant population. . . .

Bishop Heber (1783-1826) said that Elphinstone had seen more
of India than any other man and that he never ceased to promote
the training of Indians for self-government which, he believed, must
eventually come, and which would, in his own words, prove to be
"our highroad back to Europe." Elphinstone College, Bombay, was
founded under his auspices.

India was spared the particular social upheavals and racial an-
tagonisms caused by the presence of millions of European settlers
and thousands of minor officials, from which the French and Bel-
gian empires suffered when independence came, because while India's British administrators welcomed an elite of transient educated
Europeans, as leaders in administration and business, who would
retire to England, their opposition to any large-scale immigration
of settlers initiated a tradition which lasted as long as British rule.

Above all, these early British administrators had before their eyes
the havoc wrought by Aurangzeb's efforts to proselytize the Hindus.
They, therefore, proclaimed neutrality toward the social and religious customs of the country, and reinstated, and themselves took
over, the Mughal empire's traditional obligations to administer temples (as well as mosques) that Aurangzeb had flouted. Not least,
they prohibited Protestant missionaries within their territories.

This was the position around 1800-1810, when the East India
Company's officials began to feel the first breaths of the wind of
social change that was to rise to gale force over Britain.

The Nineteenth-Century Englishman

Evangelism, "the rock upon which the character of the nineteenth
century Englishman was founded,"[7] owed much of its pioneer drive
and prestige to its connection with India. Two high Company officials, Charles Grant (1746-1823) and John Shore (1751-1834),
on their retirement from India became neighbors of William Wilberforce and Zachary Macaulay (father of T. B. Macaulay) in

_____

[7] Eric Stokes, *English Utilitarians and India,* Oxford, 1959, p. 12.

Clapham, where they joined in founding the militant Evangelistic Clapham sect. Of its two aims—the abolition of the slave trade and the opening of India to missionaries—the sect considered the second to be, as Wilberforce said, "the greatest of all causes, for I really place it before Abolition." Wilberforce, personal friend of Pitt, and Grant, chairman of the East India Company in London, had influence in the House of Commons, before which the Company's Charter came up for renewal every twenty years. The link between Clapham and India enabled the sect not only to dictate policy-directives from London to the Company but to send to India succeeding generations of Evangelically minded missionaries and civil servants.

The Evangelical characteristics were consuming moral earnestness and the experience of conversion—the anguish and terror of sin, the ecstatic joy of rebirth, which made duty plain. Duty lay in preserving the state of grace by prayer and work, and in the mission to save others—to evangelize. Salvation came through knowledge of God's revealed word. Evangelicals sought therefore to spread enough education to read and understand the Bible, as the prerequisite for salvation. "To the Evangelicals . . . power carried with it an awful responsibility and duty, the evangelization of India's heathen millions . . ." whose plight was desperate, for they were "actual worshippers of false gods."[8] The panacea was an Indian counterpart of the European Reformation, setting the individual free from the tyranny of the priest. Education was the first requirement.

In 1813, on the occasion of the renewal of the East India Company's Charter, the Evangelicals launched a public campaign which succeeded in securing freedom for missionaries to work in the Company's territories. The Charter also included clauses authorizing the governor-general in council to set aside £10,000 a year for (1) "the revival and improvement of literature and the encouragement of the learned natives of India" and (2) "the introduction and promotion of a knowledge of the sciences . . ." This alarmed the Company's officials, because it would violate their policy of neutrality toward the country's social and religious customs. If, however, they could no longer prevent missionaries and others from starting

[8] Ibid.

schools, they could at least postpone *official* action from year to year. They had an arguable case. To India's traditional ruling classes, the Company was an oligarchy of upstarts, tolerable only so long as it was strong enough to prevent the ravages of war and banditry, and only so long as it followed the policy of conciliation toward the *established* religious customs and the *traditional* social hierarchy, successfully pursued by the Mughal Emperor Akbar (1556-1605) and so disastrously discarded by Aurangzeb.

The Company could not now, however, prevent the opening of *unofficial* missionary and secular schools, which co-incided with a revival of learning among a minority of enlightened Hindus inspired by a Brahman, Ram Mohan Rai (1772-1833). For twenty years he had been a Company revenue officer under a sympathetic eighteenth-century Englishman, John Digby, who had kindled his interest in English literature, which had led him to a profound study of Western science, philosophy, and religion. He founded the Brahmo Samaj, which proclaimed a rationalist, Unitarian, Socinian faith, reconciling Hinduism with Western philosophy, enabling men to worship without idolatry and cruelty. Until 1914, the Brahmo Samaj's influence persisted in the higher walks of life in Bengal and Bombay, and produced a series of great men, including the Tagore family.

Orientalists Versus Anglicists

So that when, in 1825, the Company proposed to use its educational grant (for which it *had* to find some use) to set up additional *oriental* colleges, Ram Mohan Rai protested. That he was the greatest Sanskrit scholar of his day enhanced his authority among his fellow countrymen and enabled him to protest in terms which, if Macaulay had used them, would have hammered another nail in Macaulay's coffin.[9] *Rai wrote*:

> When this seminary of learning was proposed, we understood that the Government of England had ordered a considerable sum of money to be annually devoted to the instruction of its Indian

[9] This reference to T. B. Macauley is explained on p. 143.

subjects. We were filled with sanguine hopes that this sum would be laid out in employing European gentlemen of talent and education to instruct the natives of India in mathematics, natural philosophy, chemistry, anatomy, and other useful sciences, which the nations of Europe have carried to a degree of perfection that has raised them above the inhabitants of the other parts of the world. . . . We now find that the Government are establishing a Sanskrit school under Hindoo pundits to impart such knowledge as is already current in India. . . . The pupils will here acquire what was known two thousand years ago, with the addition of vain and empty subtilties since produced by speculative men, such as is commonly taught in all parts of India. The Sanskrit language, so difficult that almost a lifetime is necessary for its perfect acquisition, is well known to have been for ages a lamentable check on the diffusion of knowledge; and the learning concealed under this almost impervious veil is far from sufficient to reward the labour of acquiring it. If it had been intended to keep the British nation in ignorance of real knowledge, the Baconian philosophy would not have been allowed to displace the system of schoolmen, which was the best calculated to perpetuate ignorance. In the same manner the Sanskrit system of education would be the best calculated to keep this country in darkness, if such had been the policy of the British legislature. But as the improvement of the native population is the object of the government, it will consequently promote a more liberal and enlightened system of instruction, embracing mathematics, natural philosophy, chemistry, and anatomy with other useful sciences, which may be accomplished by employing a few gentlemen of talents and learning educated in Europe, and providing a college furnished with necessary books, instruments, and other apparatus.[10]

The Company staved off English education a little longer, but its own desire to recruit efficient Indians, in response to London's insistence that as few expensive Englishmen should be employed as possible, helped to tilt the balance. The directors in London concluded in 1830 that higher English education must be pushed to create "a class of persons qualified . . . for high appointment in

[10] See Bureau of Education, Delhi, *Selection from Educational Records,* 1920, Part I (1781-1839).

the civil administration." It is clear that long before Macaulay arrived in Calcutta in 1834 the die was cast in favor of English education, but his famous Minute of 1835 clinched the matter. As
Thompson and Garratt shrewdly observe,[11] Macaulay was profoundly ignorant of the Orientalists' case (always an advantage,
joined to decisiveness such as his). He guessed if not the whole
truth, at any rate an essential part of it. His Minute conveys the
gusto with which it was written and is good fun to read:

> . . . It is argued, or rather taken for granted, that by literature
> Parliament can have meant only Arabic and Sanskrit literature,
> that they never would have given the honourable appellation of "a
> learned native" to a native who was familiar with the poetry of
> Milton, the metaphysics of Locke, and the physics of Newton; but
> that they meant to designate only such persons as might have
> studied in the sacred books of the Hindus all the uses of Kusa-grass
> and all the mysteries of absorbtion into the Deity. This does not
> appear to be a satisfactory interpretation. To take a parallel case:
> suppose the Pasha of Egypt were to appropriate a sum for "reviv-
> ing and promoting literature and encouraging the learned natives
> of Egypt," would anybody infer that he meant the youth of his
> Pashalic to give years to the study of hieroglyphics, to search into
> all the doctrines disguised under the fable of Osiris, and to
> ascertain the ritual with which cats and onions were anciently
> adored? . . .

> . . . I am quite ready to take the Oriental learning at the
> valuation of the Orientalists themselves. I have not found one
> among them who could deny that a single shelf of a good Euro-
> pean library was worth the whole native literature of India and
> Arabia. . . . It is, I believe, no exaggeration to say that all the
> historical information which has been collected from all the
> books written in Sanskrit is less valuable than what may be found
> in the most paltry abridgements used in preparatory schools in
> England. . . .

> In India, English is the language spoken by the ruling class
> . . . by the higher class of natives at the seats of government. It
> is likely to become the language of commerce throughout the . . .
> East. It is the language of two great European communities which

[11] E. Thompson and G. L. Garratt, *Rise and Fulfilment of British Rule in
India,* London, 1935, p. 660.

are rising, the one in the South of Africa, the other in Australasia. . . .

The question now before us is simply whether, when it is in our power to teach this language, we shall teach languages in which, by universal confession, there are no books on any subject which deserve to be compared to our own; whether, when we can teach European science, we shall teach systems which, by universal confession, whenever they differ from those of Europe differ for the worse; and whether, when we can patronise sound philosophy and true history, we shall countenance, at the public expense, medical doctrines which would disgrace an English farrier, astronomy which would move laughter in girls at an English boarding school, history abounding with kings 30 feet high and reigns 30,000 years long, and geography made up of seas of treacle and seas of butter. . . .[12]

Many Indian nationalists have bitterly assailed Macaulay for imposing an alien culture on an unwilling India. They forget that those who in the 1830's eagerly *sought* the alien culture were the newly emerging middle classes, who were to lead the nationalist struggle and to constitute the ruling classes of independent India. Paradoxically, those who resisted westernization were the traditional ruling classes, the princes, landowners, and other feudal elements, whom today's elite of nationalist politicians, civil servants, and industrial leaders—all drawn from the middle classes—despise as reactionary. The late K. M. Pannikar,[13] a great Indian scholar, who synthesized Western and Hindu culture in his own person, has this comment on Macaulay's Minute:

Divested of the narrow prejudices against Hindu civilisation, and of the shelf of books for which he was prepared to exchange the entire treasures of oriental literature . . . his main thesis of an education based on the New Learning, and through the medium of English, was . . . the most beneficently revolutionary

[12] For Macaulay's complete Minute in 5,500 sonorous words, see Bureau of Education, Delhi, *Selection from Educational Records,* 1920, Part I (1781-1839) p. 66. For the spirited reply to Macaulay made by the Orientalist, H. T. Prinsep—extremely interesting reading—see *Selection from Educational Records,* pp. 118-29.
[13] Indian historian, statesman, and ambassador to China (1948-1952), author of *Survey of Indian History,* Asia Publishing House, London, 1947.

decision taken by the British . . . The exaggerations of Macaulay's Minute do not concern us now, but the importance of the decision . . . may be gauged by considering what the results of the alternative policy would have been. The particularisms based on vernaculars would have grown so greatly as to break up even the idea of Indian unity. Much of the New Learning on which India's Great Recovery has been based would not have been available. . . . By going in for . . . English, India joined a world community . . . what was the alternative? Even the most advanced Indian languages . . . had not reached the level of literary standards for secondary education. Education up to university standards would have been impossible without decades of preparation. . . . This, after all, is what Macaulay's system has done. It developed Indian languages to standards in which a university education is now becoming (*sic*) possible. But without the universities teaching in English and producing the army of workers, such a development would hardly have been possible. The great colleges, universities, schools of India[14] . . . are the direct result of Macaulay's system.

II. INDIA'S MIDDLE CLASSES

Why Did They Emerge?

The middle classes which emerged in the mid-nineteenth century, and from which, I repeat, the political, administrative, academic, and industrial elites of independent India were recruited, are the product of British education. Why and how did they emerge?

In traditional pre-British India, the princely, priestly, warrior, and land-owning castes were, by definition, not interested in trade and industry. The literate castes, who followed intellectual professions, looked down on craftsmen. The artisan castes, who monopolized craftsmanship, were not interested in education. The trading castes were shrewd, but their education, purely practical, stopped at accounts. Occupational specialization arose from hereditary caste callings, not from higher education, which was literary and ignored the applied skills and sciences that lead to technological development. Nor did the Mughals build up a cadre (as understood in Western Europe) of trained civil servants, because they laid down

[14] Using English, under Macaulay's *Fiat,* as the medium of instruction.

neither service rules nor educational requirements: appointment depended on caste inheritance, tenure of office, or ability as a courtier.

Two developments created a demand for Indians educated in such a way as to be able to work with the British. The first was, as we have seen, the Company's desire to recruit Indians both for its civil services and judiciary. The numbers required, modest as long as the Company's rule covered only Bengal and small areas around Madras and Bombay, multiplied as its suzerainty gradually extended across the sub-continent. The second was the abolition of the Company's monopoly of trade in 1813, which, opening India to non-official enterprise, had two consequences: (a) British entrepreneurs needed more and more trained clerks, accountants, supervisors, and junior (and eventually senior) executives, and (b) since the rule of law established by the British made no distinction between British and Indian businessmen, new Indian enterprises added their own ever growing requirements for personnel educated in Western ideas, business methods, and industrial techniques. Thus, whereas in 1815 there were in Calcutta 23 European and 74 Indian firms, by 1859 there were 177 European and 322 Indian firms.

English education began, therefore, to be prized as the gateway to a career in government service or in commerce. The earlier generation of British administrators assumed that the historical natural leaders of India, the landed Hindu castes and the Mughal aristocracy, would take the lead in the Westernizing process which the rest of India would follow—this was known as the "downward filtration" theory. But *Karma,* or caste destiny, had made those who were Hindus into princes, chieftains, or warriors, while Muslims owed their authority to the right of conquest. Neither belonged to castes whose destinies or functions included letters. The depression of the old aristocracy was initiated by the Company's land revenue reforms, hastened by the substitution of the English language, laws, and ideals for the old Indo-Persian culture, and completed by their indifference to Western education.[15]

[15] Muslims were slow to realize that their indifference to Western education, and the eagerness of the Hindus for it, gave Hindus the monopoly of the services and professions. It was not until 1877 that the Aligarh college for Muslims was started. This delay of half a century was a contributory factor to the creation of Pakistan.

As eighteenth century tolerance yielded to nineteenth century Evangelicalism, the Company began increasingly to interfere in the life of the country in the name of "progress, moral and material," and when from 1848 Governor-general Dalhousie began to speed up Westernization by vast public works—by roads, railways, telegraphs, grants-in-aid to schools, by founding universities, and steady absorption (instead of preservation) of Indian principalities—the answer of traditional India to the mounting challenge to the established religious and social structure was the Mutiny of 1857. That the Mutiny failed was due as much to the refusal of the new Indian middle classes to support traditional India as to the strength of British arms.

Had traditional India driven the British out, there would have followed the re-establishment of the façade of the Mughal Empire, controlled by the princes of the Maratha states, and the destruction of the embryonic Western economy of British private enterprise and industrialization. The middle classes would have disappeared—reabsorbed in the environment from which they had emerged.

Whence Recruited?

From what castes were India's middle classes recruited?

In Britain, the middle classes began to emerge in the fourteenth century by attracting recruits from the classes above and below them. That all men were equal before the law, and that (unlike India before British rule) savings could be invested and property accumulated in safety, opened avenues to the enterprising among artisans and tradesmen and, since the eldest sons succeeded to aristocratic estates, younger sons had either to live as obscure dependents or to join the enterprising in carving out a new life away from the land—in trade or in the professions.

India's middle classes, by contrast, originated from the literary castes—Brahmans (priests, philosophers, scholars, physicians, astrologers, professional men), Kayasths (scribes), and trading castes, such as Marwaris, Banyas, Bohras (Muslim business men), Parsees, etc. All these are among the higher castes. The downward filtration theory broke down, first, because the literary castes had no wish to see their hereditary prerogatives extended to lower castes, with whom they could not mix in schools or elsewhere without pollution, which, unless purged by an expensive ceremony, meant social ostracism, inability to marry off sons and daughters, and loss of family rights and properties. Second, none of the non-literary castes —which included the agriculturists, laborers, depressed castes and their womenfolk, who constituted the bulk of the population*— could afford to spare children from herding cattle or work in the fields from their earliest years. Any children sent to school soon forgot how to read or write because they had neither books to read nor need to write. Their capacity for mental arithmetic might, on the other hand, have left some Cambridge mathematicians out of breath.

The enterprising among the literary castes sent their sons to what amounted to secular vocational training for government service, the new professions of teaching, medicine, law, commerce, and industry, and, more gradually, the slowly emerging new technical services, like irrigation and the railways. Before Macaulay's Minute of 1835 a handful of schools in Bengal, Madras, and Bombay sufficed for their needs, training but a few hundred at a time. By 1854, there are estimated to have been 180 schools and colleges dotting the whole of British India, educating some 30,000.[16]

The majority of these institutions were day schools, which were preferred to boarding schools for two reasons: first, because cost is important in a poor country; second, because, although all pupils came from the literary castes, there were sub-divisions within these castes: sitting next to anyone in class might be permissible, but to play, eat, worship, or sleep together could create difficulties. Since character is developed essentially outside the classroom in social and corporate activities, it followed that these schools were, from a British viewpoint, more places of *academic instruction* than of character training. There were, in fact, a number of boarding schools, but discussion of who attended them, and of the inter-related problems of caste status and character training, is adjourned to p. 178.

* Estimated at 150 million in 1850.
[16] *English Education and the Origins of Indian Nationalism,* New York, 1940, p. 129.

That the representative institution for Western education in India was a day school has meant that, while Western concepts have preponderantly conditioned the *intellectual* outlook of their pupils, caste feelings and loyalties have preponderated in their family relations and *emotional* life. This is a point to which I have found no references in the voluminous literature on education in India, perhaps because Indian and Western observers alike may find its importance difficult to work out. To the average Westerner, superficially acquainted with history and sociology, caste is as self-evident an evil as feudalism is to a Marxist. He can no more assess the social strengths and weaknesses of caste than the Marxist can of feudalism.[17] The Western-educated Indian shares the Western intellectual's prejudice against caste. He is, therefore, anxious to assert that its influence is vanishing, and he is unlikely to appreciate the extent to which his conduct (as opposed to his thinking) remains conditioned by it.

All this is not to say that the British had no influence on Indian concepts of conduct,[18] but it seems probable that it has come less from social training in schools and more from the example of British attitudes encountered in working together with them.

The Government Engineer: A Case Example

Insights into the personal difficulties that Indians experienced in working with the British, and the lessons that they thus absorbed, may be found in *Punjabi Century: 1857-1957,*[19] the autobiography of Prakash Tandon, who gives a vivid firsthand account of the trans-

[17] It is a common mistake to assume that the elite of the feudal barons, or Brahman priests, in a traditional society hold the villager down in misery. The stability of the social structure could not have persisted for centuries if it had been based on fear and force, if it had not been socially acceptable. The villager did not live in despair, sullenness, or apathy. It is true that he often is sullen or apathetic *today,* but it is not the traditional society but the disrupting forces that make him despair. India's villagers cling to caste, as mediaeval Europe clung to feudalism, because it provides each individual with a recognized, respected status, with customary *rights,* as well as obligations, and—barring calamities like war, famine, or pestilence—with social and economic security.

[18] I use the word "conduct" here descriptively, without implying any judgment on the values of British and Indian concepts.

[19] Chatto & Windus, London, 1961.

formation of the Punjab that followed the impact of British education on the generations of his great-grandfather, grandfather (1840-
1931), father (1876-1955), and himself (born *circa* 1912).

When in 1924, Prakash Tandon went to high school in the small
town of Gujrat, his history book ended with a chapter on the "blessings of British rule." His generation took these blessings for granted
and this chapter seemed to them mere propaganda. But to his fore-
bears, who had lived through an era in which, proverbially, there
had been "neither a rupee nor a virgin between Lahore and Pesha-
war"—the respect for life and property that the British enforced was
a new and extraordinary experience. The Tandons, an impoverished
family of high caste, rejoiced that marauders and high-handed officials of despotic rulers harassed them no longer. Since Aurangzeb,
the Tandons's caste had been denied its prerogative of posts in the
administration, but under the British, Prakash's grandfather was
able to start his family on the road back to prosperity: educated in
an indigenous village school, he knew Persian and elementary arithmetic. He soon grasped that under the new régime there would be
widening opportunities for those educated in English, so he sent his
son to learn it at the new high school at Gujrat.

In the time of Prakash's father, Ram Das, the headmasters of
high schools and colleges were still Englishmen, pioneers evolving
curricula, writing new text books, translating others. Ram Das spoke
with admiration of these men, so far from their homes, who worked
hard for small pay, because they loved India. From the seeds that
they sowed, says Prakash, sprang the rich harvest of his father's
generation. In the days of large Victorian families, many of these
school masters and college professors were younger sons of good
family and outstanding education, sent out to make their way. The
records of St. John's College, Agra, show that of the thirty-two
Principals and Vice-principals between 1850 and 1930, most were
public school men, and all were graduates (usually with First Class
Honours) of Oxford or Cambridge.[20]

From Gujrat, Ram Das went to Lahore College, then to the
Roorkee Engineering College (founded 1844), which trained Indians for the new Public Works Department. Ram Das "sometimes

[20] Cf. Rev. J. P. Haythornthwaite and T. D. Sully, *St. John's College, Agra
(1850-1930)*, London, 1932.

spoke to us of his stay at Roorkee as a dream." The thought that he
might become an engineer in a coveted government service, on a
salary that he would hardly know what to do with, spurred him. He
became the first engineer from his village and the second from
Gujrat. Ram Das's generation accepted willingly, without resent-
ment, that they would not reach the top of their service, because
they thought it right that, as teachers and leaders, the British should
enjoy the privileges of *gurus*.[21] Prakash writes:

> We were used to give our *gurus* and seniors respect. In the
> primary school . . . the boys swept the teacher's house, did his
> shopping, tended his cow, chopped wood, and brought daily
> offerings of milk and curds, vegetables, grain, and fruit . . .
> later, when fees were paid in cash, the custom of service and
> gifts continued for long. . . . Even I took milk and curds to the
> master, besides the English newspaper to which my father was
> one of the few in the town to subscribe. . . .

From the beginning to the end of his days as one of the first Indian officers of the cadre of the Imperial Service of Engineers (the
elite of his service), Ram Das was meticulously conscientious—a
perfectionist. While he took an occasional short leave for weddings
or funerals, he asked for the six months' leave to which he was entitled every five years, only once in all his thirty-five years' service.
This was characteristic of his generation. They lived only for their
work; they only talked "shop"; they envied the ability of the English
to relax and to play. Ram Das explained that the English could
afford to relax because they assumed that it was natural that they
would occasionally make mistakes. But when an Indian made a mistake the reaction was that the job was too difficult for him ". . .
after all he did not have the experience." Being always on test made
Ram Das and his generation even more punctilious.

Indians found Western science easier to learn than British ideas
of discipline—something new and alien. Prakash's grandfather recalled how the British in the 1840's appointed a village *patwari*[22]
to maintain a register of land holdings. The *patwari* was told that
he must keep a daily record of his work, but that every Sunday was

[21] Brahman religious teachers, objects of deep filial respect.
[22] A village accountant who serves as a land registrar—*Ed.*

a holiday. The idea of not working on a Sunday, to him a day like any other, was outside his experience and he never understood it. When the British officer, inspecting the *patwari's* diary, found a frequent entry "Today a Sunday was celebrated," he fired him for frivolity and incompetence. But a funeral, a wedding, an illness, a call for help from a neighbor, were caste obligations, which came before one's own work, even if they compelled several days' absence. The *patwari* was only fulfilling his obligations, using the Sunday holiday rule as a respectful bow to the customs of his employers. His dismissal puzzled and shocked everyone. Discipline, said Prakash, did not begin to be fathomed until his father's generation of men in government service, and even then it was (as it still remains) incomprehensible to virtually everyone outside, because the foundation of the caste system is the religious obligation of mutual support. Although Ram Das observed British discipline, it was with difficulty, because his relations considered it natural to go to him for favors and jobs, unnatural that he should refuse. How could they turn to others who had obligations to their own families? My experience supports Prakash's observation that the Punjabis of his father's generation had a tremendous esprit de corps, and were proud of the Punjab Services' reputation throughout India as a *corps d'élite*. Prakash justly observes that Ram Das's generation both founded the Punjabi middle class and added new values to the old Punjabi character.

Ram Das was posted from canal colony to canal colony, each of which (unlike indigenous towns with their crowded, winding lanes, dust-laden and pungent with aromas) was a model town, laid out by British architects and engineers, in rectangles with modern, electrically-lit bungalows standing in their own gardens, along broad boulevards. To these new towns, lawyers, traders, business men, artisans, of all castes, came to settle from all over the Punjab. A new society emerged, in which families married, irrespective of caste,[23] into families of the same social and educational standards.

---

[23] So claims Prakash Tandon. Before accepting it, however, I would like to see statistics compiled from the marriage registers. This looks, to my sceptical mind, like an example of the Western educated Indian's anxiety to reassure critical Europeans that caste is no more. I suspect that any inter-caste marriages—certainly at the time of which Prakash Tandon is writing—were exceptional.

Prakash accepts the commonly held view that the Englishman and the Punjabi had something in common, which enabled them to get on together from the start. Punjabis are not aloof and complex like the Brahmans of Bengal or Madras, with whom the British came first into contact. They are extrovert and adaptable and, says Prakash, ". . . the British impact was comparatively so gentle and persuasive that the Punjabi for once enjoyed the process of change and adaptation."

Education of Women

The education of women in India is a British creation. There was not one girls' school in India until, in 1819, missionaries founded one for orphans and converts. But the Magna Carta of women's education in India originated with John Elliot Drinkwater Bethune (1801-1851), a successor of Macaulay as Law Member of the Governor-general's Council, who as (spare-time) President of the Council of Education, gave £10,000 (the equivalent of £70,000 in 1968 sterling) of his own money to found the Bethune Girls' School, which still functions in Calcutta. Enrollments rose slowly not only because of strong Hindu and Muslim family objections, but also because no careers awaited women. A woman living alone in a village was unheard of. The only women who lived alone in towns were low-caste prostitutes or high-caste courtesans. The British opened the first doors by employing women as secretaries, teachers, nurses, and eventually gynecologists. As the nineteenth century went by, the influence of increasing numbers of pioneers multiplied schools until in 1936, in addition to a total of 11,000,000 boys under instruction (excluding universities), there were 3,000,000 girls in 392 girls' high schools, 413 middle English schools, 560 vernacular middle schools, and 32,618 primary schools. "If," wrote Mr. K. Natarajan, a leading Indian liberal and a Brahman, in 1937, "a person who died a hundred years ago came to life today, the first and most important change that would strike him is the revolution in the position of women."[24]

After World War I women even entered public life. Examples of

[24] *Indian Social Reformer,* Sept. 25, 1937, article on English education.

the growing numbers of Indian women, who have played distinguished roles, include Sarojini Naidu, first woman president of the Congress party and ultimately governor of the United Provinces; Padmini Naidu, first woman Governor of West Bengal; Vijayalakshmi Pandit, at various times a cabinet minister, Ambassador to the United States, and President of the United Nations General Assembly; the Rajkumari Amrit Kaur, first woman to be a federal cabinet minister and sometime President of the World Health Organization; and Mrs. Indira Gandhi, Prime Minister of India.

III. 1854 AND AFTER: MASS VERSUS ELITE EDUCATION

We come now to the Education Despatch of 1854. It is time that this document, unanimously hailed by the standard authorities as "bold, far-seeing, and statesmanlike," was reassessed. What it sought and, by contrast, what it achieved, can best be understood in the light of the differences in (1) the aims that developed between British leaders in India and those in Britain concerned with the government of India, and in (2) political and educational theory and experience in the two countries.

That, following Governor-general Bentinck's decision in favor of English education in 1835, enlightenment had not filtered downwards did not worry the British in India, because to them the idea of trying to force education on the masses seemed unrealistic. To the British in England, however, the failure of downward filtration seemed a reproach. Under the influence of the Utilitarians and the Evangelists, public opinion had come to feel that illiterates "steeped in ignorance" were a challenge to humanitarianism. That in the economy of rural nineteenth-century India, a peasant could be successful, happy, *and* illiterate, was beyond imagination.

The Utilitarians were able to use India as a laboratory for their theories because James and John Stuart Mill were officials of the East India Company in London, and the law professors of Haileybury College (where aspirants to the Company's service were trained) taught from Bentham's writings. The assumptions of Utilitarianism and Evangelism were akin. Ignorance barred men from happiness. Knowledge revealed reality and enabled them to choose rightly. But, until they were educated, a severe schoolmaster was necessary in the form of the law; for the Evangelicals, this was God's law, which punished ignorance and slew the sinner;[25] for the Utilitarians it meant that the human legislator must keep men from harmful acts by attaching penalties to them. Utilitarian logic leads to bureaucracy because it does not fear executive power in itself, and it conceives the legislature as sovereign. The end of government is not individual liberty but the greatest happiness, as conceived from on high by wise (popularly elected?) legislators, of the greatest number.

By 1854, the Utilitarian and Evangelist forces in London were agreed that to confine education in India to an elite, demanding higher education, prevented the greatest numbers from attaining the greatest happiness.

The Despatch of 1854 is a watershed because it assumes, for the first time, the state's responsibility for education in India. Its aims were the same as those of European governments when (mostly at much later dates) they came to inaugurate their national educational systems. Under the superintendance of the central government, each Indian Province was to have a Department of Public Instruction, which was to increase the numbers of schools and to improve teaching by establishing model schools at key centers, and by offering grants-in-aid to private schools—elementary, secondary, and collegiate—if they fulfilled conditions prescribed by (all-wise) government inspectors. New universities—examining, not teaching— were to be set up in Calcutta, Bombay, and Madras. European knowledge was to be "extended throughout all classes." But in India these aims encountered obstacles without parallel in Europe. India's population was not only larger than any single European state but larger than that of all Europe. Nor was it homogeneous: it was divided vertically and horizontally between many peoples, several creeds, and innumerable castes; and while the masses, in their millions, would have to be taught in twelve different major languages, the scheme of education to be introduced was to culminate in the study of a totally unfamiliar culture and science through the medium of a foreign language. With India's limited financial re-

[25] See John Wesley, Sermon XXIX.

sources, this colossal task could not be achieved,[26] and the vital factor in the relative success of the European systems—an upward demand for education from the masses—did not exist in India.

Whereas, prior to the 1854 Despatch, the increase in places in schools had remained in line with the demand for them *and* with vacancies available in government service and the professions to absorb the output, a large part of the substantially increased sums of money thereafter available were (since primary education met with mass apathy and middle-class resistance) concentrated on multiplying high schools and colleges, so that the output began to exceed the possibilities of employment.

Before 1854, there were in Bengal, for example, six government and eight private colleges, distinguished by the variety of their curricula, methods, and individual characteristics. The government colleges were under the Council of Education, an occasional *ad hoc* group of officials and local dignitaries, who looked after education as a voluntary extra to their real functions. They made decisions of policy but did not peer constantly over their headmasters' shoulders. Not so the new Departments of Public Instruction. They employed full-time educators, of the highest ideals and integrity, with platoons of zealous inspectors—and money to spend. The 1854 Despatch had emphasized that the grants-in-aid were intended to help private schools to improve standards and to consolidate themselves, after which, the grants were gradually to be diverted to mass education. In the event, higher education, particularly the departmentally controlled institutions, throve, while the masses remained "steeped in ignorance."

To understand the rising suspicions evoked among the middle classes by the several educational reforms that followed the 1854 Despatch, we must glance back.

The Charter of 1833 had laid down that no native should be debarred from the East India Company's employment, and up to the Mutiny the employment of Indians advanced. In 1857, there were 256 Indian officials in higher capacities and nearly 3,000 in clerical grades. Indian judges tried virtually all cases in the first instance. The outbreak of 1857, sudden, unexpected, bloody, created a sense

[26] It has not yet been achieved.

of insecurity among British officials. Despite Queen Victoria's re-affirmation of the 1833 policy in the Proclamation of 1858 (by which the Crown took over the responsibilities of the East India Company), they were now at pains to ensure that the Indian Civil Service (i.e., the senior executives) were all British. That this was *de facto*, not *de jure*, made the ensuing antagonism between British officials and educated Indians the more bitter.

Since a truer appreciation of the sociology of the 1857 rising is only now—over a century later—beginning to emerge,[27] it is not sur-prising, but none the less disastrous, that the contemporary British in India were muddled in their diagnoses. To many, 1857 seemed a mass movement. They therefore sought to insure against recur-rence by enlisting the support of the "natural" leaders of the people —the princes and landowners—by various concessions. Although it was precisely these elements which had led the revolt, it was argued that if their status were upheld they would feel no urge to rise again and would keep their followers in order. On the other hand, the British in India now directed their deepest distrust toward those who talked about "political advance, individual liberty, and democracy," in other words, the new and articulate middle classes. Thus it was that the British in India bolstered those who had risen in revolt against them, and who with each succeeding generation became po-litically more anachronistic, while they repressed those who had supported them in the crisis, the educated *elite* whose emergence had been regarded both as inevitable and as a source of pride to men like Munro, Elphinstone, and so many others of the earlier British administrators, whose views Macaulay crystalized in char-acteristic rhetoric:

> It may be that the public mind of India may expand under our system till it has outgrown that system; that by good government we may educate our subjects into a capacity for better govern-ment; that, having become instructed in European knowledge, they may, in some future age, demand European institutions.

[27] Notably in such works as Percival Spear, *India: A Modern History,* Ann Arbor, Mich., 1961; S. Gopal, *British Policy in India, 1858-1905,* Cam-bridge, Eng., 1966; and B. B. Misra, *The Indian Middle Classes,* London, 1961.

> Whether such a day will ever come I know not. But never will I
> attempt to avert or to retard it. Whenever it comes, it will be the
> proudest day in English history.[28]

Their studies of British philosophers, leaders, and dreamers—
John Locke, John Wilkes, Edmund Burke, Wordsworth, Byron,
Shelley, John Stuart Mill—had revealed to India's middle classes
the concepts of individual freedom and equality before the law.
Here was the beginning of an Indian counterpart of the Renaissance
for which the Evangelicals had hoped. But English studies also revealed to Indians the virtue of constitutional political agitation.

The Indian middle classes contrasted the liberal attitude toward
India that predominated in Britain, and in the Viceroys sent to
India (until Curzon), with the distrust of British officials and businessmen in India after 1857. This contrast kept alive their faith
(ultimately justified) that however much the British in India might
repress political agitation, the British at home would understand
and respond. The Indian National Congress was founded in 1883,
with the blessing of the Viceroy, Lord Dufferin, to provide a plat-
form for India's political aspirations. In his inaugural address, the
President, W. C. Bonnerjee, said:

> Great Britain had given them above all . . . the inestimable
> blessing of Western education. . . . The more progress the peo-
> ple made in education . . . the greater would be their insight
> into political matters, the keener their desire for political ad-
> vancement. . . . Their desire to be governed according to the
> ideas . . . prevalent in Europe was in no way incompatible with
> their loyalty to the British government. All they desired was that
> the basis of the government should be wide and the people should
> have their . . . legitimate share in it.[29]

The controversy that still surrounds the Hunter Commission,[30]

---

[28] Speech in the House of Commons. July 10, 1833. *Speeches and Documents on Indian Policy: 1850-1921,* Oxford, 1922, I, 265.
[29] Quoted in that form by P. J. Griffiths, *British Impact on India,* London,
1952, p. 280.
[30] So called after its president, Sir William Hunter, appointed by Lord
Ripon. Sir William Hunter, Indian Civil Service 1840-1900, was a member
of the Government Chief Legislative Council 1881-1887. The Hunter Commission was officially the Educational Commission of 1882-1883.

appointed in 1882 to review progress in carrying out the aims of 1854, illustrates how differently the facts looked in India and in Britain and explains the contradictory motives attributed to the British in India and the British at home.

In Britain, it was natural that a Liberal government in power should send a Liberal statesman, Lord Ripon, as Governor-General to India in 1880 and that he should interest himself in progressive causes, such as education, at this time in the forefront of British politics. Britain had just launched a national system of compulsory education. What was more natural than that efforts should be made to remedy the "pitiable ignorance of the Indian masses."

British officials in India, however, welcomed the Hunter Commission on other grounds: they were disturbed by educational developments since 1854. If mere numbers counted, the universities had been astonishingly successful, but degree standards were unbelievably lax, with the result that low standards prevailed all down the line: ill-qualified school teachers sent up ill-prepared pupils, so that as the years passed more and more graduates and "Failed B.A.'s" chased too few jobs.

The Hunter Commission was called upon to decide how simultaneously to provide (1) universal compulsory elementary education and (2) the highest standards of university education, for all who considered themselves able to benefit by each, in a subcontinent which, as the first census of 1871 had revealed, contained 254,000,-000 people. This is a problem which independent India (population 500 million) has not even begun to solve. The difficulty is that if state education is free it costs parents money in taxes (and, nowadays, inflation). The amount that could be raised in taxes in British India was minimal in an economy where barter predominated and money incomes had in 1857 been estimated at £2 per head per year (unadjusted for money values).[31]

[31] In 1935, elementary education in England and Wales cost taxpayers £16/17/1 per head. On this basis, free and compulsory education for India's 53 million children between the ages of six and fourteen would have cost £900,000,000 a year, i.e. eighty times the total revenues, central and provincial. Primary education in India would have cost far less than in the United Kingdom, but even to have divided the English figures by ten would still have left compulsory education beyond India's means. See *Modern India and the West,* ed. O'Malley, Oxford, 1941, p. 177.

The Hunter Commisson's Findings

The Hunter Commission found that the provincial Departments of Instruction had established government schools (as models) in the best catchment areas, so that, even where they were encouraged, private schools found it hard to compete with institutions backed by all the resources of the state, and they tended to set up in areas where the educational soil was poorer. Some Departments discouraged private initiative and fostered the traditional disposition of Indians to rely on the government as "father and mother." Where, before 1854, relations between schools and officials had been cordial, they were now antagonistic. The private schools complained that the Departments used public examinations to impose text books, and that inspectors, who held strong views (as earnest and able officials do) *and* the purse strings became the *de facto* supreme authority over a school, making it a mere facsimile of the state schools.

The Commission argued that if it was, indeed, part of the Department's job to provide direct education, its more important responsibility was to stimulate others to educate. But, it went on, to "most men it is more satisfactory to work through agents that are under complete control than through those who have views of their own. . . . the Department was instructed to manage directly one set of schools, while it was only indirectly to control another. It could hardly be expected altogether to overcome the natural tendency" to give more support to its own schools.

The Commission recommended that Government should gradually transfer its responsibilities for higher education to private bodies with liberal grants-in-aid, but that the bulk of funds available should go to educate the masses. *The excessive supply of collegiate students would thus be leveled off and economies in state expenditure on secondary schools would release funds for primary education.*

To summarize thus in two paragraphs the thousand foolscap pages of the Hunter Report conveys no idea of its quality. It is sufficient to say that every page shows sympathy with India's problems and aspirations.

Yet the report kindled Indian suspicions because the middle classes counted money spent on the masses as thrown away, the more so because the masses were indifferent to education. Above all, the middle classes connected Hunter's recommendations not with the ideals of the British Liberals in the Mother of Parliaments but with the success of four Indians in passing the Indian Civil Service entrance examination in 1869, which (Indians thought) dismayed the British in India as the first opening of the door to Indianization of the highest executive posts from which (Indians suspected) the British considered that Indians should be excluded. The Hunter Commission's emphasis on education *for the masses* was interpreted as a smoke screen to conceal a decrease in expenditure on secondary education intended to reduce the numbers of those equipped to achieve embarrassing successes in higher examinations. This suspicion was largely, though never wholly, justified in regard to the British in India between 1857 and 1917.[32] It was largely, though never wholly, unjustified in regard to public opinion in Britain. Indeed, the main achievement of the Liberal Viceroys Ripon and Dufferin, and even of their cautious successors Lansdowne and Elgin, was to reveal to the Indian middle class the possibilities of working with their rulers for political and social advance, providing that they organized an Indian lobby in London to keep interest alive.

The appointment of Curzon as Viceroy (1899-1904) is not in contradiction to this view, because Curzon was not sent to carry out the reactionary policies with which he became identified. He was sent because he seemed, on paper, to have every conceivable qualification.[33] His genius lay in administration. Among several Augean stables that he joyfully attacked, oblivious of obstacles, was the state of education. He was appalled to find that 13,969 students had, between 1864 and 1873, matriculated in Calcutta, Madras, and Bombay, and that of these, 7,385 (52 per cent) failed to obtain degrees. Of the 6,584 who made some progress, 3,503 passed their "First Arts" examination, and 1,324 of these went on to secure a

[32] For causes of the change after 1917, see p. 174.
[33] S. Gopal, *British Policy in India, 1858-1905*, Cambridge, Eng., 1966, p. 222.

pass Arts Degree. A mere 259 (3 per cent of total matriculates) secured honors.[34] And what "honors!" Questions were confined to the set books. Most answers were memorized. Examiners avoided probing for critical assessment of text book expositions for fear of failing virtually all candidates.

Curzon had no racial prejudice; he made himself intensely disliked by the British in India by severely disciplining those who maltreated Indians. But this was not simply racial tolerance: it was, in Curzon's eyes, a matter of justice and good administration. On the other hand, Curzon saw no reason to conceal his view that Indians were incompetent to fill any but subordinate government posts, and *a fortiori,* were unfit for self-government. He therefore considered that to tolerate low university standards was an offence not only against education but against political common sense, since the ever rising numbers of "Failed B.A.'s" who filled the ranks of unemployed were a political menace.

Curzon's solution was to stem the flow of unemployables by raising the standards for all examinations from matriculation to finals. Up to now, the universities had only been examining bodies with power to affiliate colleges, but with no control over their studies, professors, or students. His University Act of 1904 strengthened unwieldy governing bodies by slashing their numbers and staffing them with a majority of nominated members (usually government officials or government educationists), and by authorizing them to inspect colleges and drastically increasing their power to affiliate or disaffiliate. These measures, announced in terms needlessly offensive to Hindus, and drawn up by a Commission which included only one Indian (who presented a strongly dissenting minority report) angered the entire middle class, for it was they who were removed from the governing bodies, and who organized and staffed most of the colleges. More and more under Viceroys Ripon and Dufferin, they had come to see higher education as the gateway to power for themselves and to political freedom for their country. The whole teaching profession, students, and parents of future students, joined in vituperating the Act. Curzon's further announcement of the partition of Bengal fanned anger to white heat. The case for partition

34 Statistics compiled from B. B. Misra, op. cit. p. 300.

on grounds of administrative efficiency was unimpeachable, but it entailed reducing the Hindu majority over the Muslims in the area and, following the Universities Act, confirmed the assumption that the Viceroy supported the Indian Civil Service British in their opposition to India's constitutional advance and regarded the middle classes as a political danger to be suppressed. The result—spectacular but unintended—of Curzon's educational and other reforms was to transform the "loyal opposition," the constitutionally-minded Congress party, into resentful revolutionaries, ready for violence, tolerant of terrorism.

Technical Education

That the British failed to encourage engineering and technical education is a frequently repeated charge. The records do not, however, support it. A class in Western medicine was started in the Sanskrit College in 1792. The Medical College was opened in Calcutta in 1835 under three British doctors. To touch a dead body meant loss of caste, and a dramatic account survives of the first dissection by a Hindu, Madhusudan Gupta:

> . . . It had needed some time, some exercise of the persuasive art, before Madhusudan could bend up his mind to the attempt; but once having taken the resolution, he never flinched. . . . At the appointed hour, scalpel in hand, he followed Dr. Goodeve into the godown where the body lay. . . . The other students deeply interested . . . but strangely agitated, with mingled feelings of curiosity and alarm, crowded after them, but durst not enter the building where this fearful deed was to be perpetrated; they clustered round the door; they peeped through. . . . And when Madhusudan's knife, held with a strong and steady hand, made a long and deep incision in the breast the lookers-on drew a long gasping breath, like men relieved from the weight of some intolerable suspense.[35]

The sacred status of letters in India gave Arts subjects prestige before all others but, even if this had not been so, it would have

[35] Bureau of Education, *Selections from Educational Records 1840-1859*, p. 313.

been useless to turn out engineers and craftsmen until industry had developed to create a demand for them.

Interest in technical education quickened as, in the second half of the nineteenth century, the Government successively created new specialist services: Railways, Education, Public Works (irrigation, roads, buildings), Public Health, Agriculture, Veterinary, Forestry, Archaeology, etc. Indianization was at first comparatively slow because: (1) most of these services were launched or grew to importance after the Mutiny, and resistance to Indians in the highest posts persisted until the first World War; (2) most industrial (in contrast to commercial) enterprises were British-managed and suffered from the same post-Mutiny reluctance to promote Indians. Curzon's absence of racial prejudice and readiness to help Indians in activities for which he thought them suited showed itself in his practical encouragement to Indian capitalists, such as J. N. Tata, head of a rising enterprise that grew into what was, for long, the biggest steel works in the British Commonwealth, and in his insistence that science and teachers' training should each be given status as separate University studies.

While the British did develop technical education, they were, prior to the first World War, slow to admit Indians to the very top level of posts.[36] Prakash Tandon's autobiography[37] throws light on this. He says that the British up to around 1900 (i.e., Curzon's viceroyalty) were so busy teaching and developing the country that they apparently never gave a thought to what would happen when their pupils became responsible old hands. The day came when young engineer graduates, fresh from England, had to be given specialized training by experienced Punjabi irrigation officers, who then had the mortification of seeing their trainees start higher in the scale than Punjabis, maintain their lead, and go over their heads to the very top. After 1887, 10 per cent of posts in the Imperial Service were reserved for Indians who had studied engineering in England, while the Provincial Services were recruited from the Indian colleges. Indians resented this because it lowered the standing of the Indian colleges, although their graduates considered that their

36 For the quickening pace thereafter, see p. 174.
37 See p. 148.

knowledge of local conditions and languages made them more useful than those educated in the United Kingdom. Until then, these
servicemen had shown little interest in the Congress party politicians, whom extroverted Punjabis tended to despise as intellectuals
and indisciplined speechifiers, who never seemed to have *done* anything in real life. But now they equated the unfairness to Indians in
their service with the injustices that the politicians proclaimed. With
able Indian engineers crowding below the top, bitterness grew. They
began to read the political reports in the press with a new eye, to
wonder how long the British could carry on in the face of political
disturbances. So that it was significant that when Prakash Tandon
graduated from Lahore in 1929, his father advised him not to seek
entry into the Indian Civil Service—hitherto the acme of the educated Indian's ambition—and he went into business. Today as head
in India of the internationally known firm Unilevers he is among
independent India's business elite.

Politics Versus Discipline

Thirteen years after Curzon's university reforms, another inquiry—
the Sadler Commission (1917)—found that matriculations had
climbed over the 16,000 mark,[38] and that university governing bodies tolerated lax standards, liberal admissions, and indiscipline.

Hitherto, historians have usually blamed these evils on the nationalists who, before independence, incited students to violence in
the cause of freedom, and on the politicians who, after independence, did the same in the cause of party politics. This is a superficial
judgment: the basic causes originate in the 1854 policy, by which
the government did not inaugurate *autonomous* academic bodies,
whose independence was respected by a university grants commission, but itself assumed direct responsibility for education.
Governing bodies and teachers were not independent scholars but
"education officers" working their way up the ladder of promotion.
Incentives to research were weak because the top posts were administrative. Syllabuses were supervised, so teachers, seeing that government and students agreed in discouraging study outside approved

[38] Cf. p. 160 above.

courses, became apathetic. That, as Sir Theodore Morison[39] said, was why "Government colleges, though manned by much abler men, are so dead-alive compared with independent institutions." Furthermore, education officers were subject to transfer on promotion to higher posts. Government schools could often have made greater impact if they had enjoyed the same continuity of staff as the mission schools.[40] Before the 1854 Despatch, schools of varied individual character, staffed by dedicated pioneers, multiplied in accordance with demand and parental ability to pay. Their output, keeping in step with the development of the professions, could be absorbed. Classes were small enough for academic instruction. But after 1857, there began an increasing diversion of efforts to interest in book-learning the rural millions who neither sought nor needed it.[41] Grants-in-aid to every type of institution from primary schools to universities opened the way to bottomless expenditure and waste of limited resources on assembly line curricula, the object of which was not to cultivate critical faculties but to pass examinations. "The idea of a uniform system such that no one capable of receiving higher education could fail to get it," said T. S. Eliot,[42] "leads imperceptibly to the education of too many people, and consequently to the lowering of standards to whatever this swollen number of candidates is able to reach."[43]

Intellectuals nourish nationalism, and the stronger the nationalist movement grew the stronger the official reflex action in tightening control over senates and teachers, thereby insuring that the universities continued in the center of nationalist political strife. The Sadler Commission recommended that all government colleges should

[39] An eminent Indian educator who in 1913 fought vigorously but vainly to reverse the established policy.

[40] R. C. Symonds, *The British and Their Successors,* London, 1966, p. 256.

[41] It is, broadly, only since independence that the vital need to grow more food has created a real use for the three R's. The cumulative pressure of population has made it urgent for villagers to be able to use farm machinery and read directions for using fertilizers.

[42] *Notes on Culture and Education,* London, 1948, p. 101.

[43] There were honorable exceptions. A number of private institutions managed to maintain high standards, and Roorkee Engineering College, even though a state institution, turned out graduates, like Ram Das, of high efficiency and personal integrity.

gradually be handed over to independent bodies for administration and staff appointments, but when the 1919 Act transferred responsibility for education to popularly elected provincial ministries[44] they clung to government control, so that the universities continued to "educate for frustration."[45] On the problem of widespread student strikes and violence, which remain the despair of Indian educators to this day, the University Education Commission (appointed by the independent government of India) observed:

> . . . witnesses cited the period of the struggle for independence in which students and staff were called upon by political leaders to engage in political agitation as a cause of indiscipline. . . . Such action may have served a patriotic purpose . . . for national freedom, but such practices now . . . promote confusion and become a serious impediment to national solidarity. . . .[46]

IV. ON-THE-JOB TRAINING: BRITISH-INDIAN RELATIONS IN THE PUBLIC SERVICES

Despite the weaknesses of higher education after 1857, three major factors contributed to train an Indian elite for government service and the professions.

[44] See p. 176.

[45] In *Universities: British, Indian, African,* London, 1966, published after this essay had been completed, Sir Eric Ashby and Dr. Mary Anderson justifiably defend the good faith of Britain's pioneering export of universities to India and show that the experience gained there influenced government officials at a later date to seek to avoid the same mistakes in Britain's African dependencies. Here, the principle survives under "interdependence," that while the government may provide the money it must not interfere with its spending. Where it has been flouted an informed public opinion has reacted, in contrast to continued acquiescence in India. These findings should be studied not only overseas but in London where, as R. C. Berdahl has shown in *British Universities and the State,* Berkeley, Calif., 1959, some politicians strive for parliamentary supervision over university expenditure. In 1966, the House of Commons Public Accounts Committee began an inquiry into the question of how to make the universities accountable to Parliament for what they spent.

[46] For a review of the 1948-49 University Commission Report and of the gravity of post-independence indiscipline, see Jossleyn Hennessy, *India, Democracy and Education,* Calcutta, 1955, Ch. III.

The first was that in the 1870's a few Indians began to go to Oxford and Cambridge, and that from the 1890's their numbers rose year by year. In 1921, the first census of Indian students in the United Kingdom revealed that there were 1,450 in universities and technical colleges, studying a wide range of courses—accounting, law, medicine, arts, engineering, chemistry, economics, and other subjects. "They were" says Professor E. Shils, "always young people of distinguished qualities and many made their mark in the liberal professions, in education, and in politics."[47] From innumerable examples, I cite four internationally known names: the late Jawarharlal Nehru (Harrow and Cambridge), Sirdar Vallabhbhai Patel (barrister of the Middle Temple, London), respectively first Premier and Deputy Premier of independent India; M. A. Jinnah and Liaqat Ali Khan (barristers of Lincoln's Inn, London) respectively first Governor General and first Premier of independent Pakistan.

The second factor was that at different dates in the nineteenth century (after 1857) the Central and Provincial governments ceased to accept an Indian university degree as an automatic qualification for the various services and inaugurated special examinations of their own (in which an assessment of character by interview was important). The long controversy over Indianization of the Indian Civil Service should not obscure the fact that, apart from top-level posts, the administration had been Indianized some sixty years before independence. Indians had been appointed Deputy Collectors and Magistrates from 1833. Subordinate officers and clerical staff had virtually always been Indians. As far back as 1891, Sir George Chesney[48] described a typical district of a million inhabitants as having at most six European officials—the District Commissioner, two deputies, two police officers, and a judge. Below these came Indian Deputies and Assistants. There were in 1891 only 750 Indian Civil Service officers in India.[49] Besides these, the higher judicial and executive services had about 2,600 officers, of

[47] Foreword to A. K. Singh, *Indian Students in Britain,* Asia Publishing House, London, 1963.
[48] Quoted in R. C. Symonds, *The British and Their Successors,* London, p. 63.
[49] The Indian Civil Service (I.C.S.) was a corps of senior executives.

whom only 30 were British. The subordinate civil service had 111,000 officers of whom 97 per cent were Indians. As for the Indian Civil Service, all probationers, British and Indian, studied Indian history, law, and languages at Oxford or Cambridge before joining the Service.[50]

The third factor was that teaching in classrooms is only one aspect of education. The mingling of British and Indians not only in the various administrative services, but also in the police, army, navy, air force, in commerce and industry, and as school masters, professors, doctors, made a profound contribution to the training of elites in India. The quality of British officials was an important formative influence.

For a Briton, the material rewards of service in India were generous, the life was colorful and varied, the responsibilities challenging. Government services and private enterprises therefore attracted elite British candidates. Selectors could hold out for the best. That the characters of such men[51] and their attitudes towards their work and towards their Indian trainees made a deep impression emerges incidentally from a symposium by twenty retired Indian I.C.S. officers, who ended outstanding careers at the top level as Secretaries to the government, ambassadors, governors of states or of the Federal Reserve Bank, and as senior officials of the United Nations.[52] The object of this book, published by Indians in India, is to bring home to future generations of Indian administrators the traditions of the Indian Civil Service, which the contributors fear may be lost in the course of the vast reorganizations that have followed inde-

[50] The independent government of India ceased this practice in 1947. Pakistan continued it until 1959.

[51] Some representative British names taken at random are Sir Ronald Ross (1857-1932) of the Indian Medical Service, who identified malaria with the anopheles mosquito; Sir Albert Howard, first Economic Botanist to the Government of India, whose pioneer work on fertilizers was amplified by his Indian successor, Dr. C. N. Acharya; Sir John Marshall, Director-General of Archaeology, who discovered the Indus Valley civilization; Sir Maurice Gwyer, a great legal luminary, sometime Chief Justice of India and Vice Chancellor of Delhi University; Sir Jeremy Raisman, last British Finance Minister of India, now Deputy Chairman of Lloyds Bank, London; Sir Paul Chambers, a British Inland Revenue officer called to India to reorganize the tax system, now Chairman of Imperial Chemical Industries Ltd.

[52] *The Civil Servant in India,* Bombay, 1965, ed. K. L. Punjabi, I.C.S. (ret'd).

pendence. Relevant to our purpose are the references to their training under British seniors and their relations with the British in general. While all write appreciatively of the British officials who tutored them as probationers, it is noteworthy that as many as twelve out of the twenty dwell at length on their tutorial experiences as examples for their successors to emulate. They describe how they were taught to cultivate a sense of humor,[53] to think for themselves, to protect the people in their charge from misinformed directives issued by seniors at urban headquarters out of touch with the districts, and to realize that these seniors, from viceroys and governors downwards, would respect independence in action and judgment, provided that it showed good faith. The probationers did not learn these precepts from rule books or from exhortations, but by *doing,* by being given steadily increasing responsibilities, by being allowed to learn from their mistakes, and by seeing from day to day how their tutor coped with obstreperous people and unforeseen or dangerous situations.

Here are some typical examples. The first two illustrate that British seniors did not allow themselves to be prejudiced by any false starts by their trainees. The subsequent distinguished careers of these recruits in every case vindicated the tolerance and judgment of their tutors.

G. D. Khosla joined the I.C.S. in 1926,[54] a few weeks after his

[53] Humor differs from country to country, but in this context what these Indian I.C.S. officers are recalling is that they absorbed the Englishman's horror of a "scene" and his readiness to use a joke to avoid one. The dislike of a "scene" can be useful to those required to enforce law and order. The opposite of the British attitude is found in countries in which it is a punishable offense to treat officials in uniform with what those officials regard as inadequate respect. I myself once narrowly escaped arrest when, wishing to expostulate with him in a friendly way, I addressed a Paris police officer as "mon vieux." "Je ne suis pas 'mon vieux.' Je suis Commissaire de Police," he replied furiously.

Years later, talking to an Indian I.C.S. officer, I mentioned that psychologists say that the stimuli of rage and laughter are closely connected. "That's a thought," he said, "I must circularize my district officers: 'Tighten nuts and bolts on your car before setting out to quell a riot but keep connections loose in your head.' "

[54] After his retirement as Chief Justice of the Punjab in 1959, Khosla was a member of the Commonwealth Commission of Enquiry appointed by the government in the United Kingdom to inquire into disturbances in British Guiana. Khosla drafted the Report.

father had resigned from government service in a flurry of publicity because he could "no longer tolerate the government's oppressive measures." The Chief Secretary to whom young Khosla reported for duty greeted him with "So you're the son of the man who doesn't want to serve the Satanic government." This, he says, was the only reference ever made to the subject. Even when Khosla went out of his way to flaunt his national costume and Gandhi's picture in his home, "my British colleagues and superiors did not question my probity or my devotion to duty . . . they respected my sentiment."

> At the very beginning of my service I learnt that the first duty of a senior officer is to help the junior in becoming a knowledge-able, self-confident, and efficient civil servant. The mistakes made by the tyro were pointed out to him and then promptly forgotten lest he develop a sense of guilt or inferiority. If he displayed un-usual talents, he was given praise and encouragement. Within a few weeks of my joining the service, I passed an order sentencing a man . . . and then, at the request of defence counsel, admitted him to bail. My order granting bail . . . was at that time not permitted by law, and as soon as I realized my error I went to the District Magistrate (who) . . . with . . . paternal indul-gence, told me not to be unduly agitated . . . and sending for the lawyer . . . reprimanded him for misleading an inexperi-enced judicial officer. . . . Afterwards he told me that it was just as well to refresh one's memory of the Criminal Procedure Code before passing an order and not depend too much on the submissions of lawyers. . . .
>
> A week or two after this, I was entrusted with . . . drawing up a note on the municipalities in the district. I took great pains. . . . The file came back to me the very next day with the Deputy Commissioner's thanks and a remark that I had prepared 'a very good note indeed.' My earlier lapse had been completely forgot-ten and I was . . . patted on the back. . . .

H. V. R. Iengar, who joined the I.C.S. in 1925 and retired as Governor of the Reserve Bank in 1957, early found himself in difficulties, because he unwittingly became involved in a local Hindu-Muslim scandal. Aggrieved by unjustified suspicions, Ien-gar's relations with his superior became strained. Iengar says:

I suppose I was hot-headed. I was equally offensive and, in retrospect, it is clear that I was somewhat intemperate, considering that I was a junior officer. It says a great deal for the basic fairness among the senior officers that, in the ultimate decision that was reached, Government made no comment whatsoever about my alleged part in the Hindu-Muslim activities at Godra, but drew my attention to the fact that I had not co-operated adequately with the District Magistrate during a time of stress, and expressed the hope that I would avoid such an error in future. Looking back . . . I cannot help remarking that this was a fair judgement. . . . Almost immediately after . . . I was asked to work as Under Secretary to the Chief Secretary to Government. This undoubtedly was a promotion and made it clear that Government thought well of me.

Iengar next recalls that a file came before him which showed that a British I.C.S. officer had failed to reply to a request despite as many as eighteen reminders.

Being young and enthusiastic, I was horrified. . . . Instead, therefore, of signing another routine reminder, I wrote a curt letter to Mr. X. asking him, in effect, what he meant by his failure to reply to Government and demanding a reply by return of post.

A senior Indian I.C.S. officer, to whom Iengar recounted "rather braggingly" what he had done, pointed out that an officer could only be censured by the Chief Secretary. Iengar therefore sent the file to the Chief Secretary with trepidation.

It came back with a sealed letter from the Chief Secretary saying that no doubt my attention had not been drawn to Secretariat instructions. He was sure that in future I would not ignore them! In the meanwhile, he himself had written further to Mr. X., and had put a copy of his letter on the file. The letter began: "In continuation of the letter which I asked my Under-Secretary to write to you earlier today . . ." I have not forgotten yet the effect this letter had on me. My attitude to the Chief Secretary became one of admiration and gratitude and I therefore took particular care to see that I did not let him down. Some time later, he was appointed Home Member of the Bombay Government. During his last four weeks as Chief Secretary, he was so busy tidying up his arrears that he asked me to carry on all his current work. This was a big responsibility . . . at a farewell gathering he made particular mention of this and told the audience how grateful he was to me for having carried his burden so well.

And Iengar concludes: "This is an example of how to handle young officers."

Several contributors emphasize the *camaraderie* between I.C.S. seniors and juniors and the useful part that the old club life and field sports (at which some now sneer as part of the "sahib" complex) played in an I.C.S. officer's work. Thus, V. Isvaran, who joined in 1933 and retired in 1963, as Chief Secretary of Gujarat state, says:

> There was an intimacy between senior and juniors. . . . The training of the new-comer was accepted by the seniors . . . as their special responsibility. Merely watching the senior at work was instructive. There were innumerable discussions outside the office—at the senior's house, or the club, or in the field of sport. Valuable pieces of advice were handed over in a casual manner. The reception was thereby made more certain than if they had been passed on in a heavy-handed formal manner.
>
> In performing his task as the head of a team of district officers the Collector found it very useful to spend a little time in the evening a few days a week at the local club. This . . . served two useful purposes. First, the members, mostly government officers, could take exercise regularly and keep fit. I . . . enjoyed playing tennis or badminton every day at the club. Secondly, both during the games and sitting around afterwards, the officers got a chance of meeting each other informally in a relaxed atmosphere. This helped to build up a spirit of *camaraderie*. . . . Often official matters were discussed informally. Views were exchanged. It was useful to know the possible reactions . . . before an official move was made. . . . It also saved a lot of time in processing the cases officially . . . it is a pity that the club is dying out. . . . The level of physical fitness among officers is coming down. Inter-departmental co-ordination is now less efficient.

G. V. Bedeker, who joined in 1923 and retired in 1963 as Special Secretary to the Maharashtra Government, is another who stresses relations between seniors and juniors.

> Full scope was provided for exchange of views. . . . It was accepted . . . that all difficult questions should be settled . . . over a cup of tea. . . . The highest authorities were easily accessible to, and welcomed, junior officers, who were encouraged to discuss their problems The result was that junior officers had background knowledge and did not labor under misapprehensions.

Illustrating British good-humored common sense and the relaxed relations between seniors and juniors, K. P. S. Menon (joined 1921, retired 1961 after being Indian ambassador in Moscow) recalls that when, as a probationer, he returned from leave a day late, he asked his District Officer how the extra day should be treated officially. "Any way you like, provided you don't rouse the demented ingenuity of the Accountant General," was the reply.

A. D. Gorwala (joined I.C.S. in 1922) insists that the informal part of his training was more important than studying for examinations.

> This unofficial training was often administered quite imperceptibly. . . . The Collector . . . might ask the new Magistrate to come and have tea with him one evening a week. . . . Almost in passing he would suggest that it would perhaps be a good thing if he brought along any particular cases in which he had written judgments or in which points of evidence were perplexing him. . . . Plied with good tea . . . the touchiness and arrogance so characteristic of the intelligent inexperienced young prize-winner, to whom for some period at least all the world seems inferior, would fall off. . . . Differences of kind or race would sink to insignificance and the young man would, sometimes to his own surprise, find himself talking freely, listening with attention, proffering his work for examination, pleased at the praise, not hurt at the warning and advice.[55]

I do not suggest that life in government service was uninterrupted tea and sympathy. We were all human. But from personal observation, I am convinced that friction, when it occurred, arose from

[55] A. D. Gorwala, *Role of the Administrator, Past, Present and Future*, Gokhale Institute Lecture, 1952. Quoted by R. C. Symonds, *op. cit.*

clashes of temperament rather than of race.[56] The risk was that a clash between an Indian and a British officer could so easily be interpreted as racial antagonism. The marvel was that it was thus interpreted so rarely. If racial friction had been serious in government service, the police, the armed forces, the machinery of government would have collapsed under the stresses that it was periodically called upon to bear (e.g., political disturbances, Hindu-Muslim riots, and the Congress party's rebellion in 1942).

The outbreak of war in 1914 evoked two responses. There was a tremendous demonstration of loyalty to the empire. A million Indian soldiers fought. From the revenues of British India[57] £146 million were voted, and the Princes and others contributed generously to war funds. Second, Indians publicized their hopes that London would recognize the implications of a war allegedly fought for democracy. The British government responded with the historic announcement of 1917 that its policy was the "increasing association of Indians in every branch of the administration and the gradual development of self-governing institutions."

Two important and closely linked results followed this announcement. First was the initiation of *systematic* Indianization, according to a time schedule, of the I.C.S., other services, and the armed forces. Second, the British in all services in India thereafter accepted Indianization without reservations. A minority of irreconcilable seniors retired. Entrants knew that they would be required to make a success of the policy and would not have joined if not ready to do so.

The table shows the increased pace of Indianization of the I.C.S. Indians were also now to be trained at the Royal Military College, Sandhurst, and the Royal Flying Corps College, Cranwell. From a handful in 1918, the number of Indians holding the King's Com-

[56] I myself had a flaming row with an Indian Deputy Secretary of the Finance Department because he (successfully) impeded the working of Parkinson's Law in my Bureau. What was particularly maddening was the calm with which he dealt with me. As he explained the next day when I apologized, "There was no point in my tearing *my* hair, old boy. I knew that if I turned down your application for more staff there was nothing you could do about it."

[57] To be distinguished from the (then) 560 princely states.

Indian Civil Service

YEAR	BRITISH	INDIANS	TOTAL
1869	882	1	883
1879	907	7	914
1889	884	12	896
1899	988	33	1,021
1909	1,082	60	1,142
1919	1,177	78	1,255
1929	881	241	1,122
1939	759	540	1,299
1942	573	632	1,205

mission[58] had by 1939 risen to 400, and stood around 8,000 in 1945, when there were also over 1,000 officers in the Navy and Air Force. At Sandhurst and other English schools these officers acquired, besides the quality of leadership, the British habit of playing down potentially emotional situations by "dead-pan" or humorous understatement. In the fire and slaughter after partition in 1947, the nonchalance of Indian and Pakistani officers enabled them to collaborate smoothly in organizing the dispatch and reception of 7,000,000 refugees from each country (14,000,000 altogether). It is difficult for anyone who did not witness the bloodshed and the hatred that politicians and press flung at each other across the border, to appreciate the contribution made by the detached, matter-of-fact attitude of the officers of the two armies.[59]

The 1917 pledge[60] also led to two big efforts in the interwar years towards training Indian politicians in the techniques of administration and of parliamentary government. The first was the Act of 1919

[58] There had long previously been "Viceroy's Commissioned Officers" corresponding to Warrant Officers, a rank above noncommissioned officers and below commissioned officers.
[59] It is true that statesmen like Pandit Nehru, Sardar Patel, and Liaqat Ali Khan, jointly appealed for calm and restraint, but there was little response.
[60] See p. 174.

which, in 1921, transferred to popularly elected governments in the (then) eight provinces control over all internal subjects, except law and order. Although this Act was "far from being a complete failure,"[61] its educative effects were limited by Mr. Gandhi's "Non-co-operation" campaigns, by internecine quarrels between the left wing of the Nationalists, generally hostile to the new constitution, and the right wing, anxious to work it. Recognition among different religious and linguistic groups of Hindus and Muslims that the 1919 Act was a first step towards the transfer of greater power led to bitter struggles between them for the succession, which further impeded the smooth working of the Act.

The second effort was the Provincial Autonomy Act of 1935, which transferred to the (then) eleven popularly elected provincial governments, control over all subjects, including law and order, excluding only "central subjects" (cf. federal subjects in North America). When the Act came into force in 1937, Congress cabinets took office in eight provinces, and other parties under Muslim premiers in three provinces. Despite initial difficulties, Indian politicians came to appreciate the objective advice and constitutional co-operation that they received from British governors and British and Indian civil servants. Some piquant situations arose when a minister found himself giving orders to secretaries whose acquaintance he had first made when their roles were reversed. K. L. Panjabi (I.C.S., ret'd.) relates, for example, that many wondered how Commissioner J. H. Garrett, whose censure of Morarji Desai's conduct had led to the latter's resignation from the I.C.S., would take orders from Morarji Desai now that he had become Revenue Minister.[62] But, says Panjabi, Garrett's attitude was clear; just as he had regarded it as his duty to censure Desai, so he continued to administer the law impartially, irrespective of who was in power, and Panjabi holds Garrett up to the future Indian administrators, for whom he is writing, as typifying "one of the finest traditions of the I.C.S."

Many politicians new to office thought that ministers could issue any order they chose, and the first tutorial task of the Indian Civil

[61] For a balanced assessment, see Thompson and Garratt, *Rise and Fulfilment of British Rule in India,* op. cit. pp. 613-25.
[62] K. L. Panjabi, ed., *The Indian Civil Servant,* op. cit. p. 95.

Service, which fell alike to its British and Indian officers, was to make them realize that orders at variance with the law could be challenged in the courts. K. C. Panjabi recalls that a minister ordered him, before witnesses, not to execute certain court decrees. Panjabi said that the High Court would react severely. "Never mind," was the retort, "do as I say." Panjabi then politely suggested that it would be appropriate to send him a written order because this would enable him to advise the minister in writing of the consequences and allow the minister to decide whether he wished to face them. The minister was furious but the matter ended. Other I.C.S. tutors to politicians provide some happy footnotes to India's educational history, as illustrated in an incident recorded by S. Lall, (who joined the I.C.S. in 1920 and retired in 1955 as Assistant-Secretary General to the United Nations). His minister was nervous that a bill would evoke politically awkward hostility, whereupon Lall quoted:

MACBETH: If we should fail?
LADY MACBETH: We *fail!*
But screw your courage to the sticking place
And we'll *not* fail.

"This quotation," says Lall, "highly pleased my minister and he used it in introducing the Bill in the legislature."

Unfortunately, progress in the education of the politicians was cut short when, after the outbreak of war in 1939, the Congress party caucus instructed the eight Congress provincial governments to resign. They did so reluctantly; they were enjoying themselves. The three non-Congress ministries remained in office throughout the war.

By 1942, when there were 1,500,000 employees in all the non-military services in India, including 800,000 railwaymen, and 89,-250 postal and telegraph workers, only 5,500 were British, the other 1,494,500 were Indians. Nor were the 5,500 British crowded at the top. At the highest executive level, there were, in 1942, 632 Indian I.C.S. officers and 573 British. Ten out of every eleven judges were Indian. In the administrative services there were eight Indians to one British; in the higher grades of the engineering departments, fourteen to one. The greatest achievement of the Indian Medical

Service, as Prime Minister Attlee said when it was dissolved in 1947, had been its training of medical practitioners, of whom India had 50,000 at independence. Pakistani and Indian ex-members of the I.M.S. achieved, like those of the I.C.S., international recognition after independence as, for example, President of the World Health Assembly, President of the World Health Organization, Director of the W.H.O. Regional Office in S. E. Asia, etc.

All services were trained in the British practice whereby an officer advises his minister on matters of *undecided* policy, but once the minister has given his *decision,* the civil servant is required to carry it out without comment. This was vital to the stability of the independent governments of India and Pakistan, for it meant no loss of experienced personnel by "anti-colonial" witch-hunting. Hindu and Muslim officers carried out the policies of the new governments, as they had those of the pre-independence governments. Thus, for example, Sir G. S. Bajpai, (educated at Muir College, Allahabad, and Merton College, Oxford) who had been the (British) Indian ambassador in Washington, D.C., became Secretary of the Foreign Ministry under Jawaharlal Nehru, and Mohammed Ali, I.C.S., became Secretary-General to the Government of Pakistan. The veteran politician Sardar Vallabhbhai Patel, Deputy Prime Minister, paid tribute to the I.C.S. when he said two years after independence: "All that we have been able to achieve . . . has been possible because of their loyalty and wholehearted co-operation." And Mr. Paul Appleby, an American whom the Government of India called in as an expert adviser on administration in 1955, said: "India in these services shares with Britain the distinction of having the best body of generalist (*sic*) civil servants in the world."[63]

V. THE BRITISH "PUBLIC SCHOOLS" IN INDIA

The first genuine public school[64] was not started in India until 1935

---

[63] Quoted by N. R. Pillai (I.C.S. ret'd.) in *The Civil Servant in India,* ed. Panjabi, op. ci. p. 25.

[64] So-called because it is conducted by an independent governing body of as distinguished people as the school can muster and is not run for private profit. Its educational characteristics emerge from the discussion in the text.

because innovations in education, as in industry, only succeed if social conditions provide enterprising individuals with incentives to recognize that an unfulfilled *demand* exists or can be created.

The secondary schools before the 1854 Despatch prospered because they met the demand for vocational training in Western learning. They remained essentially places of instruction, because of the difficulties caused by caste restrictions and the need to keep costs low, and because the idea of corporate activities outside the class room was alien to Indians.

The only group anxious to send boys and girls to schools which set store on corporate activities were the Anglo-Indians[65] (who, by 1941 totaled no less than six million), for whom missionaries set up several hundred schools (day and boarding), some of which had fine buildings and grounds and attained all-India reputations. Although these schools admitted non-Christians and few attempted to proselytize, Anglo-Indians tended to be more British than the British. Neither Indian history nor languages were taught, and Indians alleged that arrogant attitudes towards things Indian prevailed. Since many of these institutions, emphasizing the British type of prefectorial system, which entrusts discipline to the seniors, took pride in being public schools, all this aroused Indian nationalist hostility to the public school system by associating it with denationalization.

The founding of "Chiefs' Colleges" fanned further suspicions. In the decade following the Mutiny, the British in India were dismayed that too few of the princes and nobility were active in public life and that political initiative was passing to the new middle classes. The obvious answer was to found schools in which, on "public school" lines, corporate activities would develop social co-operation and leadership. Lord Mayo (Viceroy 1869-1872) therefore sponsored five boarding schools known as "Chiefs' Colleges."[66] This designation revealed in itself a gulf between British and Indian ideas about education for leadership. In Britain, public schools were open to any boy who passed the entrance examination, and no qualification of birth was necessary, other than parental ability to pay the

---

[65] Formerly known as Eurasians.
[66] Two were launched later, making a total of seven.

fees. In India, caste and religious distinctions prohibited social intermingling and democratic discipline. When the Rajkumar[67] College opened at Rajkot in 1870, the chiefs of Kathiawar had recently and doubtfully been persuaded to cease the clan custom of *Bahirwatia*—going out against their enemies—and, if their sons were to go to school, each chief thought it essential to stand armed retainers outside their rooms at night. Each boy had his personal cook, other servants, and a "remembrancer" to remind him of the customary observances of his state and family. That some boys (but not all) had wives, carriages, horses, and polo ponies, created invidious distinctions within the school and made equality of treatment impossible. One college complained that it was difficult to instill "habits of cleanliness and decorum into boys surrounded, during the whole time that they were not in study, by sets of dirty and obsequious servants." Because caste qualifications narrowed the circle of families which could hope to get their sons admitted, numbers in the seven colleges remained small, ranging from 20 to 60, and this also narrowed the scope for corporate activities.

In two points alone did these colleges resemble British public schools: the munificence of the princes supplied fine buildings, ample space, and playing fields, and their English head masters promoted organized games, so that some of the most prestigious figures in English cricket, like Prince Ranjitsinhji, and his nephew Duleep, learned the game at a chiefs' college. Otherwise, these colleges had nothing in common with British public schools, in which the basis of training in leadership is acceptance by all of a common code of discipline. But their existence and identification with what India's middle-class politicians denounced as an obsolete class of feudal rulers, together with the "anti-Indian" image of the Anglo-Indian schools, hardly suggested a future for public schools in India. So matters stood until 1917 when the new policy of the increasing association of Indians in every branch of the administration and the development of self-governing institutions was announced.

No historian seems to have noticed that one important long-term consequence of this announcement was the discovery of a gap in Indian education that could best be filled by public schools. Nor was

[67] Literally "College for the heirs of rulers."

this an alien imposition on an unwilling India. The public schools emerged as a joint Indo-British private enterprise, financed by Indians without government funds, which the sponsors were, indeed, anxious *not* to have, in order to ensure that they could conduct an educational experiment without the government intervention that, past experience showed, cast education into the political arena. It happened thus:

Before 1914, most posts open to Indians in the services, public life, and industry had been limited to those for which the requirements were sound knowledge of English, Western learning and methods, efficiency in carrying out policies laid down, and personalities suited for higher subordinate command. But the new British policy gave rapidly increasing impetus to Indianization at the very top. Year by year, more and more Indians attained levels in which ideals of public service, loyalty, independent judgment, integrity, initiative, self-confidence, and leadership were essential.[68] Indians with these qualities were available: some had gone to public schools in England; very many educated in Indian schools had gone on to take degrees at Oxford or Cambridge (then recruited almost wholly from the public schools); and all their British colleagues in India were public school men. They were, therefore, thoroughly at home with the public school system; they saw its results in themselves and their colleagues; they had to train Indian subordinates for promotion and they saw the difficulties of many who had not had a public school training. Conscious of the low academic standards of so many Indian schools and their inadequate training in responsibility and self-confidence, many continued to send their sons to England. But reluctantly. They would have preferred a school in India which, though using British public school techniques, would be Indian in

---

[68] It is outside my brief to explain *how* the public schools seek to inculcate these ideals. Rupert Wilkinson, *The Prefects: British Leadership and the Public School Tradition,* London, 1964, assesses the system's aims and achievements to 1939. J. C. Dancy's *The Public Schools and the Future,* London, 1963, describes developments after 1945. My own *India, Democracy and Education,* Calcutta, 1955, outlines the "mechanics" of the system and describes (from observation) its actual working in one Indian public school and in another Indian school which subsequently transformed itself into a public school.

atmosphere. They recognized the high standards of many Anglo-Indian schools but objected to their anti-Indian image. Above all, they were appalled by the way in which Indian politicians were disrupting the academic education, and distorting the psychological development, of those who should be the elite of the nation, by involving boys and masters in political demonstrations which, more often than not, ended in bloodshed, arrests, and intermittent school closures. What to do?

In 1926, Colonel William Brown, a retired officer, pointed the way by starting at Dehra Dun a non-denominational private school open to all and run on public school lines. That Colonel Brown soon had more Indian applicants than vacancies was not lost on Mr. S. R. Das, a prominent Indian lawyer. In 1928, he founded the Indian Public Schools Society and raised £75,000 (about £400,-000 in 1968 values), but died before his plans could mature. In 1933, Mr. F. G. Pearce, energetic and imaginative head master of Scindia College at Gwalior, persuaded the *sardars* (chieftains) of Gwalior to open their college to all comers and to introduce democratic public school discipline.

In the meantime, Sir Joseph Bhore (an Indian Christian) who, after graduating from University College, London, had had a distinguished career in Indian public life, joined with Sir Akbar Hydari I.C.S., a scholar of Balliol College, Oxford, and an outstanding administrator who was to become Governor of Assam, in collecting additions to the S. R. Das fund, with which they opened a new school at Dehra Dun in 1935. As head master they appointed a 33-year-old Eton master, Arthur Foot (educated at Winchester College and Cambridge). The Doon School soon had a waiting list.[69]

The virtually instantaneous success of Brown, Pearce, and Foot had revealed an unsatisfied demand. The expense, however, of endowing fine buildings and grounds, ample enough to accommodate several hundred boys, was obvious. How long it would take, whether it was even possible, to raise the sums needed was doubtful. It was here that Pearce's example was all important. What he had done, others could. Within a few years five more fully endowed

[69] So named because it is in the valley of the Doon.

chiefs' colleges became converted to the public schools system, and an Indian Public Schools Conference had been set up.

Arthur Foot's contribution was to refuse to join! He saw that although the chieftains had abolished caste restrictions on paper, many were, in fact, insisting on privileges for their sons. The early files of the Conference sputter with infuriated references to Foot. Nevertheless, the prestige of his school was already so towering that he had no need to join and his refusal seemed such a reflection on the Conference that eventually all governing bodies agreed to enforce the public school system without qualifications of caste or other privileges. If Foot had lacked the moral courage to persist for six years (1935-41) in making himself intensely disliked by his colleagues, the chances are that the system would never have been consolidated but would have sunk into India's traditional acquiescence in lax standards and liberal admissions. When Foot retired in 1948, the Doon School's Indian governing body, anxious that the spirit of the system should be maintained by one brought up in it, appointed another Englishman, J. A. K. Martyn, who was in turn succeeded in 1966 by Christopher Miller.

Achievements

Members of the Indian Public Schools Conference rose from seven in 1943 to thirty-five schools in 1965, with 41,631 pupils (of whom 1,474 were girls) and revenues totaling £ 1,750,000.[70] The number would have risen even faster if the Conference did not insist on personal inspection to verify that (1) endowments, grants, and fees are sufficient to maintain fully adequate buildings (including ample classrooms, laboratories, sanatorium, etc.) and grounds, (2) salaries to attract masters with first-class qualifications, (3) no boy who passes the entrance examination is excluded because he does, or does not, belong to a particular race, religion, or social rank; (4)

[70] This total, small in relation to the United States or United Kingdom costs, is very high in relation to India. Fees at the Doon School, for example, are £300 a year, compared with £75 at La Martinière, top ranking Anglo-Indian college at Lucknow (not a member of the Indian Public School Conference), and down to £45 or less elsewhere. The independent government of India provides scholarships as explained on p. 188.

that all boys are treated alike, living, eating,[71] studying, and playing together.

To my request for an assessment of what the seven original public schools achieved, Mr. C. H. Barry, Principal (1933-1946) of Aitchison College, Lahore, and joint-founder, with Mr. T. L. H. Smith-Pearse of Raipur, of the Indian Public Schools Conference, replied:

> They began to set new standards of social cohesion, establishing communities in which the diverse aspects of religion and caste were minimized and in which national citizenship was engendered and encouraged.
>
> They sought to establish a concordat between the religious aspect of education and the best features of western educational philosophy and practice, stressing the ethical and social aspects of western educational thought.
>
> While paying particular importance to the teaching of English, in which high standards were achieved, at the same time they fostered knowledge of indigenous languages and did much to raise the quality of language teaching. (For example, at Aitchison College, Lahore, we not only achieved high standards in Urdu, Hindi, and Sanskrit, but also in Persian, in which we combined both classical and modern Persian).
>
> They enabled boys of considerable academic ability to take English school examinations which entitled them to admission to British universities and to technical and vocational careers demanding high academic qualifications.
>
> They encouraged the sons of the upper and middle classes to seek employment *in a much wider range of occupations than had ever been the case before, sending boys into the Defence Services, and the professions, and into industry and commerce.* [My italics.]
>
> They established a tradition of high standards in the academic qualifications and teaching capacity of the staff, offering a wholly new social and professional status to schoolmasters, many of whom went on to hold headships and other positions of importance.
>
> They were fortunate in their comparative freedom from ex-

[71] Vegetarian or nonvegetarian foods are permissible but must be eaten at the same table.

ternal influence, prejudice, or bias, and went some way towards establishing a new confidence in the integrity of education, for which many parents were hungering.

They sought to inculcate in the landowning classes a professional interest in agricultural advance, and a responsibility for the welfare of their tenants.

They aimed at encouraging a spirit of service to the community, which was one of the distinguishing hallmarks of the English Public School tradition at its best.

They fostered a sense of the importance of physical fitness and established high standards in the care of boys, and in the quality of their physical environment.

And Arthur Foot, besides endorsing Barry's points, wrote:

> From the beginning we had an Indian artist and musician and all boys for their first few years had two school periods a week with them. When we started, no Indian day schools had art or music classes.
>
> To combat aloofness from social responsibilities we adopted a village five miles away, where boys instituted and took part in various activities, by their own physical work and with money— making a pond, building a school, arranging for a villager to be trained as a teacher, and continuously visiting the village to take part in sports, celebrations and to supervize teaching at the school. . . . The boys also ran an adult education school for the school servants, and paid for a teacher. Boys used to teach those servants whose work times prevented them from going to classes. After the servants had become literate, the boys turned the school into one for their children, supervized it, organized games, etc. . . .
>
> Every boy in the Doon school is called upon for at least one quota a week of public service—construction work, work in the library, or other jobs about the school. Teaching villagers or servants counts towards quotas.
>
> From 1942, until I left we held five camps in the holidays for relief work in distressed places—the Contai district after the flood (three times), the Kosi Valley after the periodic change of the river's course, and near Port Canning in a village school after a famine. The school paid third class fares, but the boys collected funds among themselves to cover camp expenses. These and

other similar activities undoubtedly spread the idea among boys and their parents that social service was a *normal* human activity.

Those familiar with British public schools will recognize variants from British practice in the points made by Barry and Foot. They illustrate one strength of the system, namely, that it is adaptable to changing social requirements. It is interesting to note the similarity of aims and techniques in the Doon School with those of Gordonstoun in Scotland (founded within a year of each other), which seeks to identify the school with its neighborhood through the boys' regular participation in local activities, civic and social. The methods of training and social aims of the public schools have evolved both in India[72] and in Britain[73] to such an extent that much current British criticism is anachronistic to anyone who has bothered to bring himself up-to-date.

Before these facts, the hostility to the public schools of Indian nationalist politicians and press, fierce in the early years, has evaporated.

Indian Government Support

Attitudes today in Britain and India towards the public schools have been dramatically reversed. The British Left holds that opportunities should be equal for all and that parents should therefore be prohibited from buying "privileged" education for their children. Fee-charging schools should be abolished. All children should receive free education at state-controlled schools. It is unjust that independent schools can afford high salaries and small classes, because this drains the best teachers away from state schools.

It is ironic that independent India's politicians, the spiritual heirs of Harold Laski Socialism, should approve of their public schools *because* they provide higher academic standards, higher salaries, and better amenities.

In his address as chairman of the Indian Public School Conference annual meeting in 1965, Mr. R. N. Zutshi referred to the "fre-

---

[72] See Jossleyn Hennessy, *India, Democracy and Education,* op. cit. and the annual Reports of the Indian Public School Conference.
[73] See J. C. Dancy, *The Public Schools and the Future,* op. cit., who stresses postwar changes.

quent outbursts of indiscipline" in Indian schools and universities, which he agreed with educational experts in attributing to the rapid increase in numbers of students. He regretted the ensuing fall in standards but concluded:

> Public schools are happily free from these problems. They are ably manned. They are more expensive but the quality of their education is superior. Even if it is not possible to give this type of education to everybody, *let us give it to those whom we can*. These are the schools, though small in number, which impart better education and discipline. They can serve as examples to be followed by other institutions. [My italics.]

Mrs. Indira Gandhi, who succeeded her father, Mr. Nehru, as Prime Minister, and who is, as he was, a Socialist, sent a message to this meeting:

> The public school has been much criticized in our country because of the feeling that it caters only to a limited section of society and is expensive to maintain. But it is a useful institution and gives a good all-round education. The question is whether a country as poor as India can afford such a luxury. My answer is in the affirmative, for while we should like and must make every effort for education to expand all over the country and reach as large a number of children as possible, *we cannot afford to neglect quality, or else the future of the nation will be in jeopardy*. It is essential, however, to have an increasing number of scholarships so that highly intelligent children from all classes could benefit from public school education.
>
> The public school cannot maintain the standards expected of it without providing satisfactory conditions of work to its teachers, who must necessarily be of a higher standard than those in ordinary schools. I am glad the Indian Public Schools' Conference is looking after their interests. [My italics.]

Mrs. Gandhi differs from those in Great Britain who, in effect, argue that *because* the tax burden of providing the best possible secondary education for all is prohibitive, *therefore* children whose parents can afford it must be deprived of the best education available. I submit, however, that if state control of all education provides opportunities for all, it also creates monopoly of access to educational opportunity—one of the most dangerous powers that can be vested in politicians or bureaucrats—fatal to educational independence, experiment, diversity, and progress. It is good that education should be democratic, essential that it should be education.

The problem that confronts all countries is (1) how not to handicap the gifted child in a system in which all children are supposed to have equal rights but in which half the children are, by definition, below average, and (2) how to maintain equality. India's solution has been to provide state scholarships to boys and girls able to pass the public school entrance examination, but whose parents cannot afford the fees, i.e., the state recognizes that it can help in paying for education *without necessarily providing it,* and that the cash should go not to schools but to parents, who are thereby encouraged to compare the characteristics, curricula, and end-products of different schools, thus ensuring that competition maintains standards and progress.[74] India's educational authorities reject the argument, periodically heard in Britain, that the public schools attract the best teachers by offering higher salaries than the state can afford, thus impoverishing state education and keeping its standards down. In India, it is, on the contrary, appreciated that by higher salaries the public schools attract men and women into the profession *who would otherwise not become teachers at all,* and further, that every fee-paying child who does *not* go to a state school allows the state to spend more money on each child who does.*

ENVOI

To sum up, the impact of British rule and education in India produced an elite capable of filling, first, the higher subordinate ranks

---

[74] That some similar solution has not so far been adopted in the United Kingdom is not the fault of the British public schools, which have at intervals *since 1918* submitted schemes for co-operation with the state educational system. The response from Local Education Authorities has been minimal. (Cf. Sir Frank Fletcher, *After Many Days,* London, 1937, Ch. XIV, and J. C. Dancy, *The Public Schools and the Future,* op. cit. Chs. I and VI.

* The main assumption here is that fee-paying parents spend more on education than they would through added taxes if all schools became state schools. The assumption is plausible though not proven; in Britain the whole issue has been much debated recently.

and, in due course, the highest levels of government service, the professions, and industry.

The transfer of power to India and Pakistan demonstrated to all that the government services and armed forces constituted an exceptionally efficient elite, in my opinion, second to none in the world. The tragedies of 1947 originated in religious and political dissension, not in administrative breakdown. That the partition did not crumble into fragments of half a dozen or more linguistic and several hundred princely, autonomous states, and that the bloodshed was confined to border provinces, while the overwhelming mass of the subcontinent led its everyday life, was largely due to the high competence, discipline, and dedication of the service elites. While all around them many were losing their heads, the administrators kept theirs.[75]

What, then, of the political cadres? An attempt to assess the impact of British education on the political leaders requires a glance at the years since 1947. That allegations of factionalism and corruption in public life are widespread is not so much an evidence of the wickedness of men as of the clash between the obligations and values of (1) westernized secular democracy, (2) traditional Hinduism, and (3) regional and linguistic "nationalisms"—problems which would require an essay in themselves. One may, however, suggest that while education for the public services and for business began sufficiently far back to penetrate and to *consolidate itself over several generations*,[76] education for political life was, by contrast, too recent and spread over too few numbers. British and Indians

---

[75] I do not base this paragraph on documentary research but on innumerable eye-witness experiences when, as *Sunday Times* correspondent, I toured the centers of Hindu-Muslim-Sikh strife in the Punjab, watching district magistrates, police, army officers, and noncommissioned officers organizing columns of refugees along routes which would avoid hostile centers, and bringing life back to burnt towns and sacked villages, countering mob leaders by appropriate selections from their repertoire of understatements, more often humorous or rudely vernacular than by force. For a vivid personal account of joint Indo-British service team work in 1947, see Penderel Moon, *Divide and Quit*, London, 1961, Ch. IX, "Restoring Order."

[76] In government service, cf. the generations of Prakash Tandon's family cited earlier. In industry, cf. J. N. Tata (1839-1904), educated at Elphinstone College, Bombay, founder, *inter multa alia*, of the Tata Iron & Steel Works, still successfully controlled by his descendents.

alike share the responsibility. The British delayed until 1921 to give the first installment of provincial self-government and until 1937 to give the second. The number affected—about 1,900 elected representatives and 150 ministerial portfolios—were inevitably small. But if the time allowed for apprenticeship was short, Indian politicians went out of their way to cut it shorter.[77] With the prophetic vision of hindsight one sees that if the Congress party, the Muslim League, the Sikhs, the Scheduled Castes, and the others, had gone all out to make the 1919 constitution an unqualified success, and to demonstrate their ability, and above all their anxiety, to co-operate on an all-India basis, constitutional advance could have been speeded up. The Act of 1935 could have come in 1929, and if such a new Act had been worked equally successfully, independence—without partition—might have been achieved by 1939.[78] Twenty years of hard-working democracy, in co-operation with British and Indian service officers, would have gone far to consolidate secular democratic attitudes in successive generations of India's political leaders and might perhaps have averted the danger reported to threaten India today, namely, that universal adult suffrage is hastening the replacement of the urban western-educated political elite, which valued democracy and secularism, by a new generation of leaders whose roots and values are rural, indigenous, and revivalist—a development favoring centrifugal forces—religious and linguistic. This revival of traditional values conflicts with the service elite's western ideas of discipline and diminishes the attractiveness of government service to men of their caliber.

Since the universities continue to pullulate along their negative way, one turns to the public schools. Six facts offer hope that their success may not be a flash in the pan: (1) In India, these schools, although oriented towards training for leadership and based on the British prefectorial system, were not imposed by the British but spontaneously launched by Indians who, impressed by several generations' experience of the end-product, decided that, if modified to

[77] Cf. page 177.
[78] If India had attained independence in the circumstances imagined, her co-operation in World War II could have been expected. The Congress party's wartime nonco-operation was not pro-Hitler but part (however ill-timed) of the struggle for independence.

suit the Indian scene, public schools were the best to meet an urgent need. (2) Nationalist antagonism to the public schools has disappeared; public opinion approves of them. (3) Competition among other schools to qualify for admission to the flourishing Public Schools Conference is keen. (4) Numbers in public schools rise year by year. (5) Admission depends on the school's assessment of a candidate's ability, as revealed by his written papers *and* personal interview, to profit by the type of education that it offers. This is all-important, because a school compelled to admit a candidate solely on the basis of a written examination (which reveals nothing about his aptitudes and may mean no more than that he has a good crammer* and a reasonable memory), can no longer uphold its own independent and evolving standards of education, social discipline, and content of curricula, but, in the straitjacket of the state system, must move in line with the prescriptions of politically motivated Ministries of Education. (6) The demand in all walks of Indian life for public school men and women is such that they can pick and choose among vacancies in any career for which they have qualified themselves.

* A crammer is a private tutor on the fringe of the academic world, who analyzes previously set and published examination papers in the hope of working out what questions are likely to be put in the next examination. He "crams" pre-digested answers into his pupils, who may thus secure high marks although their appreciation of the subject may be full of gaps and half-truths.

ACKNOWLEDGMENTS

I am indebted to Mr. Radha Raman Pathak, headmaster of the Birla Public School since 1944 and secretary of the Indian Public Schools Conference, to Mr. C. H. Barry, Principal (1933-46) of Aitchison College, Lahore, and to Mr. Arthur Foote, headmaster (1933-48) of the Doon School, for replying at generous length to my inquiries, and for supplying invaluable documentation from their personal archives. I am also grateful to Mr. Percival Spear, Fellow of Selwyn College, Cambridge, and to Dr. Mary Anderson, joint author with Sir Eric Ashby of *Universities: British, Indian, African,* who made helpful criticisms of my manuscript. None of these authorities are, of course, responsible for my interpretation of the facts.

I am indebted to the following for permission to quote extracts from the books named:

Asia Publishing House: *A Survey of Indian History* by K. M. Pannikkar.

Chatto and Windus: *Punjabi Century* by Prakash Tandon.

H. V. Iengar, G. V. Bedeker, V. Isvaran, and Justice G. D. Khosla, contributors to the *Civil Servant in India* (Bharatiya Vidya Bhavan, Bombay).

CORRELLI BARNETT

The Education of Military Elites*

To listen to politicians and constitutional historians holding forth on the marvels of parliamentary democracy, one would not think that ours was a civilization largely born out of war and devoted to it.[1] There is an extraordinary reluctance (reflected for example in the meagre number of university departments in Britain devoted to military history and war studies) to acknowledge how deeply war and preparations for war have moulded social organization in this century, and determined technical and industrial progress.[2] However, the very politicians who congratulate themselves on the "civilian" nature of western democracy employ the metaphors of war with the abandon of frustrated field-marshals: they demand "aggressive" salesmanship to win "bridgeheads" in foreign markets; they "redeploy" workers; they seek technological and social "break-throughs"; they wage "campaigns" against drunken driving. The metaphors reflect the fact: many of our civilian institutions, ways of thinking, techniques of organization and control, were evolved first in armies or during wars. The Schlieffen Plan preceded the Marshall Plan. Staff colleges preceded business schools. The first schools of engineering and technology were military.[3]

* © Correlli Barnett 1967. Originally published in the *Journal of Contemporary History,* II, 3 (London, 1967). An abridgment was published in *New Society,* London, July 27, 1967.
[1] Stanislaw Andrzejewski, *Military Organization and Society,* London, 1954, Ch. 1, and Introduction by A. R. Radcliffe-Brown.
[2] See especially Introduction by the editor, Michael Howard, to *Soldiers and Governments,* London, 1957; Walter Millis, *Armies and Men,* London, 1958, pp. 296-302.
[3] Royal Military Academy, Woolwich, 1741; Mézières, 1749; Ecole Polytechnique, 1794-5; West Point, 1802.

The education of military elites is not therefore a matter of a specialized professional group, isolated from the mainstream of modern life. It is a subject of great interest and relevance.

The military elite historically was not only professional, but social.[4] On the eve of the industrial revolution the officer corps of Europe were the inheritors and preservers of a chivalric tradition of arms handed down from the middle ages.[5] In many cases they were the direct descendants of feudal military land-holders. During four centuries of transition from medieval warfare to disciplined standing forces and fire tactics, the nobility and gentry succeeded generally in retaining their leadership of armies. In fact there was often a kind of tacit "neo-feudalist" pact between absolute monarchies and the *noblesse,* especially the poor *noblesse.* The *noblesse* wanted a rewarding life in the open air consonant with their conceptions of honour; the king wanted a loyal officer corps. The bourgeoisie generally was more keen on the ring of coin than the roar of cannon.[6]

The military aspects of the industrial and social transformations of the nineteenth century thus impinged on an elite most unlikely to welcome them. It was a paradox that an elite rooted in pre-industrial society and traditions was henceforth required to be in the vanguard of progress—both of technique and of organization. It was a role the soldiers fought hard to avoid, because the new industrial world seemed in most aspects a threat to all they lived by, especially their privileges. Education therefore occupied a key place in the rearguard action fought by the neo-feudalist officer corps against

---

[4] Morris Janowitz, *The Professional Soldier: A Social and Political Portrait,* London, 1964, Ch. 5, and especially Table 16, p. 94; Karl Demeter, *The German Officer Corps in Society and State 1650-1945,* London, 1965, Part I and especially Ch. 3; Brigadier Sir John Smyth, V.C., *Sandhurst,* London, 1961, Appendices 3, 4, 5; Raoul Girardet, *La Société Militaire dans la France Contemporaine,* Paris, 1953; Paul-Marie de la Gorce, *La République et Son Armée,* Paris, 1963, pp. 34-5.

[5] Janowitz, op. cit. p. 23; Andrzejewski, op. cit. pp. 67-8; Demeter, op. cit. Appendix 4, and Introduction by Michael Howard, p. ix; Charles de Gaulle, *France and Her Army,* London, n. d., p. 24.

[6] De Gaulle, op. cit. p. 24. Gordon Craig, *The Politics of the Prussian Army 1640-1945,* New York, 1964, pp. 4, 10-12; Demeter, op. cit. pp. 3-6.

the advance of the nineteenth century. The higher the demanded standards of general and technical education in the army, the more the domination of the neo-feudalists was threatened. It was not only that their traditions were against books and study and in favour of a hard gallop, a gallant fight, and a full jug. The neo-feudalists often came from a poor *noblesse* scattered over the wilds of Pomerania or Provence or Ireland, where good schooling was hard to find, even if they could afford it.[7] In Prussia between 1806 and 1870 a particularly fierce battle was fought over these related questions of educational standards and the preservation of the officer corps in the hands of a social elite.[8] In Great Britain, where there was no privileged noble caste, and the army was a backwater rather than a great national institution, the contest was less defined and specific. It constituted perhaps the military aspect of another long rearguard action, that of the Tory squirearchy under Disraeli in defence of the values and influence of eighteenth-century rural society against Victorian utilitarianism. However, education was central to the contest in Britain also; several committees and commissions examined this painful question between 1857 and the Great War.[9] Whereas in Prussia the neo-feudalists feared that a demand for higher educational qualifications would often bar the poor but honest, in Britain the fear was rather of barring the rich but stupid.

The neo-feudalist case against higher technical and professional qualifications rested on belief in "character" as opposed to intellect. The history of military education to the present time has been a tug-of-war between these two qualities: between the conception of a soldier as a fighting-man and the new conception of him, born of the industrial age, as a military manager; between a traditional elite and the social changes that have gradually swamped it.

[7] Robert Laulan, *L'Ecole Militaire,* Editions Albert Morancé, n. d., pp. 14-19; Demeter, op. cit. p. 68.
[8] Excellently treated in Demeter, op. cit. Chs. 10, 11.
[9] H.M. Stationery Office, London, *Report on the training of Officers for the Scientific Corps* (1857); *Report of the Royal Commission on the Present State of Military Education and the Training of Candidates for Commissions in the Army* (1869); *Report of the Committee appointed to consider the Education and Training of the Officers of the Army* (1902). The last report is especially rich in evidence of the connections between birth, wealth, and ignorance.

Even in the bright dawn of the Scharnhorst era, in Prussia, a royal order recalled to mind that: "Education and technical knowledge are not the only things required for a competent officer; he also needs presence of mind, rapid judgment, punctuality, regular habits on duty and proper behavior. These are the cardinal virtues that every officer must have."[10] Fifty-two years later Prince Frederick Charles required "Affection, aptitude and zeal for the chosen profession, a sense of the importance and honour of the status of an officer, a mind receptive to the spirit that has always marked the Prussian corps of officers . . ."[11] In Great Britain the preference for character over intellect, for brawn over brain, has always taken the form of denigration of the staff-college graduate and apotheosis of that splendid chap, the regimental officer. Thus the Duke of Cambridge, the Commander-in-Chief, in evidence to the Royal Commission of 1868: "I prefer for the staff to have regimental officers. I am quite satisfied that the best staff officer is your regimental officer . . ." Or, as he put it less formally on another occasion: "Staff College Officers! I know these Staff College officers! They are very ugly officers and very dirty officers!"[12]

The prized quality of character was of course seen as the peculiar property of the traditional elite, in which also was seen reflected the finest virtues of the nation and the very foundation of the character of the state. In every way the problem of military education was bound up with the impact of the industrial revolution on a traditional society.[13] Nevertheless it would be wrong to conclude that the neo-feudalist case for character and against intellect and education was no more than obscurantist conservatism. There is a gulf

[10] Demeter, op. cit. p. 279, Appendix 6.
[11] Quoted ibid. p. 79.
[12] Quoted in A. R. (later Lieut.-Gen. Sir Alfred) Godwin-Austen, *The Staff and the Staff College,* London, 1927, pp. 155, 214.
[13] Paradoxically, Jacksonians and later American radicals employed similar arguments in favour of "character" against "education," similar arguments that stiffer qualifications would bar the officer corps to the social class that was the support of the state and the fountain of national virtue. They wished, however, not to preserve the officer corps for ignorant junkers, but to open it to ignorant common men. See Stephen E. Ambrose, *Honour, Duty, Country; A History of West Point,* Baltimore, 1966, Chs. 6, 10, especially pp. 193-5.

fixed between the military profession and all others. Only the soldier (or, obviously, the sailor or airman) stakes his life and limb; only the soldier must function effectively in situations of terror and panic that naturally make for least efficient action. Only the soldier has quite the same dependence on his fellows and on the adequacy of their performance; and performance not only as individuals but as a group. Recruitment of officers from a homogeneous social class gives a ready-made homogeneity to the officer corps. If that class also places high value on courage, hardihood, and leadership, a ready-made military quality is also imparted to the officer corps. Homogeneity means cohesion and understanding in times of stress— qualities of crucial functional importance on a battlefield or in a hard-pressed headquarters.

Nevertheless, as the technical demands of war become steadily more sophisticated, they could be resisted only up to a point, other- wise all armies would have been reduced to the absurdities of the British in the Crimea. Formal military education was born out of these technical needs and has kept faltering step ever since. The requirements first become obvious in gunnery and military engi- neering. France, Prussia, Russia, and Great Britain had all set up schools for the artillery and engineers by the middle of the eight- eenth century. However, the beginnings of reform of a professional education for officers in general usually followed only upon some notable defeat or disaster. In Prussia Scharnhorst's reforms were the consequence of the collapse of the Frederician system at Jena and Auerstädt. In Great Britain the foundation of the Royal Mili- tary College (Junior and Senior Departments) owes much to the lamentable display of ignorance and ineptitude of British officers in the Netherlands in 1793-4.[14] France owes the *Ecole de Guerre* to her defeat in 1870.[15]

It often needed men of vision and personality to overcome the apathy of most soldiers towards education. The *Ecole Polytech- nique* owes its existence to Carnot, Monge, and Lagrange, as well as to the national emergency of 1794; the character of West Point

[14] See Hugh Thomas, *The Story of Sandhurst,* London, 1961, p. 20, for eyewitness account of British performance in the Netherlands.
[15] *L'Enseignement Militaire Supérieur,* Librairie de l'armée, Paris, 1955, pp. 10, 13.

derives essentially from Thayer; Sandhurst and the Staff College from Le Marchant. In the case of Carnot and Thayer, they were able to create so well that their schools ran on like machines, giving excellent performance for generations without requiring spasmodic overhauls. In Britain, however, the military colleges tended to relapse each time into stagnation after each brief nervous trial of reform.

When the main battle was being fought in the mid-nineteenth century between the neo-feudalist social elite and the effects of the industrial revolution, between the character of the warrior and the professional knowledge of the military manager, the sponsors of military education weakened their case by the aridity, pedantry, and remoteness of their syllabuses.[16]

The Sandhurst final examinations of the period required as obligatory subjects Euclid, military surveying, and higher mathematics, and three more optional subjects selected from: conic sections, attack and defence of fortresses, general history, Latin, French, or German.[17] It is not easy to see such a curriculum as a functional preparation for a subaltern's work in the regiment of the day, whether at home or in India. The British Staff College (until 1857 the Senior Department at the Royal Military College, Sandhurst) was even more formidably mathematical and geometrical. Everything needed to turn out surveyors was included; but military history was hardly studied at all. The Prince Consort himself noted this fatal gulf between academic abstraction in the military schools and the real work of handling men and situations as an officer: "What is to be gained by making the officers of the army, and the Staff in particular, abstract *mathematicians* instead of scientific soldiers? . . . it is well-ascertained fact . . . that mathematicians, from their peculiar bent of mind, do of all men show the least judgment for the practical purposes of life, and are the most helpless and awkward in common life . . ."[18]

---

[16] For a full account of the organization, teaching methods, and syllabuses of the military schools of France, Prussia, Austria, and Sardinia at mid-century, see *Report on the Training of Officers for the Scientific Corps together with an account of foreign and other Military Education,* H.M. Stationery Office, London, 1857.

[17] Thomas, op. cit. p. 86.

[18] Godwin-Austen, op. cit. pp. 62-3, 102.

If an enlightened fellow like Albert could express such senti-ments, how much more easily and crudely could the neo-feudalists in the regimental messes sneer at formal professional education.

In the end, it was the inner elite (the general staff) of one of the most caste-bound and privileged officer corps in Europe—the Prus-sian—that was the first to succumb to the new world of industrial change, and transform itself into a group of "industrial" managers and technicians. The reasons were several. In the Prussian army the intellectual tradition typified by Scharnhorst and Clausewitz had never been entirely extinguished; nor was the officer corps immune from the contemporary climate of philosophical and scientific en-quiry in Germany. The *Kriegsakademie* (founded 1818) and the general staff continued to foster a professional approach to prob-lems of war. But it was not so much these continuing influences that swamped the simple soldiers, as the irresistible demand of mass modern armies. Railway transport, swift mobilization, and new equipment called for a high degree of technical skill and compe-tence. Education and intelligence in conscripts required the same attributes in officers. Above all, the Prussian army, in the era of Moltke, Roon, and Bismarck, was the key to Prussian unification of Germany; neither the officer corps nor the nation could afford it to be less than efficient and modern. By 1870 the revolution was al-most complete; the first European army of the modern era had been seen in action in three swift wars.[19]

In this enforced modernization of the German officer corps there remained a paradox: the junkers had modernized themselves pro-fessionally without changing their outlook, values, or code of hon-our. They remained spiritually true pre-industrial neo-feudalist warriors. And these characteristics they succeeded in imparting to the new bourgeois officers who came flooding into the officer corps right up to 1914, inevitable result of expansion of the army. Indeed, the neo-feudalists succeeded under Wilhelm II in imparting their values to the entire nation.[20]

The new German conception of organizing and planning opened the modern epoch of war. Nothing like the minutely dovetailed

[19] Michael Howard, *The Franco-Prussian War,* London, 1961, pp. 18-27, 455.
[20] Demeter, op. cit. pp. 246-7.

plans, routes, and timetables of the mobilization and *Aufmarsch* of 1870 had been seen before. Thus an army had become the professional and organizational peer of modern industry.

In the person of Moltke, the intellectual, educated soldier triumphed over the pre-industrial qualities handed down by such as the Old Dessauer; and all other armies had now to follow suit, however reluctantly. It is this process after 1870, and even more after 1900, that constitutes the contemporary history of military education.

At this point one must distinguish between the education and indoctrination of the entire military elite—that is, of the professional, regular officer corps—and of the inner elite, that is, the staff and high command.

There were at the beginning of the twentieth century and there have remained wide national differences in the organization and conception of training of the young officer. These differences stem partly from the national systems of civilian education. In France, Britain, and America the key to the character and personality of the military elite has been the military academy. In the case of France, gunners and engineers used to enter the *Ecole Polytechnique;* cavalry and the line the *Ecole Spéciale Militaire de St.-Cyr.*[21] Today few officers pass through the *Ecole Polytechnique;* gunners and engineers now receive their first training in common with other cadets at St.-Cyr. Until 1947 in Great Britain there were also two schools: the Royal Military Academy, Woolwich (gunners and engineers), and the Royal Military College, Sandhurst. Today, as in France, cadets for all arms pass through a single school, the Royal Military Academy, Sandhurst. The United States Military Academy too, West Point, trains all arms. Although in each of these three armies the national military school trains only a portion of the en-

[21] John W. Masland and Laurence I. Radway, *Soldiers and Scholars: Military Education and National Policy,* Princeton, 1957, are in error in their footnote p. 77, linking the founding of West Point with the founding of St.-Cyr. West Point was intended as a school for engineers—like the *Ecole Polytechnique,* not St.-Cyr, which was founded as a general cadet school. In any case the general conception that a school of engineers should be established at West Point had been settled several years before the founding of St.-Cyr.

trants to the officer corps, nevertheless its personality deeply marks the officer corps, because its graduates remain a cohesive body. In the words of a French officer, "The St.-Cyriens are the core of the army."[22]

Leaving aside the detail of curriculum and method, the essential and constant factor common to all three national academies is the indoctrination with tradition: potent emotional conditioning in military myth, habits, and attitudes. There are the physical symbols and reminders: engraved tablets of the glorious dead; the museums; the assembled iconography of illustrious graduates; statues; guns. There are the evocative names: *le cour Rivoli* and *le cour Wagram, le carré de la Victoire* in the old St.-Cyr: Blenheim, Waterloo, Alamein, and other "victory" companies at Sandhurst. At West Point and St.-Cyr there were—and are—uniforms dating from pre-industrial war. At all three academies there are songs, slang, customs and ceremonies that link each annual class together for the rest of their army life, and to a slightly lesser extent link all old graduates. There is the ceremony of "the Triumph" at St.-Cyr to mark the graduation of the senior class, and "the Baptism" of the junior class at the end of its first year. At West Point there is Graduation Day Parade; at Sandhurst the Sovereign's Parade, and the Adjutant's ride up the steps of the grand entrance.

This indoctrination has grown out of history rather than been artificially created, but it may be doubted whether psychologists or sociologists could improve on it. Upon this mental sub-structure, purely neo-feudalist with its emphasis on glory, gallantry, honour, duty, and patriotism, is built functional and technical training, both concurrently at the academies, and later in schools of application. But it is this indoctrination, together with drill and discipline, that turns civilians into soldiers. Without it there would be no difference

[22] Colonel P. Duplay, currently French military attaché in London, in an interview with the author. The author wishes to express his gratitude to the following for granting him extensive interviews and furnishing documentation: Major-General P. M. Hunt, CB, DSO, OBE, Commandant of the Royal Military Academy Sandhurst, and his Directing Staff; Major-General M. A. H. Butler, CB, CBE, DSO, MC, Commandant of the Staff College, Camberley, and his Directing Staff; Colonel P. Duplay of the French Embassy; Colonel Hans J. Kraaz of the German Embassy; and Colonel F. Lash of the United States Embassy.

between a general in a defence ministry and a high executive in a business cartel. In terms therefore of creating the common character of the military elite, this constant factor of conditioning inside cadet colleges has been of greater importance than the changing detail and emphasis of academic curriculum and military training.

It is of interest that, whereas the severity of discipline and general harshness of life at Sandhurst and St.-Cyr has greatly relaxed since 1939, West Point remains proportionately far less changed: still, as it ever was, more Prussian than the Prussians. It is difficult to decide whether the reason for this is simply the inertia of conservative tradition, or whether West Point faces a special problem with its intake.[23] The human raw material at St.-Cyr and Sandhurst comes from homogeneous, old nations, and at Sandhurst especially from roughly common educational and home backgrounds and standards. The new cadets have already experienced discipline—or self-discipline—at the *lycée,* public school, or grammar school. West Point has to deal with young men from all over a continent, from a wide variety of home and social backgrounds;[24] young men from a school and home life much more permissive than in Europe. West Point continues to feel the need to break down its assorted raw material into a common malleable stuff in the course of the "Plebe" year, before proceeding to mould that stuff into the West Point graduate.

Equally, West Point has always had a four-year course, as against two years for St.-Cyr and Sandhurst. West Point rates as a university (college) and grants degrees to its graduates; it must be remembered that until the second half of the nineteenth century it was a leading engineering school rather than an academy primarily to supply officers. The length of course is partly determined by the academic standard of the eighteen-year-old American, which, although comparisons are difficult, appears to be about one year behind the English entrant to Sandhurst.[25]

The best balance between academic study and military training in a military academy has always been difficult to judge. In Britain

[23] See Masland and Radway, op. cit. Chs. 9-11, for an account and critique of US service academies.
[24] Janowitz, op. cit. pp. 92, 100; Ambrose, op. cit. p. 329.
[25] Edmund J. King, *Other Schools and Ours,* London, 1951, pp. 55, 132.

before 1939 there was a heavy emphasis on drill and smartness to the detriment of intellectual stimulation. However, two short-lived attempts were made at Sandhurst between the wars to broaden the training; one in 1929-32, when Edward Tollemache was Assistant Commandant and Chief Instructor, and the other after 1934, while B. D. Fisher was Commandant. Since 1945 the balance at Sandhurst and at St.-Cyr has shifted in favor of general intellectual preparation. At Sandhurst the academic atmosphere is relaxed, encouraging to the development of individual resourcefulness—perhaps somewhere between a British public-school sixth form and a university. However, although it carries the students forward from the General Certificate of Education, Sandhurst does not deliver them at the next stop, a degree. St.-Cyr has perhaps the highest academic standards of the three national academies; its students enter at a later age (20-21 as against 18), having spent two years after the *Baccalauréat* reading for the entrance examination, which counts as the first stage in a degree course, which is then completed within the school. Not unexpectedly, the educational atmosphere is rigorously academic, with characteristic concern for developing powers of logic and abstract reasoning. At West Point there is less room for personal work and thought than at St.-Cyr or Sandhurst; the leading theme is the provision, and assimilation, of a staggering quantity of information by means of a comprehensive machinery of instructions.

"It includes an almost completely prescribed course of study, close supervision of students' work, a concern for uniform and fairly frequent grading, and extraordinary devices to help all men assimilate the great quantity of material placed before them." And: "Explicit and detailed instructions are given. Elaborate manuals and syllabi direct attention to key facts or concepts. Little is left to chance."[26]

This system is partly traditional, derived from Thayer, but partly the product of the basic modern American approach to training and education, which is reflected even in higher military education for staff and command. Masland and Radway comment: "They look upon military education as a mass distribution of information rather

26 Masland and Radway, op. cit. pp. 223, 230.

than as an individual inquiry for knowledge and understanding."
Here they reflect a development in American public education generally. So far as West Point is concerned, it is hard not to agree with
Masland and Radway when they conclude that "The cumulative
effect of the methods and attitudes . . . is a greater tendency than
we think desirable towards conformity, rejection of the unorthodox,
and acceptance of the *status quo*."[27]

In Prussia (and later in Germany) there never developed a single
national military academy putting a single stamp on the officer
corps. The structure of a young German officer's education was entirely different, and remains so today. Until 1918 there was, it is
true, something of an equivalent of Sandhurst, St.-Cyr, or West
Point in the cadet schools: three in Prussia and others in each of
the larger German states. They had been created to give poor noblesse, military orphans, or sons of officers free or assisted state
education; and although they supplied only a minority of the officer
corps, the style and personality of the cadet schools pervaded the
whole elite. However, the age of entry to the German cadet schools
was between 12 and 14. At the time, therefore, that a Briton,
Frenchman, or American was *entering* a military academy, the
young German from the cadet school was being commissioned, having already received a long indoctrination in military discipline,
attitudes, and values. The German cadet schools in particular used
history as a source of the right kind of moral indoctrination; rather
less emphasis than in France, Britain or the United States was
placed on unique ceremonial.

After 1918 the cadet schools were abolished and all German
officers entered the army by the same route as the majority *before*
1918—the ranks. The aspirant officer, or *Fahnenjunker,* received
his basic military training with other recruits, thus, in the German
view, acquiring an essential understanding of the men they were
to command. Although officers were later segregated into a special
squad during the rest of their first year's training, the emphasis remained that officers trained alongside men, and had to prove their
capacity to lead by their performance at common tasks. Whereas

[27] Ibid. pp. 509, 244.

in military academies cadet NCO's commanded other cadets, in Germany they commanded other recruits. The emphasis was thus strongly on functional capability and on close intimacy with the soldiers rather than on separate status. After this basic training, the German aspirant officer attended an officer school, which was entirely professional training in the duties of an officer, not an indoctrination. Practical training was given in the functions of a platoon commander in a particular arm of the service, but general study covered all aspects of professional knowledge up to command of a battalion, including all arms and services. This system has endured from 1918 to the present time. It is impossible to say how well it would work with other nations. Primary training in the ranks worked well enough in the British army during conscription. On the other hand, the French tried giving their officer-candidates preliminary training in the ranks before the Great War and it proved a failure. The presence of ordinary recruits, instead of acting as a spur and serving to give psychological insights, seemed to have been an embarrassment to the aspirant officers, if not actually a bad influence. What can be said is that in both world wars the German officer enjoyed a closer understanding and comradeship with his men, and was thus able to give them more effective leadership, than the French[28] or the British.[29] Certainly St.-Cyr and Sandhurst today place great emphasis on training cadets to be *leaders*, not simply givers of commands. The broad trend in most armies has been to diminish the element of status in the officer and enhance that of function. Part of the pressure has come from conscription, because a cross-section of a nation has been found less amenable to the simple distinctions and rough discipline of old regular armies, where the officers were "gentlemen" and the other ranks peasantry or riffraff. Part of the change has come from the loosening hold of the "neo-feudalists" on the officer corps: in France the proportion of general officers with the class-distinctive *"de"* in their names (like

---

[28] See Pétain's Instruction of 2 June 1917, in Lieut.-Col. H. Carré, *Les Grandes Heures du Général Pétain,* Paris, 1952, p. 133.
[29] In the Great War a British battalion was considered to need a higher complement of officers than a German, especially in attack. In the Second World War German companies stayed in the line without relief for long periods when down to twenty men; an unrivalled achievement.

de Gaulle) fell from 25 per cent in 1898 to 7 per cent in 1939. Since then the proportion of upper-class cadets, or of sons of officers, at St.-Cyr has continued to fall. In 1966, 50 per cent of entrants were sons of warrant officers or sergeants. In the case of entrants from civilian families, 36 per cent were sons of workers or salaried staff. The sons of workers, salary-earners, warrant-officers and sergeants, together accounted for 30 per cent of the entry to St.-Cyr in 1965, and 42 per cent in 1966.[30] There is therefore now little class basis to the French officer corps, and certainly no class "style." In Great Britain the number of entrants to Sandhurst furnished by leading public schools fell from 255 (including entrants from private crammers, the preserve of wealthy parents) out of 339 in 1891, to 266 out of 777 in 1961.[31] However, among modern armies the British officer corps remains the last donjon keep of neofeudalism because the manners, values, and attitudes of the aristocratic past have become institutionalized. After ten years in the British army, the grammar-school boy is to be distinguished only by the expert, if then, from the son of a country gentleman educated at a famous public school. Indeed, the grammar-school boy may well —quite understandably—adhere even more closely to the neo-feudalist ideal than the true "gentleman." In the British army perhaps alone, therefore, the old battle between the professional manager, the technician of war, and the gentleman, continues; not so much in education and professional performance, but perhaps more in psychological tensions within the officer himself. In Germany the noble proportion of the officer corps fell from 40 per cent in 1898 to 20 per cent in 1932.[32] After 1933 breakneck expansion and Nazi social radicalism went hand in hand to demolish finally the "apartness" of the officer corps.[33] Yet a further cause of diminishing social distance between officer and other ranks in all armies, in favour of a

[30] Guy Chapman, in Michael Howard, ed., *Soldiers and Governments,* op. cit. p. 71, n. 18. 1965-66 figures supplied by the French military attaché in London.

[31] Smyth, op. cit. App. 3, 5.

[32] Janowitz, op. cit. p. 94.

[33] Blomberg's instruction on the Army and National-Socialism, 25 May 1934, in Robert J. O'Neill, *The German Army and the Nazi Party 1933-1939,* London, 1966, p. 64, and further instruction of 16 April 1935, p. 66. Brauchitsch's order of 18 December 1938, pp. 67-8.

relationship founded on function, was the nature of modern war, which is fought by small isolated groups.

In contrast to this narrowing of the social distance between officer and man in western armies (though least in the British), and the liberalizing of the education at cadet schools, the officer corps of the Red Army, designated instrument of the working classes, and recruited exclusively from vetted working-class backgrounds, has felt it necessary to sharpen distinctions between officer and man, and to create and maintain a high formal status for the officer corps that rests on a severe disciplinary code.[34] There is not space here to discuss this, but enough to say that it shows that an intellectually conceived blueprint of military education and discipline cannot be imposed successfully against the grain of national character and tradition. To sum up briefly the general change in the basic education of the new officer in the West since 1900, the branding of the traditional, pre-industrial mark of the warrior—his code, manners, and habits—remains a fundamental task, although perhaps only the British try to inculcate the style of the "gentleman." The acquiring of general knowledge and education comparable to that of other elites, as well as of basic professional skills in modern war equipment and man-management, has grown enormously in importance.

The education of the inner elite—staff and high command—has followed a parallel transformation. Generals no longer emerge because of neo-feudalist warrior qualities alone; staff officers no longer receive a narrow technical training. Instead they are exposed throughout their service lives to a process of rigorous selection for higher and higher categories of education, giving not only technical mastery of all complexities of modern defence, but understanding and knowledge of all the fields into which defence now extends: foreign policy, economics, politics and social questions, science and research.

The German General Staff under Moltke began this transition

[34] John Erickson, *The Soviet High Command*, London, 1962, includes some passages on military education. See also Basil Liddell Hart, ed., *The Soviet Army*, London, 1957, Chs. 17-19, 22, 34-6.

from the simple world of Raglan or Bazaine. The *Kriegsakademie* preceded the business school in teaching top management its techniques. The *Kriegsspiel* was a great gift to modern professional education. However, the education of the German staff officer remained limited to his own professional sphere; he was not encouraged to consider the wider political implications of his work. Both the Schlieffen Plan itself and the unhappy role of the German general staff in the July crisis of 1914 were the tragic results of this too narrow professionalism. After the Great War Seeckt tried to broaden the understanding of his officers by means of secondment to universities and technical schools, and through his "Thursday lectures" given by visiting authorities in all kinds of fields. Seeckt's first instruction on education stated that "officers must be trained to have an eye for broad issues." His Order of the Day of 11 October 1920 referred to "the need for knowledge and understanding of social and political life."[35] Certainly men like Beck and Fritsch displayed greater understanding of Germany's political and economic position than Hitler, or their own predecessors before 1914 and their successors after 1938. Regrettably, they did not enjoy Schlieffen's or Moltke's pre-eminence in the state.[36]

France followed the German example by opening the *Ecole Supérieure de Guerre* in 1878. Under Lewal, its first Commandant, and a directing staff including Maillard and Bonnal, the course was closely professional and functional, aiming at preparing students for staff and command work in a future war. The teaching was based on minute study of the war of 1870, and on the solution of specific problems in tactics and organization; not so much a higher military education as solely a higher military training. In Maillard's words, the new school intended "to place officers face to face with the eventualities of war, with the unexpected, in order to form their judgment."[37] This was realistic but limited. When the teaching of the *Ecole de Guerre* did broaden out to encompass general ideas after the turn of the century, under Foch, it fell into a characteristic French pitfall—the desire to extract from historical example (especially the pre-industrial one of Napoleon) a fundamental law or

---

[35] Quoted in Demeter, op. cit. p. 105.
[36] See O'Neill, op. cit. Chs. 9, 10, 12.
[37] Quoted in *L'Enseignement Militaire Supérieur*, p. 14.

doctrine of war, a symmetrical intellectual system.[38] Great emphasis was attached to developing the student's capacity for abstract reasoning. The gulf between abstraction, however logically impeccable, and reality, was uncovered in 1914-15.

In Great Britain the neo-feudalist attitude to senior responsibility survived along with pre-industrial techniques or organization for war until the Haldane reforms after the Boer War. The creation in 1906 of a General Staff gave an importance to the Staff College and an incentive to officers to pass through it that had never before existed. In the syllabus the old emphasis on mathematics, geometry, and fortifications finally gave way to the study of the organization of bases, lines of communication, mobilization, large-scale movements by railway, and to the general study of strategy based on modern campaigns as well as on history. Under Robertson as Commandant, special importance was laid on the practical aspects of staff duties in the field. Theoretical study and discussion of a problem was followed by the drafting and issue of dummy orders in the field under simulated war conditions.[39] The fruits of this work were seen in the unprecedented faultlessness of the British move to France in August 1914, and the skill of the British retirement from Mons.

Thus until the Great War the scope of instruction at all staff colleges remained limited to the conduct of war itself in modern conditions: that is, to armies and battles. The penetration of staff and command functions by the whole range of industrial, social, and political questions took place during the war itself, as did the reverse process of penetration of almost every aspect of national existence by the demands of defence. By 1916 it had become clear that national survival in the modern world involved a total and indivisible commitment of all resources. In Professor Michael Howard's words, "Thus the scope of the military interest expanded enormously . . . leaving virtually no aspect of national life in which the military leaders might not be legitimately concerned. No longer was the soldier simply the hero to whom a people turned to

---

[38] Ibid. p. 15. Unfortunately, there is not space to discuss the influence on the education of officers in different armies at different epochs of such unofficial writers as Grouard, Colin, de Gaulle, Burgoyne, Fuller, or Liddell Hart.

[39] Godwin-Austen, op. cit. pp. 241-5, 255-7.

lead it to battle; he was now technical adviser whose views had constantly to be given weight in almost every branch of policy, internal and external . . ."[40]

The Great War was in this as in so much else a revolutionary turning-point. The effect on the education of inner military elites was seen in the 1920s in the creation of higher schools of combined military and civilian study above the service staff colleges. In Great Britain the Imperial Defence College was opened in 1927,[41] while in France, the *Centre des Hautes Etudes Militaires* (CHEM), although founded in 1910, took over questions of grand strategy from the *Ecole de Guerre*.[42] Study groups employing the well-tried devices of the syndicate and the *Kriegsspiel* tackled the entire field of national existence. "The technical developments of warfare made soldier and civilian entirely interdependent, dissolving the old distinctions between civil and military responsibility."[43] In France, after 1945, a new institution was established above even CHEM, the *Institut des Hautes Etudes de Défense Nationale,* to consider national policy on the level of government. Disastrously, no such comparable institutions were founded in Germany, except the short-lived and ineffective *Wehrmachtsakademie* in 1939.

The French *Ecole de Guerre* fell into a sad stagnation after the victory of 1918 under the deep shade of ageing *grands chefs* like Pétain. Having yielded the big strategic questions to CHEM, it busied itself with the narrowest and minutest possible study, from the point of view of a corps or a division, of the stage-management of a set-piece battle like Malmaison. After the resulting catastrophe in 1940, the French system of higher military education was reorganized and given a new spirit and direction in 1945. A new school, the *Ecole d'Etat-Major,* provided a five-month course in functional training for staff duties. The *Ecole de Guerre* concerned itself again with the wider study of strategy and the conduct of war in the political, social, and industrial setting of the contemporary world. At the opening of the inaugural session in 1947 Marshal de Lattre de Tassigny gave the school its new objective:

[40] Howard, *Soldiers and Governments,* p. 19.
[41] T. S. Chegwidden, in *Public Administration,* 1947.
[42] *L'Enseignement Militaire Supérieur,* p. 16.
[43] Howard, *Soldiers and Governments,* p. 18.

"This school must know how to take the lead in this evolution [of war under the impact of technology] in order to adjust in time to the needs of the moment." He told the staff: "You will engage [the students] resolutely in the ways of the future, there where the spirit of foresight should be exercised, since the lessons of the past remain unable to cast light on the progress of science."[44]

From St.-Cyr to CHEM the French system today is still marked by extreme intellectual rigor and competition, by emphasis on powers of reasoning, and on the approach to topics as an academic study. Excellent though the system is, there may be a danger that a gap will open between theoretical study and practical application, as it has in France in the past. In the British Staff College, there is perhaps better integration of the academic with the actual, and more emphasis on the individual's powers to apply his knowledge and judgment to specific problems. Periods of work against the clock, in simulated war conditions, alternate with leisurely periods for personal study and reflection.

The aims of modern staff colleges are roughly similar: to train in the technique of high command and staff work; to inculcate the capacity for rapid analysis of complex problems; to evolve solutions by both logic and imagination; to present the solutions clearly; but also to broaden general understanding of all aspects of world affairs and the role of defence forces in them. This is a long way from the neo-feudalist soldiering that even now is often the stereotype held by public opinion.

In France and Britain this transition has taken place against a background of diminished power, both absolutely and relatively, but also against a background of a long earlier history of gradual military development (this is also true of Germany until 1939). But the United States presents a strikingly different pattern, which lends peculiar interest to the American system of higher military education.

Until 1914 the American army was smaller even than the British. In 1967, however, its regular officer corps is more than three times the size of the German officer corps in 1911—numbering some

44 *L'Enseignement*, p. 18.

50,000. This staggering expansion in the United States army as a peacetime force really dates only from Korea in 1950, although there were temporary rapid expansions in both the world wars. The importance of such speed and scale can hardly be over-emphasized, either from the point of view of its psychological and social impact on a nation so resolutely anti-military throughout its history, or from the point of view of organizational and technical problems— such as reconciling quantity of officers with quality.

Although the continued—though diminishing—domination of the officer corps by West Point graduates (especially in senior ranks) injects traditional military characteristics and attitudes, the intellectual and psychological climate of the United States establishment owes much to General Motors and its fellows. In the colossal joint services-science-research-industry-university American defence complex, the line between soldier and civilian has become even more blurred than in Europe; almost a hybrid mind has resulted. As an American soldier enthusiastically put it during the Second World War, "We go at this thing just like it was a great engineering job."[45] Or as a German sailor more recently expressed it: "One has the impression that the military profession does not consist of a self-contained corporation within a society, but is completely blended with civilian society as a group with civic duties like any other."[46]

Given the problem of raising mass armies from a very small regular base and the American cast of mind, it is not surprising that the solution should have been found in the appropriate application of the principles of production engineering. Not only were the camps, equipment, and weapons thus produced, but the trained officers and men as well. The training task was broken down into components like the components of a car, and mass production similarly organized. "They have developed a vast assortment of instructional techniques and devices by which they have reduced the training of thousands of individuals to something approaching assembly line operations."[47]

[45] Quoted in Janowitz, op. cit. p. 35.
[46] Fregattenkapitän F. Forstmeier, in an article in *Wehrwissenschaftliche Rundschau,* September 1963.
[47] Masland and Radway, op. cit. p. 53.

It is one thing to apply the "kitting-out" approach to other ranks in particular trade skills; quite another to apply it to the higher education of officers, where judgment and understanding is the aim. Yet even in the Command and General Staff College, Fort Leavenworth, the Army War College, and the National War College,[48] the flow-line processing system, with its packaged predigested judgments, doctrine, and information, is applied as a basic approach, though of course progressively modified the higher the institution. Compared with a European staff school, Fort Leavenworth has a packed curriculum which grips and directs the student throughout, and demands fearsome cramming of facts. "The manuals, directives, faculty lesson plans, and other study materials . . . are prepared with meticulous care." Although group projects and group discussions form, as in Europe, an important part of the study, such exercises "are subjected to close review by the faculty and frequently are followed by a critique, in which a preferred solution is offered."[49] Compare this with the British Staff College's Charter, which says that students are not expected or desired to have a readymade Staff College answer to each problem.[50]

Even at the Army War College, where officers destined for the highest commands study national defence questions, there is some confusion between cultivating individual understanding and imagination and providing a piece of intellectual equipment. "In spite of stress upon the importance of individual initiative, none appears willing to let the student alone for long periods to study as he wishes. On the contrary all [service war colleges] are characterized by a standard course of study utilizing a compact, carefully calculated schedule . . ."[51] Attempts are made to liberalize the atmosphere by free discussion and lectures by distinguished outside speakers, but clearly it is the system itself which is at fault—if it is at fault. For in the long run nations evolve, naturally, the kind of systems that suit them. To externalize the inner human qualities of insight and wisdom as a piece of equipment and a technique, then

[48] For a good account of the structure of American higher military education, see Masland and Radway, op. cit. Parts 4, 5, 6.
[49] Masland and Radway, op. cit. p. 283.
[50] Lieut.-Col. F. W. Young, *The Story of the Staff College,* Camberley, 1958, p. 7.
[51] Masland and Radway, op. cit. p. 330.

to be employed on finite, measurable problems, is not peculiar to the army in the United States, but permeates the approach of a practical nation of engineers to many fields where Europeans might think it sometimes inappropriate.

Nevertheless, because of the responsibility that the United States bears in the world, and because politico-strategic situations are at base subtle, uncertain questions of human nature, there is room for doubt whether the "technique" approach is not less fruitful than the professionally informed and cultivated insight that European military elites try to inculcate in their senior officers. One American strategic commentator has indeed criticized "the American tendency to treat psychological and political problems as if they were primarily technical compounds . . ."[52] The American type of higher military education, as Masland and Radway point out,[53] also makes for orthodoxy and conformity, qualities that before 1914 seriously weakened the effectiveness of the Royal Navy, and before 1940 ruined the French army. It is no secret that European soldiers, while admiring the unmatched technical expertise and resources of the American army on "an engineering job," sometimes feel that the American officer does display undue respect for orthodox doctrine, and an unwillingness to deviate on his own responsibility from standard procedure or from orders from above; or even to accept responsibility if access can be had to an officer higher up the chain of command. It is possible that in the field of the education of military elites, from cadet academy to National War College, America may have useful lessons to draw from Europe. It is also possible that, like Britain in the late Victorian era, she may feel too self-sufficient to wish to do so.

The education of military elites is a vast subject in which much work remains to be done, not least in England. Here I have only been able to indicate some of the principal lines of development since the nineteenth century in a few selected armies, and to hazard some hypotheses that I hope may be fully explored by other scholars.

[52] Henry A. Kissinger, *The Troubled Partnership*, New York, 1965, p. 21.
[53] Masland and Radway, op. cit. pp. 389-91, 504.

Elites and Effectiveness

CRITERIA OF SUCCESS

How may one judge the effectiveness of a governing elite's selection and training? I will confine myself to those standards whose underlying values would be given some prominence in the culture concerned.[1] This rules out absolute ethical standards of the sort which are incomprehensible in certain cultures. The view, for example, that elitism is intrinsically wrong, and that therefore "the less elite, the better," will not be discussed here. "Social integration," on the other hand, represents something that is valued in virtually all cultures, although we must allow for cultural differences in the way it is measured and treasured.

At the outset some distinction should be made between *direct social functions* of the elite selection and training system, and its *indirect governing functions*. The first set of functions includes those ways in which the elite selection system relates as a social institution to other components of society, and its effect on the social order. Henry Selby's chapter deals very much with this kind of function: he shows how elite selection systems can contribute to social integration by helping to allocate roles in a way satisfying to the individual and harmonious for society. To some extent the system reflects a larger cultural pattern determining how elite and

---

[1] "Given some prominence" is vague, but the formulation must be a rough one. "Values held by most people" would give a western democratic bias to the matter; on the other hand, I do not wish to include standards held by eccentrics when those standards are not really part of the culture.

non-elite roles are shaped and filled, but in an immediate sense elite selection may be viewed as a shaping factor "in its own right." (To what extent and in what sense institutions, like individuals, can be seen as free of surrounding and preceding cultural patterns is a complicated problem in conception alone, quite apart from the matter of proof. Whatever the answers, the assumption here is that institutions can be viewed as functional or dysfunctional in terms of cultural ends.)

Another, if overlapping, criterion of a successfully performed, direct social function is the fulfillment of social and cultural wants. When, for example, a population's economic demands are rising, a governing elite system may be relatively unsuccessful if it directs too much talent away from entrepreneurial and technological roles in favor of governing roles. I have argued elsewhere that this criticism can be made of the Victorian-Edwardian "public" schools in Britain.[2] However, in an industrializing country, it is no simple matter to obtain the right balance between recruitment into economic and technical roles, and the recruitment of political leaders. Likewise, an elite selection and training system may have to honor, or at least not dishonor, a range of cultural values if it is to be judged successful. In a society where the fruits of artistic creativity or technical invention are desired or respected, successful elite training systems will not define political virtue and leadership in a way that deprecates private invention to the point of retarding art or science.[3]

To some extent, however, an elite system writes its own rules by influencing the cultural values, or ends, against which it may be judged. The prestige of the system, the values implied by its education, and the articulateness of its educators will often combine to

[2] Wilkinson, *Gentlemanly Power*, New York, 1964 (London edition, *The Prefects*, 1964).

[3] It has been suggested, however, that scorn by socially dominant convention can sharpen creativity, if not pushed too far. Despite the tendency of many nonconformists to establish their own conformities, creative pursuits may be nourished by rebelliousness, an outsider's skepticism, and the freedoms and discoveries beyond mainstream convention. Consider the disproportionate number of leading American writers in the 1920s who came from midwestern small towns; consider again the Huguenots, Jews, and Overseas Chinese.

affect the attitudes of non-elite as well as elite. The system, of course, will also influence the general public through the behavior of its graduates in high position. This brings us to the second type of function of an elite selection system: the indirect governing functions.[4]

These functions embrace the various effects of elite selection and training on the society, through the public leadership which it helps to shape. The question here to ask is: how successfully did the system select and prepare future leaders for their roles? To answer this question, one must ask another: how effectively did the graduates of the system in fact govern? At first, such a question may seem unfair, for it implies that qualities of government are wholly attributable to the education and selection of leaders. But if one expands the concept of selection and education, so that it includes both the family backgrounds recruited from and the informal elite training received in government, then the objection is diminished. It may still be argued that government institutions have a momentum of their own which influences the effectiveness of government somewhat independently of personal abilities and aptitudes. But these institutions form part of the circumstances with which the leaders have to deal. One may ask how effectively they dealt with them, while recognizing roughly that some eras and situations have demanded more ingenuity of public leadership than have others.[5]

What, then, are the criteria of successful or effective government as measures of elite systems? At the farthest, Machiavellian point there might be included the power and identity of the governing elite itself, particularly when it is given, and gives itself, a moral value so that its vitality becomes an end. By this standard, Hitler and his "Old Fighter" group could only be judged unsuccessful when they pursued policies which led to their own weakening and

[4] Since this book focuses on *governing* elites, the indirect governing functions are dealt with more fully. All the criteria used for assessing these functions might be called subcriteria of "the fulfillment of social and cultural wants," the broad criterion already used.

[5] One should, of course, allow as much as possible for differences of education and background among government groups and individuals responsible for different policies.

destruction. A second criterion might be the long-term integration
and survival of the society. This would include security from un-
wanted invasion. I stress "long-term" integration because too
tight and rigid an integration in the short-term may weaken the
society's ultimate capacity to survive. This is especially so in conditions of flux, when narrow conformity may block adjustment of
organization, techniques, and behavior. It is obvious that a governing elite's policies and decision-making may affect social integration, stability, and security; but they will also help to define what is
generally *considered* integration, stability, and security. Here then,
the elite itself, like the system which produces it, takes a hand in
writing the rules by which to judge its success. Far short of an-
archy, lie conditions which may be viewed either as acceptable
change or as a disintegration of social order and cultural identity, a
distinctive and precious way of life. How they are viewed will depend in part upon how "peace and order" and the cultural identity
are defined. As influential persons, the members of a governing elite
may play a large part in determining the definitions used. And yet,
governing elites do not entirely rig the tests of their performance.
Although they may largely learn their standards of effectiveness
from an elite system of training, this training must itself be shaped
by wider cultural forces. By their own standards, too, some elites
in history may be considered failures at preserving social cohesion.
This function, it should be added, is not always compatible with
preservation of the elite itself. In times of social change, an elite
may preserve social order, in effect, by phasing itself out (as with
some colonial elites)[6] or by so widening its recruitment that its
nature is fundamentally changed. The latter case illustrates the
two-way relationship between a governing elite's selection and its
behavior. As political decision-makers, members of an elite may
substantially alter the selection and training system through which
they rose.

A more positive and demanding criterion of successful government is the solution, forestalling, or diminishing of public prob-

[6] From the standpoint of the (former) colony, the elite terminates itself as
a social force, whether or not it returns to join its own in the former parent
nation.

lems—phenomena which are clearly judged in the culture to be both undesirable and a matter for public resources. This includes but often goes beyond the preservation of social unity, security, and identity. Here again, the governing elite (and its educators) partially rigs the test of performance by influencing general opinion and thus helping to determine what is considered a public problem. On this point, the distinction between "good" government and "effective" government becomes very plain. By some absolute ethical standard—say, the desirability of alleviating economic hardship—a government may do good in helping to identify a pocket of distress as a public problem; yet by this very act, it adds to the tests which it must pass in order to be considered effective. On the other hand, early identification of what will anyway become a public problem may favor effective government, if early action would make the problem-solving easier.

The most advanced criterion of successful government is the extent to which it helps groups in the society to realize whatever is culturally defined as the "good life." A government's understood responsibility for this varies from culture to culture, but in most societies, at least, such responsibility is implicitly recognized, if only to help preserve for *some* groups those conditions in which the good life may be sought. In many instances, this function may demand little more than solving or forestalling public problems, as already mentioned. But in other situations, problem-solving may clash with responsibility for the good life. This can happen when cultural values are changing or divergent. For example, towards the end of the Hoover Administration, demands that the federal government assume a more direct responsibility for economic problems clashed with concerns for preserving a competitive and self-helping way of life. But again, in some situations it is not so much the good-life concept itself that clashes with problem-solving as the *means* which convention declares necessary for the good life's attainment. In Imperial China, there was often a governing assumption that rulers could best promote a good society by devotion to an exemplary self-cultivation. Sometimes this helped to inhibit the Emperor and his officials from energetic problem-solving (irrigation, for example) as well as the maintenance of peace and order:

social integration. Yet at other times, Imperial China had active central governments, despite a persistence of the same social and moral philosophies. So governments and governing elites sometimes enjoy a certain leeway in which to select those means to the good life which clash as little as possible with other requirements of effective government. Governments may also have to choose between, or arbitrate, conflicting good-life demands from different social groups, and to do so in a way which preserves social integration as much as possible. Under these circumstances, a degree of social integration must represent the first test of successful government, since minimal social cohesion and survival is usually the prerequisite of any good life.[7] The successful government, however, will try to define both the good life and the requirements of social cohesion to make its task easier.

This discussion, it must be reiterated, is entirely amoral. To preserve social cohesion and *general* harmony, a government might tolerate local power groups which were quietly abusing a minority in a way not greatly recognized as a public problem. To interfere with these power groups might gravely divide the society, especially if the local power groups could count on allies and supporting traditions from elsewhere in the realm. At some point, "successful" governing, as I have described it, might no longer be worth it by humane standards. Fortunately for the oppressed, the kind of choice involved here is seldom a clean either-or. A government may preserve some social cohesion without making success in these terms its paramount end. It may also persuade itself, and persuade others, that dealing with the local bully is in the long-run interests of social harmony: that, for example, revolution may result if nothing is done. And this may indeed be the case. But alas for the oppressed, it is not always the case. The Mississippis of history have not always had their civil rights acts, and we know that civil rights acts are not always enforced. More cruelly still, the governments which neither make nor enforce their civil rights acts may in many respects be very successful.

To conclude: governments are successful and effective to the extent that they do what they are culturally supposed to do; yet

[7] Even hermits have often counted on considerable resources from a hinterland community, and they have inevitably drawn from a social background.

even within this cultural framework there may be clashes between the criteria of success. A very successful government will then try to define the criteria and the means of meeting those criteria so that they do not clash so much. Where it cannot avoid such a conflict, it will promote a clear notion as to what aspects of successful government have priority over others. Except for the preservation of a minimal social cohesion, no criterion of successful government has intrinsic priority.[8]

So much for the criteria by which to test the *indirect governing functions* of an elite selection system. It remains to be said that these functions may not be well supported by the system's *direct social functions*. Imperial China again provides a case in point. Its elite educational system was overloaded. The country stretched over great variations of geography, and in the absence of a strong legal tradition (minimized by moral teaching itself), much depended on education to hold the society together and give it a common moral stamp. This may well have reinforced the conformist tenor of the neo-Confucian education and examination system whose prime constituencies were elite "gentry" classes. Yet the same system had to produce officials with the resource to govern a huge nation. The conformist traits induced by the education served the needs of effective government in some ways, but when imagination was called for, they did not help. Here then, the direct integrating function of the system did not seem to be wholly compatible with the requirements of effective public leadership.

ELITE EDUCATION AND SOCIAL EFFECTIVENESS: A GENERAL ASSESSMENT

The complications met above suggest that rather little can be said about a general relationship between (1) the social effectiveness of

---

[8] The terms "successful" and "effective," used synonymously here, have been deliberately chosen rather than "efficient." The latter entails the effective performance of a function with relatively little effort and resources. Insofar as efficiency frees resources, enabling a system to serve cultural ends more effectively or to serve *more* cultural ends than it otherwise would, "efficiency" contributes to "effectiveness" as used above. But in this broad context, the term "efficiency" used by itself involves further problems of measurement and relative values.

the way public leaders are selected and trained—effectiveness, that is, at reaching culturally prescribed goals—and (2) the extent to which the selection and training forms a special system highly geared to a governing elite. What one can do, however, is to list potential strong points and weaknesses of such a system, remembering that these are but general tendencies and are not the entire list. I will confine myself to systems comprised of schools and/or colleges which provide the main supply of their respective governing elites, giving a distinctive education to selected individuals in childhood, youth, or early adulthood.[9]

These systems as a whole would seem to have at least four broad advantages. First, they enable educational resources to be concentrated on those who are to assume crucial tasks of government. In a more general way, too, elite concentration can ensure that standards of personal excellence valued by the culture as a whole are served and honored. This may give added moral focus to the society and cohesion to the culture. Second, in a complex society it may often be easier, politically and administratively, to make needed changes in the education of leaders when that education is the charge of relatively unified elite institutions. (This applies at least when all education is not under such tight control by a central authority that planners can shape the training of leaders whether or not the training is concentrated in a few places). In the third instance, a close link between elite education and government recruitment will enhance the status and allure of high government careers; and this effect may be particularly useful in capitalist societies where private money-making and other pursuits will tend to draw a wealth of talent away from public service. Fourth, a shared elite training can give leaders a "common language," mutual respect, and general sense of unity which often facilitates action and, by minimizing political division, contributes to social cohesion.

The chief liabilities seem to be threefold. First, the recruitment

[9] To the extent that a given brand of educational elitism forms part of the society's mores, an educational system cannot be viewed simply as a more or less effective *means,* for education includes values and values represent ends. But these ends may be intermediate: to this extent they may be judged for their utility in reaching broader and more fundamental goals of the society.

of public officers through a formal elite system will always exclude
some potential leaders who might have contributed to government.
Even a system strongly devoted to selection by demonstrated
"merit" will tend to penalize the late-developer, especially the person who does not show the required aptitudes until well into adulthood. And the in-group mystique which elitist institutions develop
can inhibit the formulation of new conceptions of merit, which
might minimize waste in the leaders' selection. One answer to this
is to base the recruitment of public leaders on more than one elite
educational system (as with Britain's public schools and grammar
schools); but then the systems may imitate rather than complement
each other's methods, while giving the impression of casting a wider
net than they really do.

The second liability is that elite education closely linked to government service may direct and train too much talent away from
certain creative occupations in favor of government and related
professions. This liability has already been noted, and it is the
shadow of advantages contemplated above: educative concentration on future public leaders and the enhancement of public careers. As far as business occupations are concerned, the Japanese
kobun system and the French *grandes écoles* have minimized the
liability by preparing leaders for careers in which many eventually
move from government to business. But in other economic contexts
it may be doubted whether the same training is the best for both
civil servants and businessmen. Does a long preparation for bureaucracy do much for the entrepreneurial nerve and mind?

A third liability is the lack of social and intellectual ventilation.
Elitism tends to cut a group off from other groups, and therefore
from some sources of ideas and facts. In a democratic or socialist
society this raises special problems of responsibility and trust, and
to the extent that elitism itself generates widespread dissatisfaction
and cultural conflict, the system is not effective. More generally,
however, the social isolation of a governing elite may reduce the
effectiveness of its government. This liability may not materialize
in a simple, unchanging society; but complex organization makes it
difficult for an elite to be responsive to its social environment when
it does not draw its members from varied educational backgrounds.

On these grounds it may be argued that the American federal bureaucracy has had advantages over the British civil service. A related liability is the potential antagonism between the questioning, innovating mind and the strong loyalties and mystique of the group which elite education tends to develop, however much it may also develop certain types of well-trained intelligence. Again, this liability is particularly pronounced when social change puts a premium on the innovating mind. It must be conceded, however, that populism as much as elitism can abhor imagination as subversive. The informal systems in many American high schools have been no less anti-intellectual than the "muscular Christianity" of the Victorian public schools.[10]

In conclusion one may doubt that there is any cross-cultural relationship, positive or negative, between social effectiveness, and the extent to which public leaders are trained in an elite education system. So much depends on the particular wants, requirements, and traditions in the society concerned, and on the kind of elites which have emerged. In advance of more empirical study, it is safe to suggest that a very high degree of educational elitism—that is, a very special training and group feeling imparted to nearly all the future public leaders—tends to serve government and society badly in an advanced industrial society marked by rapid technical change. But some degree and form of elitism may be useful in these conditions.[11]

[10] I have discussed elsewhere the tension between certain kinds of loyalty and intelligence, with particular reference to Jesuit traditions: Wilkinson, op. cit. Ch. 14.

[11] As conceived of here, degree of educational elitism involves more than one dimension: the distinctiveness of the training; the feeling of specialness induced; the length of special training (how far back it reached in the individual's life); and the proportion of public leaders produced by such a system.

Index

225